Please return / renew by date shown.
You can renew at:
norlink.norfolk.gov.uk
or by telephone: 0844 800 8006
Please have your library card & PIN ready.

nmL/so

28-10-06

19 APR 2008

28 JUL 2008

13 OCT 2008

NORFOLK LIBRARY
AND INFORMATION SERVICE

LETTERS FROM A SUBURBAN HOUSEWIFE

LETTERS FROM
A SUBURBAN HOUSEWIFE

by
Mark Eden & Bill Hill

MARKHILL PUBLISHING
Golden House, 29 Great Pulteney Street, London W1F 9NN

THIS IS A TRUE STORY.

All the characters who appear in this book were actual people.

All the major events and incidents described herein actually took place.

The trial is an edited version of the transcripts from The Crown v Edith Jessie Thompson & Frederick Edward Francis Bywaters, at the Old Bailey in December 1922.

All Edith Thompson's letters reproduced here are authentic.

It is only where there is no way of knowing what was actually said in certain situations that the authors have employed analysis, conjecture and imagination to help tell this remarkable story.

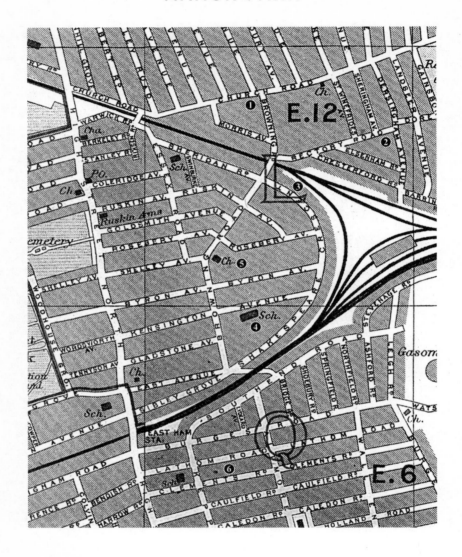

❶ The Avenue Hotel

❷ Freddy Bywaters's house until 1919

❸ 231 Shakespeare Crescent – Edith's family home

❹ Kensington Avenue School – attended by the Graydon and Bywaters children

❺ St Barnabas Church – where Edith and Percy married in 1916

❻ Percy Thompson's family home

ILFORD

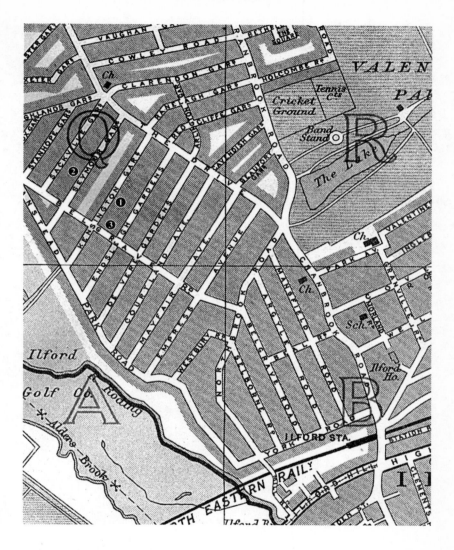

❶ The Thompson's home – 41 Kensington Gardens

❷ Richard Thompson's home

❸ Murder spot

Chapter 1

In the already-fading light of a bleak December afternoon in 1922, a crowd of some several thousand had gathered outside the Old Bailey to await a verdict.

A throng of men, women and children of different backgrounds, ages, classes and creeds, buttoned up against the bitter cold of that momentous day all intent on playing a role, however small, in the high drama being enacted in the amphitheatre of Court Number One.

Inside the court, the clock stood at 3.30 as the Judge, Mr Justice Shearman, concluded his summing up at the end of a sensational trial - The King v Edith Jessie Thompson and Frederick Edward Francis Bywaters.

The two defendants had been jointly charged with the wilful murder of Percy Thompson, Edith Thompson's husband. They had been tried together on the same charge, in the same dock, throughout a five day trial that had become a cause célèbre.

As Edith descended the steep stone stairway to the cells below to await the jury's verdict, she glanced over her shoulder at her co-defendant and lover, Freddy Bywaters. If he felt any apprehension, it was not apparent in his demeanour. He stood, ramrod-straight, staring straight ahead, his face betraying no emotion.

Sitting in the gathering gloom of her cell, Edith had every reason to feel confident - sanguine even - about her chances of acquittal. She had taken no part in the crime nor had she wished the deed to be done. That *must* have been obvious to everyone.

Her counsel, Sir Henry Curtis-Bennett, had conducted her defence with immense skill and eloquence - his closing speech being a paradigm of impassioned rhetoric tempered with reasoned argument.

He had been a tower of strength throughout. His reassuring manner, resonant voice and sturdy physical presence being, as she saw it, a bulwark against those intent on her destruction.

That *she* would walk free, Edith was in no doubt. Now it was only for the jury to find her innocent. With poor Freddy, it was a different story. He had admitted everything and could only be found guilty as charged.

To his eternal credit, Freddy had done his utmost to shield her from the accusations made against her, stating over and over again that she had no foreknowledge of the murder of her husband nor played any part in it.

Poor, dear Freddy. The best he could hope for now was that, because of his youth, his sentence would be commuted to one of life imprisonment.

Edith shook her head in an effort to banish this distressing thought from her mind. She had to think in a positive way now, and plan for the future. Having been away from her home for almost three months there would be much that needed doing. Her birthday, Christmas Day, was less than two weeks away. Christmas would be a difficult time. But in the New Year she would sell number 41 and leave Ilford, perhaps. Move abroad for a while, France possibly. Get a job in a boutique de chapeaux, improve her French and use the experience she had acquired during all her years with Carlton & Prior. Revert back to her maiden name, Graydon. Yes. That's what she would do. Start again. Afresh. Anew. After all, she would only be 29. The prime of her life. Yes. A new beginning. A new life. Then, after a few years, perhaps return to England and...Edith suddenly felt drained. The mental torment of the past three months had been almost too much to bear. She lay back on the hard bunk and closed her eyes. Soon it would be all over.

As the sounds and voices around her receded, the strains of *One Little Hour*, a popular song of the day, came into her head. It had been *their* song, *their* words, *their* future. *"One little hour of moonlight, one little night of bliss, two lovers meeting, tenderly greeting, what can be wrong in this?"* With the words of the song going round in her mind, Edith Thompson slowly drifted off into an unquiet sleep.

Chapter 2

"We have found our 'Retreat' at last.
Now for what may come."

The consensus of opinion among family, friends and neighbours was that the proposed marriage was a splendid match.

Percy Thompson was 26; a good looking, well dressed, thrifty young man with a steady, well paid job as a shipping clerk in the City of London. And, if perhaps a little on the dull side, was still considered quite a 'catch' for any young lady. Edith Graydon was not 'any young lady'.

By any standards she was a remarkable woman. At 23, she was attractive, intelligent, vivacious and talented. On the face of it, the antithesis of her husband-to-be. But that was no bad thing. A marriage of opposites quite often fares far better than those of the like-minded.

While Percy sat behind his desk in the City, sedulously plotting marine movements, Edith was queen bee at Carlton & Prior, a wholesale milliners in Aldersgate Street.

She had joined the firm in 1911 as a book-keeper but had soon established herself as a fine sales co-ordinator; a role she doubled with her efficient handling of the accounts.

The proprietors, Mr Carlton and Miss Prior, had been delighted with her progress and she was in line for a senior position in the firm. For Edith and her husband-to-be the future looked promising.

For others, there was to be no future.

January 1916 saw the conflict in Europe entering its seventeenth month. With the Western Front bogged down in a bloody war of attrition, hundreds of thousands of young men were leaving England never to return.

Against this sombre background, with the war already condemning a whole generation of young women to spinsterhood, the bride and groom had good reason to count themselves lucky to have found each other.

They had first met in 1909 when Edith was 15 years old and Percy 19. Percy had noticed Edith many times at local dances and on the westbound platform of East Ham, District Line underground station and had been attracted by her elegance and poise. She wasn't a beauty in the classical sense but, with her deep brown eyes and thick auburn hair, she was certainly an attractive girl, and many was the time he had sat in the same carriage, gazing at her in tongue-tied admiration, unable to pluck up the courage to engage her in conversation.

Percy had worked at O.J. Parker & Co in Eastcheap as a shipping clerk since he had left school, always getting off at Monument station near London Bridge. But one morning, by now consumed with curiosity, he followed Edith till she eventually reached Aldersgate station. Dogging her footsteps, he observed her arriving at the offices of Carlton & Prior at 168 Aldersgate Street before dashing back to Eastcheap to face a ticking off for being late.

Eventually ardour overcame his natural reticence and he did, at last, manage to talk to her. One morning, sitting opposite him on the train into town reading a book, she glanced up, and noticed him looking at her. Realizing it was now or never, Percy managed to ask her about the book she was reading. One thing led to another and eventually they discovered they had mutual acquaintances from the public dances they attended. Then, with Monument station hurrying ever near, he threw caution to the winds and, in a voice he barely recognized as his own, asked if she would care to accompany him to a Sunday League concert in a few days time. To his amazement, and delight, she accepted. Arrangements were hurriedly made and names and addresses exchanged before Percy alighted from the train with a song in his heart and a noticeable spring in his step.

From the start they got on well together. In Percy, Edith saw a personable level-headed young man with a future. For his part, Percy was delighted to be seen in the company of such a sought-after and vivacious young lady.

In the following weeks they went everywhere together: the theatre, dances and concerts. They joined an amateur drama company, took elocution lessons, went for long walks in Epping Forest...and fell in love.

Within three months of their first meeting each had introduced the other to their families and Percy had asked Edith's father for permission to 'walk out' with his daughter.

William Graydon had taken to Percy Thompson from the outset, as had Ethel Graydon, Edith's mother. They both found him a likeable young man, well-mannered, respectable, hard working and sensible. Their only reservation about the relationship was Edith's tender age. They felt that 15 was rather young to start courting, but, that aside, they were happy to trust him with their beloved daughter.

It was to prove a long courtship.

Percy was determined not to marry until they could afford to buy their own house and he could provide himself and his wife with a comfortable standard of living.

It was to be five years before they first made love, and six before he felt financially secure enough to ask her to marry him.

It was in the summer of 1914 that Edith lost her virginity during a holiday they shared with friends in Ilfracombe. She was 20 years old.

In Europe, storm clouds of war were gathering as the unthinkable was fast becoming the unavoidable. But to Edith and Percy, all such sombre thoughts were set aside as their love for each other was finally consummated.

On the morning of January 15th 1916, a small group of neighbours and well-wishers gathered outside Edith's family home at 231 Shakespeare Crescent, Manor Park to welcome the happy couple on their return from church.

The wedding had been held at St. Barnabas, with the reception at the bride's family home, and it was common knowledge locally that Bill Graydon had 'put his hand in his pocket' to ensure a fitting send-off for his elder daughter. Edith's wedding dress in pale cream satin had been specially made, as had her sister Avis's bridesmaid dress and, when the beribboned Austin 16 car pulled up, and the newly-weds emerged, they were greeted with a shower of confetti and good wishes. As they made their way up the short pathway to the house, a young lad stepped forward, holding a small bunch of flowers.

He was wearing his Sunday best suit, with his fair, wavy hair parted carefully in the centre and brilliantined.

'Freddy Bywaters!' Edith exclaimed. 'My word, don't you look smart.'

The young lad took a deep breath and spoke his well-rehearsed lines. 'Please, Miss Graydon,' he said solemnly. 'We'd like you - mum and me that is - would like you to accept these flowers with our very best wishes for your future happiness'. With a stiff bow he presented Edith with the bouquet, which she graciously acknowledged.

'What a kind thought,' she said, smelling the flowers. 'Thank you.' Then, turning to Percy, 'This is Freddy Bywaters, dear, a friend of my brothers.'

'Hello, young fella-me-lad.' Percy patted the boy paternally on the shoulder. 'Are you coming in for some pop and a piece of cake?'

Within the modest confines of 231 Shakespeare Crescent, Mr Graydon had indeed 'put his hand in his pocket'.

The two downstairs living rooms had been opened up to accommodate the thirty or so expected guests. A trestle table had been set up along one wall with, on one side, cold meats, salads, sandwiches, tinned salmon, sausage rolls, cheeses and pickles and, on the other, jellies, trifles, blancmanges and fruit salad. In the centre of the table, in pride of place, stood a magnificent three-tier wedding cake, made to order at the local Co-op shop.

There were crates of bottled beers, bottles of whisky, gin, sherry, port wine and, for the children, lemonade and ginger beer.

He'd even had the piano tuned.

It was to be a joyous occasion, only slightly marred by the rather aloof attitude of the Thompson family.

Privately, they had never thought Edith 'quite the thing' for Percy, and although his brother Richard had agreed to be best man at the wedding, the bridegroom's family more or less kept themselves to themselves during the celebrations afterwards.

There was no such reticence from the distaff side.

Mrs Graydon never needed much coaxing to sit down at the piano and was soon thumping away, making up in enthusiasm what she lacked in expertise.

Percy sang a song and Mr Graydon sang a song, with the rest of the Graydons and guests joining in the chorus, while the Thompsons refrained.

When the time came for the happy couple to leave on their honeymoon everyone was agreed that Bill Graydon had done his daughter proud.

Edith, on her way out, saw Freddy sitting alone in the kitchen, and went over to him.

'Freddy, are *you* still here? Your mother will be wondering where you are.'

'No, she knows where I am. I wanted to see you leave. Are you going away with Mr Thompson?'

'Of course, he's my husband now. We're off to Southend for a couple of days.'

'When you come back, will you still live here?'

'Yes, until we find our own home.'

'When you do, won't I see you anymore?'

Edith laughed and put her arm around his shoulders.

'Of course you will, silly. We won't be moving to Timbuktu, you know.'

Freddy stood up and wiped his hand on his trouser leg before offering it to Edith.

'Goodbye then,' he said, holding out his hand.

Edith opened her purse and took out a shiny new sixpenny piece. 'That's to buy yourself some sweets,' she said, pressing the coin into Freddy's hand. 'Thank you for the flowers. I shall be taking them to Southend with me.'

Percy called from the doorway. 'Come on, Edith. The taxi's outside with the meter running.'

Edith kissed Freddy on the cheek and joined Percy at the door before looking back and giving Freddy a little wave. As the honeymooners walked down the path to the waiting taxi, a snowstorm of confetti and a chorus of good wishes followed them.

Once inside, Edith blew a kiss to the wildly waving crowd as the taxi pulled away. To Freddy, standing slightly apart from the main group, that kiss had been meant for him, he was sure of it. She had looked straight at him when she did it, so it must have been. As he watched the taxi disappearing down the road, he made two promises to himself. First, he would *never* spend the sixpence Edith had just given him - it would be his good-luck piece and would go with him everywhere, always. Second, and far more importantly, he vowed that one day, he and Edith would be together. He had no idea how, when or where, but it would happen. Of that he was absolutely certain. Then, folding the sixpenny piece carefully in his pocket handkerchief, he turned and started to walk home.

Inside the taxi, as it honked its way through the traffic to Fenchurch Street Station, Percy put his arm around his new bride as she settled her head on his shoulder. 'I think,' he said, smiling, 'young Freddy Bywaters has got a bit of a crush on you.'

Edith laughed. 'Oh, dear, I hope not. I can do without a fourteen year old admirer.

Percy kissed the top of her head. 'He hardly took his eyes off you the whole time. Mind you,' he added, 'I couldn't take my eyes of you either.'

'Then,' said Edith, archly, 'you are obviously both gentlemen of impeccable taste.'

Almost as soon as they returned from their honeymoon, Percy felt constrained to enlist in the army. With losses on the Western Front mounting daily, the pressure on young men to volunteer was enormous.

Everywhere the stern visage of Lord Kitchener, the hero of Khartoum, stared out from hoardings, his finger pointing accusingly with the unequivocal message: 'Your Country Needs **YOU**!!!'. Women had taken to handing out white feathers to any young man whom they felt should be walking into a hail of machine gun bullets with a sixty pound pack on his back, rather than strolling through the park with a girl on his arm. Recruitment rallies were held in all parks and open spaces with a military band and a moustachioed Sergeant Major on hand to shame or cajole young shavers into joining up.

'You, young fella,' he would bark, pointing at some hapless lad with his swagger stick. 'Make your lady friend proud of you. Step up, join up, and we'll make a man of you.' And, as the callow youth, grinning sheepishly, signed on, the band would play and people would clap as yet another young man signed his own death warrant.

Against this background and with conscription only a matter of time, Percy joined the Royal Scots Guards and was stationed at a temporary camp in Richmond Park. But after completing his basic training and while the regiment was awaiting orders to leave for France, he began complaining of pains in his chest. A medical examination found an unspecified 'heart disorder' and he was discharged from the army as medically unfit. What this mysterious ailment actually *was* nobody seemed to know.

There were dark mutterings among his comrades-in-arms about Thompson somehow having 'worked his ticket'. But whatever the reason, the fact remained that Percy Thompson would be taking no further part in the war.

Curiously enough, after an initial wave of relief at the news, Edith had felt a stab of resentment. With her two younger brothers at sea, and her other brother, Newenham, fighting on the Somme, she and her family lived in constant dread of the telegram boy knocking on the door. Later on, she became even more disappointed in her husband when, in his cups one night, Percy boasted about how he had 'wangled' his way out of the army by smoking fifty cigarettes a day instead of his usual pipe.

Percy enjoyed a drink. Unfortunately, he also possessed a very low tolerance to alcohol, which meant that after three pints of Bass, he became garrulous and after four, pie-eyed! A failing which didn't endear him to Edith, who always became hot with embarrassment when it happened in company.

His already tarnished image took a further knock, as far as Edith was concerned, when bombs started to fall on London.

With the war in Europe locked in stalemate, Germany decided on an aerial bombardment in an effort to break the deadlock and the first Zeppelins were despatched to London. The bombing itself was haphazard and wildly inaccurate but, with the deliberate attacking of civilian targets, it signalled a new and sinister departure from the accepted rules of war.

As the fear of further bombing raids increased, Percy became more and more terrified. At the time they were living with the Graydons who, like most Londoners, refused to be intimidated by the hateful Hun and were determined to stay put. But Percy was made of weaker stuff and implored Edith to move with him out of London.

Edith resisted the move for as long as she could but eventually, very much against her will, they moved down to Westcliff-on-Sea and took rooms in a street called, appropriately enough, Retreat Road.

Meanwhile, in direct contrast to Percy's pusillanimity, Freddy Bywaters, still only 15 but looking older than his years, had tried to enlist in the Royal Navy, only to be rejected when his mother informed the authorities of his true age. Undeterred, he immediately joined the Merchant Navy as a cabin boy and spent the last year of the war braving German U-boats on a troopship.

By the time the war was over Freddy had made up his mind to pursue a career in the Merchant Navy, and had signed on as a ship's writer on the *SS Plassy*, a cargo ship of the P&O Line. Not the most glamorous of jobs perhaps, but it enabled him to see the world and sample delights in foreign parts, not usually to be found in the environs of Manor Park.

It was four years after their marriage that Percy and Edith decided they could afford to buy their own home. But finding such a place proved to be more difficult than either of them had anticipated. Both had decided they would like to stay in the area to be near their families but found that houses in the better parts of the borough were usually out of their price range. By the standards of the day they were well off. Edith had been given a rise in salary at Carlton & Prior which had increased her wage to £6 a week - only fifteen shillings less than Percy's take home pay. With a combined income of almost £13 a week, they considered themselves virtually middle class. All they needed to lift them up the ladder another rung was a nice house in a sought-after road.

Number 41 Kensington Gardens, Ilford, was a fine double-fronted terraced house with two large reception rooms, four bedrooms, a morning room, kitchen, bathroom, a small front garden and a spacious rear garden. Perfect in every respect, except one - a Mr and Mrs Lester and their daughter Nora, occupied three of the rooms of the house with use of the kitchen and bathroom. The situation was further complicated by the fact that Mr Lester was an invalid and confined to the house.

After much agonizing, they eventually bought the property jointly for £250 and immediately gave the Lesters six months notice to quit, hoping that in that time they would be able to find somewhere else to live.

It was the mid summer of 1920 that the Thompsons moved in and named their new house "The Retreat" - an echo of their wartime stay in Westcliff.

From the outset, it was not the happiest of co-habitations. It soon became apparent both families needed to use the bathroom and kitchen facilities at roughly the same time each morning, so a timetable had to be drawn up and strictly adhered to. As it had been Mrs Lester's custom to prepare a saucepan of porridge for her own family every morning, it was agreed that she should also do the same for the Thompsons, thus avoiding congestion in the kitchen during that crucial early-morning period. After six months, the Lesters were still there but the situation had eased somewhat in that everyone had settled into the daily routine quite well. Which, if not entirely satisfactory, was at least tolerable.

Percy had not held the Lesters to their six months notice. He understood how difficult it could be to find a suitable accommodation, and did not wish to be unreasonable. On a more practical level, he found the seven and sixpence a week rent they paid a useful addition to the household finances.

As Edith and Percy were settling into their new home in salubrious Ilford, the Bywaters family were also adjusting to new surroundings.

They had left their house in Rectory Road, Manor Park, after Freddy's father had finally succumbed to the after-effects of being gassed in the war, and moved to South Norwood, where Mrs Bywaters opened a draper's shop at 15 Westow Hill.

With Mrs Bywaters, Freddy, his two sisters and younger brother all sharing the cramped little flat above the shop, it was not the most comfortable of re-locations, but they managed well enough.

Freddy was now 18 years old, a handsome, personable young man, a rather snappy dresser, and something of a ladies' man.

When his ship docked at Tilbury, he would collect his back pay and go out on the town with his lady friends. One of the women he was seeing at the time was Avis.

Another was Edith.

Since he had reached maturity, Edith had become more aware of, and interested in, Freddy and, unbeknown to Percy, had met up with him several times, either during her lunch hour or after she finished work, when they would have tea together at Fuller's tearooms in Fann Street, off Aldersgate Street.

To Edith, at that time, Freddy was no more than a 'divertissment'. He was fun to be with and knew how to please her by pandering to her vanity. But while *he* was completely enamoured of *her*, Edith, although flattered by the attentions of a handsome young man eight years her junior, had a husband, a home and a secure future to consider and nothing would be allowed to jeopardize that.

Chapter 3

"Do you remember the Shanklin times when neither of
us had any cares or worries, personal ones I mean, altho' we
hadn't learnt to know ourselves or each other..?"

In the summer of 1921, Edith and Percy planned a group summer holiday for the first week of June. Their destination was to be Shanklin on the Isle of Wight and the party would consist of Edith and Percy, Avis, and Norman and Lily Vellender. Lily worked with Edith at Carlton & Prior and was a close friend. Norman, her husband, had become a drinking pal of Percy's, and Avis got on with everyone. As it happened, Freddy was on leave at the time and Edith suggested that Freddy might wish to join them as a companion for Avis. Avis, who was quite sweet on Freddy, was delighted.

However, Edith had her own reasons for planning the holiday in such a way. For a whole week she would be in close proximity to the young man who, more and more, had been occupying her thoughts of late.

They booked into the Osborne House hotel, a medium-sized, family-run establishment overlooking the pier and beach at Shanklin. The terms were three pounds twelve shillings a week full board with afternoon tea extra at sixpence per person, per day.

On the Sunday, the first full day of their holiday, they woke up to a cloudless, cobalt-blue sky and a sparkling, tranquil sea.

After breakfast Norman and Lily left to visit relatives on the island, Freddy and Avis went off to buy some postcards, while Percy and Edith made their way down the stone steps at the side of the pier to the beach below. Once there, they commandeered a couple of deck chairs and staked out their claim on the sands.

Percy was no sunbather, so he contented himself with taking off his shoes and socks and rolling up his trousers, removing his collar and tie, and undoing a couple of shirt buttons. Then he unfurled the *Daily Sketch* and settled down for a pleasant morning on the beach. Edith was wearing a light summer frock and a sun hat, and had brought along a book to read, a romantic novel entitled *"Garden of Allah'*, by Robert Hichens. Edith loved the escapism of books, identifying herself strongly with the heroines and living out her fantasies through them.

It was the same when she visited the theatre, always making a strong identification with one of the characters and taking a long time to come back down to earth after the enchantment of the magic world of make-believe.

When she had been younger, everyone had said she should become an actress and for a while, she had seriously considered it, but wiser counsel and parental disapproval had prevailed, leaving Edith with only wistful dreams of what might have been.

She had managed to read only five or six pages before they were joined on the beach by Freddy and Avis who insisted on taking a snap of them on her box Brownie camera before going in for a swim. She had just bought an Ilford 120 film from the chemists and was eager to record the first day of their holiday.

Posing for one of Avis's group photographs was always a 'bit of a palaver', with the group being formed, broken up and reformed several times before she was happy with the composition.

With the smiles on their faces rapidly congealing into rictus-like grimaces, exasperation was beginning to surface among the sitters.

'Buck up, Avis.' Percy was becoming impatient. 'We're only here for a week you know!'

Finally, Avis was satisfied.

'Say 'cheese',' she called, still hunched over the view-finder.

Edith and Freddy said: 'cheese'. Percy said: 'Gorgonzola', and to everyone's relief, the ordeal was over - until the next time.

Avis and Freddy were wearing their bathing costumes underneath their clothes and were soon discarding their outer garments, eager to get in the water.

Edith's first sight of Freddy in his costume caused her to catch her breath. She had always suspected that he possessed a good physique, but now she couldn't help but notice just how well-built he was; the close-fitting bathing suit leaving very little to the imagination. Only ever having known one man - in the biblical sense - she found it all rather disconcerting and to cover her confusion she adopted a cockney accent.

'Oooh, I say!' she trilled. 'Look at the muscles on your young man, Avis. Fair makes you want to swoon it does, and no mistake.'

Edith was a good mimic, and everyone laughed.

'Come on,' said Avis taking Freddy's hand. 'Let's go for a dip.'

Freddy looked at Edith. 'What about you, Edith? Coming in?'

'She can't swim,' Avis interjected.

Freddy laughed. 'Can't swim?'

'I never learned,' Edith said ruefully.

'Then I'll teach you.'

Edith looked up at Freddy, shielding her eyes from the dazzling sun. 'Could you?'

'Of course.'

'Freddy's a super swimmer,' Avis said, proudly.

Edith turned to Percy. 'Would you mind, dear?'

Percy shook his head. 'Not at all,' he said. 'I'd teach you myself, only...'

He tapped the left side of his chest meaningfully.

'Have you brought a costume?' Freddy asked.

'In my bag.'

'Alright, get changed. I'll see you in the water.'

Freddy and Avis ran down to the water's edge, hand in hand, and waded out into the sea.

As Edith got to her feet and picked up her bag, Percy looked up from his newspaper.

'Where are you going?'

'Back to the hotel to get changed.'

Percy put down his paper. 'There's no need for that. I'll hold a towel up. Nobody's going to see.'

Edith was indignant. 'I will do no such thing,' she said, primly. 'The very idea!' And with that, trudged off across the sand towards the steps.

Watching her go, Percy smiled to himself and shook his head then, realizing his pipe had gone out, re-lit it.

In the privacy of the hotel room Edith stood at the window for a few moments, completely naked, looking down at the beach where she could see Freddy and Avis splashing around in the water, then turned away and put on her swimming costume.

Five minutes later she was back on the beach beside Percy and slipping out of her dress when Avis came storming up the beach towards them, obviously in a rage.

'What's the matter?' asked Edith as Avis threw down her bathing cap and began to towel herself down.

'Ask that silly little boy down there,' she snapped, indicating Freddy.

As Edith walked down the beach towards him, Freddy was standing waist-deep in the water, hands on hips with a cheeky grin on his face.

Edith called from the shoreline. 'What did you do to upset Avis?'

'She's cross because I ducked her under the water.'

'You *know* she hates that. Why did you do it?'

'I thought you wanted to be alone with me,' he said, and winked.

'If you were a gentleman you'd go after her and apologize.'

'Well I'm not,' he said, 'I'm a bounder. So you'd better watch out.'

Freddy regarded her for a moment with undisguised admiration before holding his hands to her. 'Come to me, Edie Peidi.'

Edith waded out to where he was standing and took hold of his hands.

'I didn't know you couldn't swim,' he said.

'There are a lot of things you don't know about me,' she replied, looking him straight in the eye.

'Right,' he said. 'First lesson, learning to float. Turn round.'

Edith turned her back to him.

'Now,' he said, 'lean back and I'll catch you.'

Edith looked up the beach to where Percy was sitting and suddenly, despite the warmth of the sun, gave an involuntary shiver.

'Are you cold?' Freddy asked.

'No,' she said. 'I think someone just walked over my grave.'

'Come on,' he said. 'Fall back and I'll catch you.'

'You won't let me go?'

He came up close behind her and whispered in her ear.

'I'll never let you go, Peidi,' he said.

As she leaned back towards him, Freddy put his arms under her armpits and gently lowered her into the water, supporting her body with his own.

'That's good,' he said. Then, shifting his position slightly, cupped his hands over her breasts.

'Your hands are where they shouldn't be, Freddy,' she said calmly.

'Sorry,' he said, laughing. 'I thought you were wearing a pair of water-wings.'

Edith became concerned. 'Freddy, take your hands away! Percy might see you.'

'Righto,' he said, and let go of her completely. With a shriek Edith sank beneath the water. When she emerged seconds later, gasping for breath, Freddy was making his way to the shore where he stood laughing.

'You beast! You rotter!' she spluttered, much to the amusement of a gaggle of small boys larking about in the water nearby.

'I'll get you for that. You see if I don't.'

Later, after Freddy had apologized profusely and bought everyone ice cream cones, they lazed around on the beach discussing their plans for the next few days.

One of the attractions they all agreed ought not to be missed was an all-day, round-the-island tour in an open-topped motor coach, which they had seen advertized in the lobby of the hotel. The tour departed at 9.30am from the pier entrance, returning to the same spot at 5.30pm. The cost was two shillings and sixpence per person, lunch not included.

Later, when the idea was put to Norman and Lily over a drink that evening, they were keen to be part of what everyone agreed should be a topping day out.

The following morning, a group of around twenty people had assembled at the pier entrance where the clock showed 9.25. Among them were Norman and Lily, Avis and Freddy, and Percy but, as yet, no Edith.

The hotel had provided them with packed lunches in a wicker basket, into which Percy had prudently added several bottles of Bass and two bottles of lemonade. As they waited for the coach to arrive, the conversation was mostly about the wonderful weather they were having, with temperatures consistently in the high eighties, today being no exception.

'Going to be another scorcher today.'

'Hottest June in living memory, they reckon.'

'Is that right?'

'That's what they said in the paper.'

'I can believe it.'

'Ah! Here comes the charabanc now.'

As the coach hove into view, Percy glanced anxiously up to the window of their hotel room on the first floor, directly across the road. When he had left, Edith had said she would only be a couple of minutes. That was almost ten minutes ago and now here was the coach but no sign of her.

The coach lurched to a stop beside them and the driver clambered down from his cab. He was a short, portly man with a round, florid face. Because of the heat, he had divested himself of his uniform jacket but had felt constrained to retain his peaked cap - a rather grand affair with the words 'Golden Rod Tours' in gold letters round the hat band and a piping of gold braid around the peak.

He took off his cap, mopped his glistening brow with a red and white spotted handkerchief, and wiped the inside of the hat band before replacing it on his head.

'Boarding now for the round-the-island trip,' he wheezed. 'Have your tickets ready, if you please.'

As the group began to file aboard, Percy again looked back at the hotel entrance in the vain hope that Edith might suddenly appear.

'What is she *doing* up there?' he groaned.

'You know our Edith,' Avis said. 'Everything has to be just right before she'll show her face.'

Norman consulted his pocket watch. 'The coach leaves in three minutes,' he said, gravely.

'Oh, Lord!' Percy was annoyed. 'I'll have to go up and get her.' He started across the road.

'Freddy!' he called back. 'Don't let that coach go without us.'

'Don't worry, Percy, I'll lay down in front of the wheels if I have to.'

Percy ignored Freddy's flippancy and pressed on with his mission.

Freddy approached the driver. 'Bit of a hold-up with one of the ladies,' he said, nonchalantly. 'Hang on for a bit, there's a good chap.'

'Well I dunno about that,' the driver began, 'see, if I lose time at the start...'

Freddy cut him short.

'Here's something for your trouble,' he said, pressing a sixpence into the driver's sweaty palm.

'Oh! Right you are,' he said, touching the peak of his ornate cap before slipping the coin into his trouser pocket.

When Percy entered the hotel room he was stopped in his tracks by the sight of Edith standing in front of a mirror trying on a hat

'Edith! What on earth are you doing?'

'I can't make up my mind which of these to wear.' Edith held up two straw hats of contrasting styles. 'What do you think, this one or this?'

'Never mind about hats,' Percy fumed. 'There's a coach full of people waiting for you down there.'

'Then,' Edith said tartly, 'I must make sure I am properly dressed, mustn't I?'

Percy looked at his pocket watch.

'If you don't buck your ideas up my girl, that coach is going to leave without us and I'll be five bob out of pocket.'

Edith put on one of the hats, secured it with a hat-pin, and headed for the door.

'Please don't address me as 'my girl',' she said called back to him. 'It's fearfully common.'

As the late-comers crossed the road towards them, a ragged, ironic cheer went up from the passengers already on the coach which Edith acknowledged with a regal wave of her hand.

Once aboard, the driver climbed back into his cab and, with a honk of the horn, the journey began.

On the coach Norman and Lily were sitting together, as were Freddy and Avis. Edith and Percy were sitting slightly apart from the others behind a small boy and his mother.

As the coach left Shanklin and headed out onto the coastal road, the little boy turned round and looked at Edith. 'Please Miss, are you a film star?' he piped.

Edith laughed.

'No sonny,' said Percy, 'she just behaves like one.'

'Are you Paula Niggly?' the little lad said, kneeling up on his seat to get a better look.

'*Pola Negri*,' Edith said, smiling.

'Cor,' said the boy. 'I've got a cigarette picture of you indoors. Can I have your autograph?'

The boy's mother intervened.

'Manners, Cyril,' she admonished. 'Stop bothering the lady.'

'It's alright.' Edith smiled at the boy. 'Later on perhaps, when we stop at Alum Bay.'

The boy resumed his sitting position and looked up at his mother. 'That's Paula Niggly,' he said.

After visiting Ventnor and Freshwater Bay it was around noon when the coach pulled up on the cliffs above Alum Bay. As the passengers began to descend the steps that led down to the beach, the Ilford party stood for a moment taking in the magnificent view from the clifftop.

'Isn't it wonderful,' Lily said, throwing wide her arms as if to embrace the vista.

'Absolutely breathtaking,' Edith agreed.

'I bet the view's even better from up there.' Freddy pointed to the crest of a hill at the top of a steep, chalky path. 'Anyone game?'

Percy shook his head. 'You wouldn't catch me climbing up there. Not in my state of health.'

'Me neither,' agreed Norman. 'Anyway, it's lunch time.'

'I thought we were going for a swim,' Avis said, plaintively.

'Plenty of time,' Freddy replied. Then, turning to Edith. 'What about you, Edith? You willing to give it a go?'

Edith looked at Percy. 'Would you mind, dear?'

Percy puffed out his cheeks and exhaled. 'Rather you than me. Watch your step now.'

As the others made their way down the beach, Freddy and Edith started to climb to the crest, with Freddy leading the way.

As they neared the top, Edith got into some difficulty so Freddy took her by the hand and hauled her up the last few yards to the summit where they sat down on the grass and enjoyed the spectacular view of Alum Bay.

After a moment Edith removed her hat and laid back on the ground looking up at the cloudless blue sky. Freddy lay back beside her.

'What's going to become of us, Peidi?' he asked.

'What do you mean?'

'I'm in love with you,' Freddy said simply. 'Have been since I was twelve years old.'

Edith sat up. 'Don't talk rot,' she said sharply.

'And if I can't have you I might end up doing something desperate.'

'Now look here...' Edith began, but Freddy interrupted her.

'I mean it, Peidi,' he said seriously. 'Without you my life isn't worth living.'

Edith took a deep breath. 'Freddy, stop this kind of talk. You're eighteen years old for Heaven's sake! I am twenty-seven, a married woman, with a comfortable home, a good job and a loving family.' She paused for a moment. 'Do you really think I would jeopardize all that? My family would disown me, I would lose my job, and be branded a scarlet woman; then where would I be?'

'With me,' said Freddy.

'Oh, for Goodness sake talk sense.' Edith studied him for a moment. 'Percy may not be the most exciting man in the world, but he's decent, reliable...'

Again Freddy interrupted her.

'Tight-fisted and as dull as ditchwater! Oh, Peidi. How can you possibly want him rather than me?'

'Because he's *safe*, that's why.'

'And I'm not?'

'No, you're dangerous.'

'I thought you liked that?'

'Well you were wrong.'

Freddy suddenly grabbed her tightly by both wrists and pushed her back down on the grass.

As Edith struggled to get free, he forced her arms back over her head and lay on top of her.

'Freddy! Stop it!' she gasped. 'You're hurting my arms.'

'You like that too, don't you?' he said, looking down at her.

As Edith turned away from him, he released her wrists, grabbed her face with both hands, and kissed her. Edith squirmed and struggled to get free but Freddy held her firm. Then, as his kisses grew in intensity, Edith felt her resistance ebbing away and, abandoning all restraint, began to respond with a passion she had never thought herself capable of.

By now, Edith was in a ferment of sexual excitement and found herself unable to resist when Freddy began to unbutton the bodice of her frock.

As he began feverishly kissing her exposed breasts Edith dreamily opened her eyes - and froze.

'Oh, my God!' she cried, pushing Freddy away from her and struggling to cover herself up.

Freddy scrambled to his feet and looked around in alarm.

Looking down at them, his face a picture of innocent puzzlement, was Cyril, the young boy from the coach.

'Please, Miss,' he said, holding out a piece of paper and a pencil, 'can I have your autograph now?'

When they joined the rest of the party on the beach, Edith was still trembling; almost unable to believe what had just happened to her and trying to come to terms with the strength of her feelings towards Freddy.

Freddy, seemingly unperturbed, had gone off for a swim with Avis, and Norman and Lily had decided to go for a walk along the foreshore, leaving Percy and Edith alone.

As Edith was eating an egg and cress sandwich from her lunch pack, Percy suddenly remembered something.

'Did that little boy catch you?' he asked.

Edith was so startled she almost choked.

'Came looking for you,' Percy continued. 'Wanted your autograph, he said, so we told him where you were. Did he find you?'

'Yes,' she said, making a mental note to sit as far away as she could from young Cyril on the return journey.

'Nice little chap,' Percy said filling his pipe. 'Perhaps we'll have a lad like that one day.'

'Perhaps,' Edith said. But, in truth, nothing, absolutely *nothing*, was further from her mind. The whole idea of starting a family appalled her.

'Neither of us is getting any younger.' Percy lit his pipe. 'And twenty-seven is cutting it a bit fine, you know. Don't want to leave it too late, do we?'

Edith smiled wanly at Percy and, as she looked away to where Freddy was splashing around in the water with Avis, felt the first sting of jealousy

Friday night was always amateur talent night at the Osborne House. "Eddy" Edwards and his wife, Beryl, the owners, were a popular couple and their talent night, held in the hotel ballroom, had become a regular feature over the years.

Mr Edwards, resplendent in frock coat, frilly shirt and floppy bow tie as the jovial chairman, introduced each act with as much alliteration and grandiloquence as he could muster, invariably calling upon Mrs Edwards to close the proceedings by singing a popular song of the day in a rather wobbly contralto.

For the Ilford party the following morning was their departure day so, in order to make a special night of it, Freddy and Edith unbeknown to Percy, had arranged to take part in the show.

With the help of Mr Edwards, they had managed to borrow two costumes from a local Pierrot show and had been secretly rehearsing a song and dance routine.

On the night of the show, they had great difficulty persuading Percy to attend. He kept calling it a 'peep into purgatory' and tried to promote the idea of going to the 'Mariners Arms' where there was a piano and they could have a sing-song.

Having been out-voted by the rest of the party, who were all in on the secret, Percy reluctantly agreed and at 7.30 they duly took their seats.

Up on stage, a pianist, drummer and violinist, all in evening dress, sorted out their music and prepared themselves for their weekly ordeal.

Almost immediately, Percy's worst fears were realized when a little girl with pigtails came out and sang a song from 1900 called *'The Boers Have Got My Daddy'*. He was already looking longingly at the exit when she was followed by a Mr Pilbeam who launched into *'On The Road To Mandalay'* in a bass-baritone voice so resonant that it set the glasses rattling.

With escape impossible, Percy sought solace in alcohol and proceeded, slowly but surely, to get pie-eyed.

It was in the middle of a rendition of *'Because'* by a large lady in a pink frock that the drink began to take effect and as she reached, not entirely successfully, for a high note, Percy winced.

'Oohh! Somebody trod on the cat's tail,' he said, rather loudly.

'Sshh, Percy,' Avis hissed. 'People can hear you.'

It was at this juncture that first Edith, then Freddy, excused themselves and left the table - a departure that went unnoticed by Percy who was now in his cups.

'Why don't we all go down to 'the Mariners'?' Percy enquired loudly. 'Be quieter down there. Beer's cheaper too.' Again, he was hushed into silence by the others.

As the large lady's contribution came to a merciful end, Mr Edwards stepped out onto the stage applauding.

'Thank you, Miss Truscott,' he called. 'A truly memorable rendition I'm sure.'

'Well, it's one I won't forget in a hurry,' said a pixilated Percy, this time under his breath.

'And now, ladies and gentlemen,' Mr Edwards paused for effect, 'the penultimate performance on the programme. What seaside entertainment would be complete,' he asked rhetorically, 'without a Pierrot show? For your delectation and delight - Pierrot and Pierrette!'

The trio struck up the introduction to a wistful ballad called *'Feather Your Nest'* as Edith and Freddy appeared, dressed in pierrot make-up and costume.

Freddy sang the opening line.

'Oh sweetheart mine, it's wedding time
The whole world seems to say...'

Percy's jaw dropped open.

'Is that Freddy?' he asked, incredulously.

'Yes,' Lily whispered

'Good Lord! What on earth..?'

Edith sang the next few lines.

'Summer days are fading
Into loveland let us stray.
Hear the love birds sigh,
In the tree tops high.
Sweetheart they hum messages
Just for you and I...'

Percy's jaw had dropped even further.

'That's never Edith, is it?' he asked, unable to believe his eyes.

'Of course it is,' Avis said. 'Special surprise, just for you.'

'Well, I'll be blowed,' said Percy, a smile spreading across his face.

Edith and Freddy sang the song through once, did a brief soft shoe dance reprised the chorus, and took their bows to heartfelt applause.

Percy, quite carried away, was standing up shouting 'Bravo' rather loudly, clapping at a faster rate than anyone else and continuing to clap long after everyone else had stopped.

When the two arrived back at the table, bright-eyed with excitement, they were greeted with a chorus of congratulations.

Percy was overcome.

'Edith,' he said, emotionally, 'I am *so* proud of you, my dear. Proud as Punch. What a remarkable woman you are to be sure.'

Percy turned to the people on the next table. 'Talented woman, my wife, don't you think?' Then he turned to the table behind. 'She's a wonderful woman, my wife. What a lucky blighter I am. Don't you agree?'

Then, turning back to a highly embarrassed Edith, he leaned over to kiss her, lost his footing, and was only prevented from falling by the quick reflexes of Freddy, who caught him as he stumbled and helped him into his chair.

'Tripped over the cat,' Percy said, grinning foolishly.

Norman took Edith to one side.

'Percy's a bit worse for wear. I think the best thing would be to get him upstairs to bed, don't you? He'll be better off there.'

'Better off where?' Percy demanded, having caught the last part of the conversation.

'In bed,' Norman said. 'Early start tomorrow morning don't forget.'

'Norman's right, Percy,' Avis agreed. 'We could all do with a good night's sleep.'

'Bloomin' marvellous, isn't it?' groaned Percy. 'Just when I'm getting in the mood to enjoy myself, everyone wants to go to bed! Edie, you don't want to go to bed do you?'

'I think perhaps it might be best, Percy. Go on, dear. I'll be up presently.'

Percy rose unsteadily to his feet and squared his shoulders.

'Then your wish is my command,' he slurred. 'Gentlemen,' he turned to Norman and Freddy, 'would you be so kind as to escort me to my bedchamber? Stopping off at the throne room en route, if you please.'

As the two men led Percy away, Edith watched them go with some concern.

'I do wish Percy wouldn't drink so much,' she said sadly.

'He'll be alright.' Lily was reassuring. 'Good night's sleep and he'll be as right as rain in the morning.' Then, changing the subject. 'You two were jolly good up there tonight, you know,' she said nodding in the direction of the stage. 'How did you manage to get it off so pat in such a short time?'

'Well, we both knew the song, and Freddy picked up the dance steps in no time. He's a good dancer that boy.'

'Not like poor old Percy then. Two left feet?'

'Sometimes it feels like *three*!' Edith said, and they all laughed.

Their conversation was interrupted by a loud drum roll and a clash of cymbals heralding the entrance of Mr Edwards.

'And now, ladies and gentlemen, to conclude a superb evening's entertainment, here to sing for you *'One Little Hour'*, your hostess, and my own dear lady wife, Beryl.'

As the band played the introduction to the song and Beryl made a majestic entrance, Avis stood up.

'That sounds like my cue to leave,' she said.

'Don't go off to sleep too quickly, Avie,' Edith said. 'I want to have a chat with you before you go to bed.'

'Alright, but don't leave it too long. I'm all in.'

Just as Avis was about to leave, Freddy came back and joined the three ladies at the table.

'Percy is all safely tucked up,' he said.

'Thank you, Freddy,' Edith said, touching his arm.

'Norman's called it a day as well,' he said to Lily. 'He's off to bed.'

'I might as well go too, then.' Lily stood up. 'Early start tomorrow,' she reminded them.

'I'll come up with you.' Avis picked up her handbag.

'Good night, Freddy,' she said, kissing him on the cheek.

'Good night, old thing.'

Freddy watched as she and Lily walked off towards the door marked 'Residents Only'.

'You know my sister's gone on you, don't you?'

Freddy looked at Edith smiling up at him archly and sat down opposite her

'It's not your sister I want - it's you,' he said lowering his head despondently.

'What's the matter?' Edith asked.

'You know what's the matter,' Freddy said, gloomily. 'I love you and I can't bear the thought of going back tomorrow - me to Norwood, you to Ilford. Back to hole-and-corner meetings in pubs and tearooms. It's not enough any more, Peidi, I just want to be near you all the time.'

Edith smiled enigmatically.

'Perhaps that *could* be arranged,' she said.

Freddy looked up, a glimmer of hope in his eyes. 'How do you mean?'

Receiving no answer, he raised his voice.

'Peidi, what are you saying?'

'Ssshh!' Edith put her finger on his lips. 'Be patient, my love,' she whispered. 'I have a plan.'

On stage, as Beryl Edwards was rendering *'One Little Hour'*, Edith joined in. Leaning forward she sang quietly to Freddy.

'One little hour of moonlight
One little night of bliss.
Two lovers meeting
Tenderly greeting
What can be wrong in this?'

Upstairs in her room, Avis was sitting in her nightdress in front of the dressing table mirror, brushing her hair. when there was a knock on the door.

'That you, Edie?' she called softly.

'Yes.'

Avis opened the door and Edith came in. 'All ready for bed?'

'Just brushing my hair.' Avis sat down at the dressing table and resumed her toilet.

'Let me do that for you.' Edith took the brush from her and began to brush Avis's hair. 'I used to do this when you were little, remember?'

Avis nodded, smiling.

'You know Freddy is sweet on you, don't you?' said Edith, matter-of-factly.

'Do you think so?' Avis looked anxiously up at her sister's face in the mirror.

'Of course he is, he just told me so downstairs. And, if I'm not mistaken,' she went on, 'you are rather keen on him as well, aren't you?'

Avis chewed her lip.

'Come on, Avie,' she laughed, 'you can tell *me*.'

'Yes I am, Edie,' she confided. 'I like him a lot, but...'

'But?' Edith looked at her quizzically in the mirror.

'It's just that...well, sometimes I get the feeling he's just stringing me along.'

'Avie, how can you say that?' Edith chided. 'Why do you think he came on holiday with us? To spend more time with *you*, get to know you better.'

Edith could see her sister was not entirely convinced.

'Now, you listen to your big sister,' she ordered. 'The biggest problem you two have is one of separation. He's away at sea for three quarters of the year, then, when he does come home, he's in Norwood and you're in Manor Park. What he wants to do, and he's just told me this, is to find lodgings somewhere near to you, so that when you want to meet, it doesn't entail a long train journey across London.'

'Is that what he said?'

'Yes. Now listen. I have got a plan that will bring you closer together.' Edith paused before continuing. 'What if Freddy rented a room in *our* house?'

'Is that a possibility?'

Edith nodded.

'Percy's been talking about taking in a lodger when the Lesters move out and Freddy would be ideal. What's more,' she added, 'I'm sure Percy wouldn't say no to a bit of extra income.'

'Are the Lesters really going to move out?' Avis was beginning to warm to the idea.

'They're under notice,' Edith replied. 'It's only a matter of time before they find somewhere. And in the meantime, Freddy could have the little room at the back.'

'It's a topping idea, Edie.' Avis was enthusiastic. 'When will you talk to Percy about it?'

Edith hesitated momentarily.

'I thought,' she said slowly, 'that it might be better coming from *you*.'

'Me?' Avis was mildly surprised.

'Percy's very fond of you, Avie. He might find it harder to refuse you than he would me. I'll back you up of course.'

'Edie, you're a brick.' Avis held Edith's hand in hers for a moment.

'Just giving young love a leg-up, that's all,' Edith said, smiling.

Edith put down the hair brush and looked at Avis in the mirror.

'Look at that,' she said, running her hands through Avis's chestnut hair. 'Shiny as a conker.'

Edith slipped into bed beside a comatose Percy, and lay for a while listening to the ebb and flow of the surf on the beach below the window.

She was enormously fond of Avis and regretted having to use her in her scheme, but 'needs must when the devil drives'. Edith was shrewd enough to know that although Percy was not the most perspicacious of men, he was no fool. Any suggestion coming from her might have aroused suspicion and possibly ruined the whole plan. If her plan *did* succeed, she had little idea what the future would hold. She hadn't thought that far ahead. First things first. It was enough for the moment that, if everything worked out as planned, she would see her own dear, sweet boy every day when he wasn't at sea and that, for now, was all she wanted.

As Percy turned over with a grunt beside her, Edith smiled to herself. She was beginning to enjoy the thought of an illicit liaison with its, as yet faint, but heady scent of danger. She found it exciting, exhilarating. She was no longer an ordinary suburban housewife but a femme fatale planning an intrigue.

It was like a novel she had read recently entitled *'The Divided Heart'* in which a lady of high birth and social standing had given up everything for the love of a young man who worked as a gardener on her husband's estate; eventually running away with him and living in a crofter's cottage on a remote Scottish island. Not *quite* the same storyline as her own but one she could identify with risking everything for love, because that is what she was about to do.

The next morning Edith got up early, had breakfast and finished her packing quickly. She wanted to be out of the way when Avis sounded out Percy, so she set off for one last walk along the sea front, dropping in on her on her way out to say that now would be a good time to approach Percy.

It was another glorious morning with an unblemished, azure sky and bright sunlight dancing on an almost motionless sea.

As she wandered along the promenade, the sands below were already filling up as mums and dads staked out favourite spots, set up deck chairs, unpacked beach bags while children splashed in the shimmering water or, with bucket and spade were busy digging a moat for the biggest and best sand-castle on the beach.

Edith walked along the front a little further, found an unoccupied bench and sat with her hands in her lap looking out to sea.

On the distant horizon she could see the tiny speck of a ship. Looking at it reminded her of Freddy, and she wondered how Avis's talk with Percy was progressing.

She watched until the ship completely disappeared, leaving behind a thin ribbon of smoke hanging on the still air. Then, hearing a clock strike ten, she stood up and started to walk back.

When she reached the hotel, their baggage was stacked in the foyer and Percy was sitting in the residents' lounge reading a morning paper.

'Enjoy your walk?' he asked, as Edith sat down beside him.

'Lovely,' Edith said. 'Makes me wish we were staying a bit longer.'

'Avis popped in just after you left,' said Percy, putting down his paper. 'Wanted to know if we'd consider having Freddy in the house as a paying guest.'

Edith nodded.

'She mentioned something to me about that last night. I told her then, I didn't think it was very likely, but to talk to you about it.'

'Seems she wants her and Freddy to live closer to one another, or something of the sort,' he said.

'She's got a bit of a rave on him, you know,' Edith confided.

'More fool her,' Percy said, bluntly.

'Percy!' Edith was reproachful. 'That's not a very nice thing to say about my little sister.'

'I didn't mean...' Percy began. 'It's just that young Freddy strikes me as a bit of a gadabout, that's all.'

'I think you're being a bit unfair, dear,' Edith said. 'After all he's only eighteen.'

They sat in silence for a moment.

'What did you tell her?' Edith asked, trying to sound disinterested.

'I said I'd think about it.'

Edith's heart leapt. 'Oh! Yes, I suppose the extra income *would* come in useful. What do you think could we charge?'

'All found?' Percy asked.

'Twenty-five shillings a week?' Edith speculated.

'Twenty-seven and six, more like.' Percy was strict when it came to money matters.

'Come to think of it,' Edith mused, 'perhaps it's not such a bad idea after all. I mean, he'll be away at sea for at least nine months of the year, so it's not as though he'd be under our feet all the time.'

Percy nodded. He was beginning to warm to the idea.

'It might even force the Lesters to move out,' he said. 'Then we'd have the whole place to ourselves.'

Edith stood up and looked out of the window.

'Yes,' she said, 'it could be the answer to all our prayers.'

Chapter 4

*"There can never be any pride to stand in the way -it melts in
the frame of great love. I finished with pride oh! a long time ago -
do you remember? When I had come to you in the little room."*

The Lesters were an old fashioned, respectable working class family. Always paid their rent on time, never got into debt and kept themselves to themselves.

Mrs Lester was a small, energetic woman of fifty-two with a careworn, sharp-featured, pale face and greying, dark hair pulled tightly back and wound into a plaited bun at the nape of her neck.

Although never uncivil, Mrs Lester did not really get on with Edith. In her opinion she was too lah-dih-dah, thought herself a cut or two above her neighbours, and had too many airs and graces for someone who hailed from Manor Park!

Mr Lester was 60 years of age, but looked much older. A lifetime of smoking had left him with chronic bronchitis and emphysema; an affliction he bore stoically, and occasionally even with a sense of humour.

Their daughter, Nora, was an unmarried, shy, retiring woman of twenty-five who never seemed to leave the house except to go to work. Being the only bread winner in the family was a responsibility she had shouldered for some time and had come to accept as part of her lot in life.

Immediately after the party returned from the Isle of Wight, Freddy was invited round for Sunday tea and to have a look at the room.

It was a warm, sunny afternoon and Edith had decided to have tea in the garden, and Mrs Lester was giving her a hand.

As they were laying the table, Edith occasionally glanced up at the window of the little room that would be Freddy's bedroom if everything went according to plan.

Mrs Lester had not exactly welcomed the idea of someone else in the house, not with the toilet arrangements being as they were, but it was not her place to say so. 'A seaman you say, Mrs Thompson?'

They had finished laying the table and Mrs Lester was smoothing the wrinkles from the tablecloth,

'Merchant Navy.'

'Be off on his travels quite a bit then, I expect?'

'Every so often he will, yes.'

'Ah, here they come,' said Mrs Lester, as the two men came through the french window.

'Perfect timing,' Edith said. 'I was just about to call you. Freddy, this is Mrs Lester who shares the house with us. Freddy Bywaters.'

'Pleased to meet you, Mrs Lester,' Freddy said cordially, and extended his hand.

'Likewise, I'm sure,' said Mrs Lester as they briefly shook hands.

'I'll be off now.' Mrs Lester smoothed down her dress. 'Enjoy your tea,' she said as she went back into the house.

'Thank you for your help, Mrs Lester,' Edith called after her. Then, turning to the two men. 'Well, what's the verdict?'

'Pleasant room. Nice view of the garden.' Freddy paused. 'I think I'm going to be very happy here.' Then, unseen by Percy, he gave Edith a lascivious wink.

Edith managed to contain her excitement

'All settled then is it?'

'All settled *and* paid for!' Percy held up a five pound note. 'Young Fred has coughed up a month's rent in advance.'

Edith was aghast. 'Oh, Percy, you didn't..?'

'Wasn't my idea, it was his,' said Percy holding the fiver up to the light and examining it closely. 'I just hope it's a good one, that's all.'

'It should be,' Freddy rejoined, 'I made it myself this morning!' and all three laughed; Edith and Freddy because their plan had succeeded, and Percy because holding a five pound note in his hand always made him happy.

Freddy's introduction into the household went quite smoothly. Not having to get up early when on leave meant he was not part of the early-morning queue for the bathroom; a small blessing but an important one.

It wasn't very long, however, before Percy began to have second thoughts about the decision he had taken. Having an energetic young man about the house meant that Edith now had a tennis partner, and she and Freddy would often play on the courts in Valentines Park leaving him sitting on the sidelines. It seemed to Percy that everywhere they went, Freddy went along too; a presumption which had begun to irritate him a little.

He had also begun to feel that Edith was paying far too much attention to the young lodger; directing most of her conversation to him, laughing immoderately at his jokes,and asking his advice on subjects on which Percy felt he was far better informed than Freddy.

So much so, that after a while, a small seed of resentment began to germinate in his mind. His only consolation was that Freddy would be sailing out of Tilbury on September 3rd, some six weeks away.

Fortunately for his peace of mind, he had no idea of the intrigue going on behind his back, with Freddy and Edith meeting regularly at lunch times near her place of work and sometimes in the evening.

It was before one of these assignations that Freddy, finding he had plenty of time on his hands, decided to buy a new hat.

As he was coming out of Dunn's, the hatters and gentlemen's outfitters in Cheapside, sporting a new grey homburg, he bumped into Molly.

Molly was eighteen years old with a pretty, over made-up face and a broad cockney accent.

'Freddy Bywaters!' she squealed, throwing her arms around his neck and almost knocking off his new hat. 'Ooh, I say,' she said, pulling a posh face. 'You do look a toff in that 'at.'

Freddy re-set his hat to a jaunty angle.

'Just bought it,' he said. 'Gives me a certain *je ne sais quoi*, don't you think?'

'Ooh, 'ark at you with your parley voo,' she said, nudging him in the ribs with her elbow.

'Tell me,' Freddy said nonchalantly, 'what are you doing in Cheapside?'

'Never mind about that,' she retorted. 'I've got a bone to pick with you.'

Freddy grinned.

'What have I done now?'

'It's what you *'aven't* done, you dirty rotter.' Molly wagged a finger at him. 'When you went away you said you'd write to me from your ship every week. That was six months ago, and nothink - not a sausage.'

Freddy shrugged. 'Well, you know how it is.'

'Oh, I know how it is alright,' she said, narrowing her eyes dramatically. 'Once you get what you want off a girl you go and leave 'er in the lurch.'

'Molly,' Freddy said, insincerely. 'Would I do a thing like that to a nice girl like you?'

'You already 'ave, you beast.'

Freddy put his arm round her.

'Tell you what,' he said, 'let me buy you a glass of port at the Chapter House to make up for it.'

'My, we are splashing out today, ain't we?' she said, giving him a saucy look. 'A new 'at *and* a drink at the Chapter. 'as your ship come in or somethin'?' she said, and hooted with laughter at her witticism.

'Come on.' Freddy took her arm. 'It's my birthday on Monday. You can drink my health.'

As they walked off down Cheapside, Molly slipped her arm into his. 'You still livin' over at Norwood with your mum?'

'No. Got myself a new berth in Ilford now.'

'Oh I say. Goin' up in the world ain't we?' Molly said, laughing

Carlton & Prior was a wholesale milliners with premises at 168 Aldersgate

Street in the City of London.

Run by Mr Carlton and Miss Prior, the establishment boasted a liveried doorman named Jim, a showroom, workrooms and a sales department headed by Mr Dunsford while Edith, assisted by Lily Vellender and Rose Jacobs, took care of accounts and retail sales. Old habits died hard at Carlton & Prior, and although Edith had been married for over five years, she was still referred to as 'Miss Graydon'.

After the directors, Edith had by far the most important role. One reason was that she could speak French quite well - a valuable asset in the shop where a small, but significant number of wealthy clients were French or spoke French. And it was a measure of the directors' regard for Edith that she had been given her own 'office' with a frosted glass-panelled door, and just big enough for a desk, a chair and a hat stand.

It was approaching lunch time as Edith finished serving a Madame Dannier with a hat for an important garden party and was showing her to the door.

As soon as Madame Dannier had left, Edith glanced up at the big clock on the wall above the counter. It was almost one o'clock.

'I'll have that word with Miss Prior now, I think,' she said to Lily. 'Then I'll go to lunch. Sure you don't mind?'

Lily shook her head.

'Meeting, someone special?'

'Just a chum.' Edith smiled at Lily before going over to a door marked 'Private', and knocking.

'Come in.'

When Edith entered, Miss Prior was sitting at her desk, sorting through some correspondence.

'Miss Graydon,' she said, removing her pince-nez, 'I trust Madame Dannier left a happy woman?'

Miss Prior was a slim, elegant lady in her late fifties with iron-grey hair swept up in a chignon and secured with a tortoise-shell comb.

'I believe so.' Edith was a little tense.

'Miss Prior,' she began, 'I was wondering if I might have next Monday off? There are certain things of a personal nature I have to attend to, and I thought Monday, being a quiet day normally, might be the least inconvenient time to...'

Miss Prior interrupted her.

'My dear, Miss Graydon, there is no need to explain. Permission granted.'

Edith took a deep breath. 'Thank you very much, Miss Prior.'

'Not at all, my dear.' Miss Prior smiled at Edith, replaced her pince-nez, and returned to her letters.

Edith went back to her office and put on her outdoor clothes. As she was adjusting her hat in front of a small mirror she was thinking about the coming

Monday. All she had to do now was to somehow get Mrs Lester out of the house and the stage would be set for...exactly what she wasn't sure, but just thinking about it set her pulse racing.

To celebrate his 19th birthday on Monday 27th June, Freddy had booked a table for four at the Café Marguerite, a popular French restaurant in Oxford Street, with a small dance floor and a resident three piece band.

The four were to be: Percy and Edith, himself and Avis.

On the Sunday night, Percy was sitting up in bed waiting for his wife to join him.

Edith was sitting in her nightdress, slowly brushing her hair, with a faraway look in her eyes

Percy looked at the alarm clock on the bedside cabinet.

'Buck up, Edith,' he said impatiently. 'I've got to be up at seven.'

'Go off to sleep then.' Edith's mind was elsewhere.

'You know I can't sleep with the light on.'

Edith sighed a deep sigh and put down her hairbrush.

'It's alright for you,' Percy went on, 'you've wangled the day off tomorrow. Some of us aren't so lucky.'

Edith closed her eyes briefly, before replying. 'I did not *wangle* anything!' she said, an edge creeping into her voice. 'I was owed some time off and thought tomorrow would be a good time to take it, seeing that we're going out to supper in the evening.'

'I don't know where he gets his money from,' Percy sniffed. '*I* couldn't afford to take four people to the Café Marguerite, not with the prices *they* charge.'

Edith got into bed beside him.

'I don't see why *we* have to go along anyway,' Percy said. 'Why can't he just take Avis? I thought they were supposed to be walking out together.'

Edith shook her head. 'Percy, we can't back out now, it's all arranged.'

Percy was resigned. 'Alright, we'll go. But in future I think we ought to try to distance ourselves from Freddy a bit. Not in an unpleasant way, you understand, just keep him at arm's length so to speak. I mean, it's not as though he's one of the family is it?'

Edith leaned over and switched off the bedside lamp. 'Anything you say, Percy. Good night dear.'

She turned her back on him and snuggled down.

Percy sat thinking for a moment, then leaned over and kissed her bare shoulder.

Edith shrugged him off. 'Please, dear, not tonight,' she yawned. 'I'm very tired.'

Percy was hurt. 'You don't seem to have much time for me these days,' he said plaintively. 'What's the matter?'

'Nothing's the *matter*.' There was irritation in her voice. 'I have a full time job *and* a house to run. It isn't easy for me you know.'

Percy weighed up his words carefully before speaking. 'Then perhaps the time has come when you should think about *giving up* your job.'

Edith struggled to a sitting position and switched on the light. 'Give up my job?'

'Yes,' he said. 'It's no sort of married life with you gadding off to work every day.'

Edith was aghast. 'For Heaven's sake, talk sense.' She shook her head in disbelief. 'I'm earning as much as *you*! How could we possibly manage without my salary?' She paused for a moment, almost lost for words. 'You're talking absolute rot, and you know it.'

She switched out the light and burrowed down, pulling the bedclothes up tightly around her neck.

Percy settled down beside her, lying on his back. 'Well I'll tell you this, Edith,' he said, quietly. 'I'm beginning to feel a bit left out of things.'

After a restless night, Edith got up early and had breakfast with Percy, then saw him off to work.

As soon as he had gone, she went to the sideboard in the morning room where they kept their best china and took out part of a Royal Doulton "English Rose" tea set which had been a wedding present from Percy's mother. She put the crockery on a tray, took it into the kitchen and began to prepare breakfast for Freddy - two boiled eggs and toast and marmalade.

When it was ready, she popped a birthday card against the teapot and carried the tray up to his room.

After knocking and getting no reply, Edith went in and put the tray down on the end of the bed.

As she was opening the curtains, Freddy hauled himself up, rubbing the sleep from his eyes.

'Happy birthday, darling boy,' she said *sotto voce* as she set the tray down on his lap.

'I say! Breakfast in bed.' Freddy looked up at her and grinned. 'Whatever next?'

As Edith went to touch his face he tried to grab her hand but she snatched it away coquettishly. 'Patience, mon brave,' she whispered, and walked to the door.

At the door, she turned and blew him a kiss, as she had seen people do in countless plays. 'A bientôt,' she whispered, and made her exit.

Sitting in the morning room, Edith watched the hands of the clock on the mantelpiece move slowly around the dial to 10 o'clock and Mrs Lester still hadn't left the house. Edith couldn't imagine what was keeping her. She had offered to keep an eye on Mr Lester, giving Mrs Lester the rare opportunity to get out of the house for a few hours, something she seldom did now, and all the while time, precious time, was ticking away.

She got to her feet and went out into the garden where she stood, eyes closed, her face uplifted to the warming sun.

'Cooee! Mrs Thompson?'

It was Mrs Lester, at last, calling from the hallway. Edith made herself walk slowly through the morning room and out into the hall where Mrs Lester was waiting.

'Off now, Mrs Lester?'

'Yes. Be back about 2 o'clock, if that's alright?'

'Of course. No hurry. Take your time.'

'It's ever so good of you, Mrs Thompson. I don't get much chance to get out and about these days.'

'Off you go then,' Edith said briskly. 'I'll look after Mr Lester, don't worry.'

'I've left some soup on the gas stove for him,' Mrs Lester said. 'If you could warm a drop up for him about 12 o'clock time I'd be much obliged.'

'Yes, of course.' Edith was becoming impatient.

'Haven't seen Mr Bywaters about this morning.' Mrs Lester was rummaging in her handbag.

'No, it's his birthday so he's having a lie in.'

'How old is he now?' Mrs Lester had found the key she was looking for.

'Nineteen, I think.' Edith went to the front door and opened it.

'Still wet behind the ears then,' Mrs Lester said pleasantly as she stepped outside. 'Ta-ta, then.'

Edith closed the door, went into her front room and watched Mrs Lester's retreating figure until she was out of sight, then turned to look at herself in the oval mirror above the fireplace.

As she began to take the combs out of her hair, she could see that her hands were shaking. She shook out her hair, took a deep breath, climbed the stairs to Freddy's room and knocked on the door.

'Come in, Peidi,' Freddy called.

When Edith entered the room, Freddy was sitting up in bed, bare chested. The breakfast tray was on the bed beside him. His birthday card was standing on the bedside cabinet and his pyjamas were lying in a heap on the floor.

'Mrs Lester gone out?'

Edith, who was having trouble breathing, nodded her head.

'So we're alone in the house?'

Edith nodded again.

'Come to me, Peidi.' Freddy held out his arms, but Edith was so nervous she found herself unable to move. Freddy smiled. 'Alright then, I'll come to *you*.' He got out of bed and walked towards her.

Edith stared at him with a combination of fear and fascination. She had never seen a naked man before; let alone one in a state of sexual arousal. Percy was unduly modest when it came to nudity, and it was an unspoken arrangement between them that he invariably went upstairs first to get undressed and into his pyjamas before Edith came up.

She had no such qualms but, out of deference to Percy, had devised a method of undressing by taking off her outer garments, putting on her nightdress, and then removing her underwear.

Now, here was a young man with the body of a Greek god, sublimely unselfconscious, standing before her, smiling, and it was something of a shock. So much so that her legs began to tremble and she was forced to sit down on a chair.

Freddy came over and stood directly in front of her. 'What's the matter, Peidi?'

Edith shook her head.

'It's just that...you see, Percy is the only man I've ever...known...in that way, and I don't...I'm afraid I might...disappoint you.'

She looked up at him and smiled apologetically.

Freddy leaned down, helped her out of the chair and began to undo the buttons on the back of her frock.

'But you don't love Percy, you love me. Don't you?'

Edith's dress fell to the floor.

Suddenly she was no longer nervous.

Freddy continued talking to her as he removed her underwear. 'One day, Peidi, you and I will be together somewhere, I promise you.'

As Edith stepped out of her cami-knickers, Freddy swept her up in his arms, carried her over to the bed and threw her onto it, sending the breakfast tray crashing, unheeded, to the floor as he leapt on top of her.

During the next hour or so Edith's life was to change irrevocably.

The lovemaking between them was rapturous and uninhibited; by turns unbearably tender and agreeably rough.

By the time they both lay panting and perspiring in euphoric, post-coital exhaustion, a shift of seismic proportions had taken place within the heart, mind and body of Edith Thompson.

She was now an adultress and things could never be the same for her again. It was a thought that at once frightened and exhilarated her.

As she lay staring trance-like at the ceiling, Freddy passed his hand across her line of vision a couple of times to break the spell.

'Where have you been?' Freddy was smiling down at her.

'Over the hills and far away,' she said, dreamily. 'But I'm back now.'

'Good.' Freddy was reaching into the drawer of his bedside cabinet. 'I've got another little treat for you.'

He took out a battered tobacco tin, opened it up and showed Edith the contents. Inside were a number of hand-rolled cigarettes with the paper twisted at one end.

Edith took one out to examine it more closely. 'I didn't know you rolled your own cigarettes,' she said, surprised.

'I don't.' Freddy took the cigarette from her. 'These are special. They're what I call my 'funny fags'.'

The expression on Edith's face made him laugh. 'They contain hashish, my dear,' he whispered into her ear.

Edith's eyes widened. 'You mean they're doped?'

Freddy laughed again. 'Yes. Dreadful, isn't it? And what is more, you and I are going to share one right now. After which I shall have my wicked way with you.'

Freddy struck a match, held it to the twisted end, inhaled deeply and passed it over to Edith.

'I don't usual smoke during the day.'

'This isn't smoking, this is puffing. Just swallow the smoke and let it find its own way out. Go on,' he said, as Edith hesitated.

Edith put the cigarette tentatively between her lips, sucked in some smoke, and handed it back to Freddy.

'That's the idea,' Freddy said encouragingly.

After two or three more inhalations, Edith began to experience a wonderful feeling of well being coupled with an urge to laugh, which continued until the cigarette was finished when, true to his word, Freddy re-ignited the flame of passion still glowing inside Edith, and the merry-go-round began to revolve again.

The clock on the bedside cabinet showed a little after twelve and rain was running in jagged rivulets down the window pane as the two lovers lay asleep, entwined in each others arms.

Down below, slightly muffled, the street door banged.

Edith sat up with a start. 'What was that?'

She sat listening intently and heard another door open and close. 'Oh my God!' She leapt out of bed and began frantically dressing.

Freddy sat up. 'What's going on?' he said sleepily.

Edith put her finger to her lips. 'It's Mrs Lester,' she whispered hoarsely - 'She's come back early. She'll be up looking for me any minute.'

'Well, she won't come in here, will she?' Freddy seemed unconcerned.

'She'll see me coming out of your *room*,' Edith hissed. 'I know her. She'll be nosing around everywhere.'

Edith came over and sat down on the bed with her back to Freddy. 'Button up my dress,' she snapped. 'Quickly!'

As Freddy did up the buttons, Edith slipped on her shoes. Now fully dressed, she dashed over to the mirror trying vainly to do something with her hair.

'Mrs Thompson?' Mrs Lester was calling from below.

'Damn the woman!' Edith said vehemently.

She smoothed down her hair, picked up the breakfast tray, took a deep breath and opened the door.

'Time you were out of bed, young man,' she said closing the door behind her.

'Ah! There you are, Mrs Thompson.'

Mrs Lester was standing at the bottom of the stairs, an inquisitive gleam in her eye.

'You're back early, Mrs Lester,' Edith said, descending the stairs.

'Yes, it came on to rain and I didn't have a brolly with me, so I thought meself might as well get the bus back home.' Mrs Lester studied Edith for a moment. 'Mr Bywaters still in bed then, is he?'

'Yes,' Edith said, brusquely.

'Alright for some, eh?'

'I'm afraid,' Edith said, 'I haven't had time to give Mr Lester his soup yet.'

'Oh, don't you worry about that. I'll do it meself now I'm back. Oh!' Mrs Lester had noticed something amiss on the tray. 'You've broken one of your best cups.'

Edith had been unaware of this until now but dissembled adroitly.

'Yes, stupid of me,' she said. 'I put the tray down on the edge of the bed for a moment and it slipped off.'

'Tsk, tsk, tsk!' Mrs Lester made a sympathetic clucking noise with her tongue. 'What a shame. Still, accidents *will* happen, won't they?'

'Indeed.' Edith was abrupt. 'Now if you'll excuse me, I must get on.'

As Edith walked away, Mrs Lester noticed that buttons on the back of her dress were done up wrongly. She thought about it for a moment, then looked up the stairs at Freddy's bedroom door. When she turned back again a frown of suspicion was wrinkling her brow.

Chapter 5

"I feel so proud - so proud to think and feel that you
are my lover and, even though not acknowledged, I can
still hold you - just with a tiny 'hope'."

The night at the Café Marguerite proved to be a great success. Going 'up West' was always something of an event and everyone had dressed up to the nines for the occasion.

Edith, looking radiant, was in sparkling form, and she and Freddy turned a few heads when they took to the dance floor for a tango. In spite of his misgivings, Percy enjoyed the evening; even allowing himself to be coaxed into dancing with Edith, and managing to get around the floor without too many stumbles.

He was inordinately proud of her, and watching her that night brought home to him once again, his extreme good fortune in having such a delightful woman as his wife.

At the end of the evening, emboldened by several glasses of unaccustomed wine, his feelings towards her were such that he could hardly wait for her to join him in bed.

When he did finally attempt to press his intentions upon her, he was immediately rebuffed. Once again, Edith pleaded tiredness, but the real reason was she could not bear the thought of being touched by her cuckolded husband. When Percy persevered, Edith became annoyed.

'Percy, for Heaven's sake,' she said, pushing him away, 'have a little consideration.'

'A little consideration' was exactly what Percy felt *he* was entitled to but he did not pursue the matter and, once again, found himself lying awake in the dark feeling hurt and resentful.

Lying beside him, Edith's thoughts were all of Freddy. Was he, she wondered lying awake thinking of her?

Only a few yards away, Freddy was indeed lying awake, but thinking only that he would need to stop spending money at this rate or he was going to be broke well before his next trip.

The following morning, Edith and Percy were sitting on the opposite sides of the breakfast table awaiting the arrival of the porridge Mrs Lester was preparing.

Percy was hidden behind the *Daily Sketch*, which was fine by Edith who didn't feel like talking anyway. She was gazing out of the french windows when Mrs

Lester came bustling into the morning room carrying two steaming bowls of porridge.

'There you are,' she said, putting the bowls down in front of them. 'Line your stomach all morning, that lot will.'

Mrs Lester set great store on the nutritional merits of a bowl of porridge. She watched as they poured on milk and sprinkled sugar before speaking.

'Enjoy your meal out last night, did you?'

'Yes, very nice.' Edith was in no mood for a cosy chat with Mrs Lester.

'French, was it you said?'

'Yes,' Percy was more forthcoming. 'Not the sort of thing you'd want to eat every day of course, but it made a nice change.'

'You wouldn't catch me eatin' that sort of thing.' Mrs Lester folded her arms across her bosom in a gesture of defiance.

'French cuisine isn't all frog's legs and horse meat you know, Mrs Lester.' There was a hint of sarcasm in Edith's voice which did not go entirely unnoticed.

Mrs Lester was not to be put off. 'Give me the roast beef of old England any day,' she said patriotically, and walked over to the door. 'Oh, by the way.' She turned back, a glint of malice in her eye. 'My Nora says you can get them cups in Gamage's.'

'Cups?' Percy looked up from his porridge.

'The Royal Doulton, same as the one Mrs Thompson broke. Mind you,' she added, 'they're not cheap.'

Edith felt a rush of anger at Mrs Lester's interference but remained outwardly calm.

Percy turned to Edith 'How did that happen?'

Before Edith could reply Mrs Lester delivered the *coup de grâce*. 'Doing a good turn, would you believe? Giving Mr Bywaters his breakfast in bed. Just shows you, doesn't it? Ah well, I'll be off now.'

As soon as the door had closed behind Mrs Lester, a heated exchange of views took place, *sotto voce*.

'What on earth were you thinking of?' Percy wanted to know, 'going into that young man's bedroom.'

Edith sighed. 'Percy, all I did was take him his breakfast in bed as a birthday treat.'

'Don't you see how easily something like that can be misconstrued?'

'Oh for Heaven's sake!' Edith feigned exasperation. 'It was all perfectly innocent, I can assure you.'

'*I* know that,' Percy said, 'but it's Mrs Lester. You know what a dreadful old gossip she is.'

Percy went back to his porridge, and breakfast continued in silence.

Upstairs in the bathroom Freddy was standing at the wash basin shaving and singing quietly to himself:

'All the nice girls love a sailor
All the nice girls love a tar.
For there's something about a sailor
Well you know what sailors are?'

He splashed some cold water on his face, looked up and winked at himself in the mirror.

Later, as they were walking to the station together, Percy returned to the subject of Edith's indiscretion. 'I'll tell you straight, Edith,' he said firmly, 'I'm not at all happy with the amount of attention you pay young Bywaters.'

Edith looked up at him and smiled. 'Why, Percy Thompson,' Edith slipped her arm, into his, 'I *do* believe you're jealous.'

'Nonsense,' Percy said stiffly. "It's just a matter of decorum, that's all.'

As they walked arm in arm along Belgrave Road, Edith realized that any further assignations with Freddy would have to take place somewhere well away from the beady eye of Mrs Lester.

In fact, she and Freddy had already arranged a lunchtime rendezvous at Fuller's tearooms in Fann Street.

When Edith arrived there, slightly breathless and pink-cheeked with excitement, Freddy was sitting at a corner table waiting for her.

As soon as she had settled, Edith opened her handbag, took out a lilac coloured envelope, and pushed it across the table to Freddy.

'What's this?' he asked.

'A billet-doux.'

'A what?'

Edith leaned across the table.

'A love letter from a mysterious lady admirer,' she whispered conspiratorially.

Freddy grinned.

'I'll read it later,' he said putting it in the breast pocket of his jacket.

'Don't forget to destroy it afterwards, darlint,' Edith said, picking up the menu. 'We don't want to leave any incriminating evidence lying about, do we?'

It was a measure of the esteem in which Edith was held at Carlton & Prior that Mr Carlton had offered her the loan of his car.

He had heard Edith and Lily discussing a picnic trip to Epping Forest at the weekend and been prompted to make the offer which had been eagerly and gratefully accepted.

Lily's husband, Norman, was an experienced driver and he was at the wheel of Mr Carlton's dark green Vauxhall open tourer when it pulled up outside number 41 early on a fine Sunday morning in July.

As Lily and Avis sat in the back chatting, Norman gave a couple of honks on the horn before getting out and lifting the bonnet to check the oil and water.

The sound of the motor horn brought Mrs Lester to her front room window. She had heard all about the trip from Percy and could barely contain her curiosity.

Looking through her net curtains, she watched as Percy appeared carrying a hamper which he stowed in the boot of the car.

Then Edith made her entrance, walking down the pathway to the car in a mincing manner, twirling a parasol over her shoulder.

'There she goes,' Mrs Lester said to her husband, propped up in an armchair behind her. 'Miss High and Mighty, full of herself as usual. Couldn't go on the bus like everybody else, could she? Oh no, not Lady Muck. Gets her boss to lend her 'is car, she does.'

Mrs Lester watched as Edith got into the back of the car with Avis and Lily and give a regal wave to the empty street.

'Well, with *all* her airs and graces she's no better than she ought to be, you mark my words.'

With Percy sitting up front with Norman, the car moved off up the road.

Mrs Lester turned from the window. 'How about a nice kipper for your breakfast, dad?'

As the car thrummed along on the road to Epping, Norman glanced towards Percy. 'I'm surprised young Bywaters isn't with you.'

He had to raise his voice to be heard above the noise of the engine and the rush of the wind.

'For this relief, much thanks!' Percy shouted back.

Norman laughed. 'He does seem to cling on to your coat tails a bit, I must say.'

'A *bit*?' Percy raised his eyes heavenward. 'Sticks to us like blooming fly-paper!'

'Where is he today?' Norman asked.

Edith leaned forward from behind. 'He's gone over to see an aunt of his in Theydon Bois,' she said. 'But he might try to catch up with us later on.'

Avis leaned forward. 'Do you think we *will* see him?'

'Not if I see him first!' Percy retorted.

'Don't be so beastly,' Avis said, and playfully pulled his cap down over his eyes.

One of the objectives of their trip to Epping was to visit a church with a derelict graveyard Edith had come across once during a school ramble and had always wanted to explore more fully.

They parked the car on the outskirts of the forest and made their way through the trees and undergrowth to where Edith thought the church might be located.

It was a warm day and Percy, who was carrying the hamper, stopped for a moment to wipe his brow. 'How much further?' he wanted to know.

'Nearly there. Don't despair,' said Edith who had appointed herself leader of the expedition. 'I think it's just beyond the next clearing.'

While the group had stopped,they were unaware that a shadowy figure had been watching them from behind a nearby thicket of bushes, and that as they moved off again, the 'watcher' was steathily following them.

It wasn't long before Edith found what she had been looking for.

There was now very little of the church left standing, and the graveyard was badly overgrown, with most of the tombstones having either fallen over or leaning at precarious angles.

Graveyards had never been high on Percy's list of fun places to visit so, leaving the rest of the party to wander around the cemetery, he found himself a convenient family vault with a flat top and perched himself on the edge.

He was beginning to wonder how much longer it would be before they reached The Forester's, when a figure with a hideously deformed face reared up beside him emitting a blood-curdling shriek.

Percy let out a cry of fear, lost his balance and fell off the gravestone onto the ground.

As the rest of the party looked round in alarm, the 'apparition' removed a joke mask - to reveal the laughing face of Freddy.

'Oh, Percy, you should have seen your face!' Freddy did a grotesque impersonation of Percy's horror-stricken face.

As the rest of the group tried to suppress their smiles, Percy scrambled to his feet, scarlet faced with anger and humiliation.

'You damned young ass!' he roared. 'What the Hell do you think you're playing at?'

Freddy was taken aback by Percy's furious reaction. 'Keep your shirt on, Percy. 'It was only a joke.'

'A *joke*?' Percy was spluttering with rage.

'A damn silly one if you ask me.' Edith felt she ought to support her husband.

'Don't you know Percy's got a weak heart?' added Norman.

Freddy was abashed. 'Sorry, Percy. I didn't think.'

'No, that's your trouble, my lad.'

Percy was still furious.

'I've said I'm sorry. What more can I do?'

'I'll tell you what you can do,' Percy said, fixing him with a look. 'You can carry this hamper for a start. And when we get to The Forester's, the drinks are on you.'

This imposition was greeted with a chorus of approval.

Freddy grimaced. 'I say, that's a bit thick.'

'Yes,' Percy said, poking Freddy in the chest with his finger, 'just like you,

Sonny Jim.'

When the others laughed at this, Percy was mollified to some extent. He had put Freddy in his place and regained some lost dignity. He even allowed himself to be cajoled into posing for the inevitable group photograph by Avis. But as he stood with a rather strained smile on his face, a feeling of animosity had begun to ferment inside him. Apart from a few reservations, Percy had always rather liked Freddy. Once he had even spoken up for him when he had got himself in trouble with the P&O Line for leaving his ship without permission to attend a New Year celebration at 231. But now, the tide that had been turning for some time, was in full flood, and resentment was replacing tolerance. Percy was determined that somehow or other when Freddy went off to sea on his next trip, he would not be returning to the Retreat.

Chapter 6

"I suppose we must make a study of deceit for some time longer.
I hate it. I hate every lie I have to tell to see you because
lies seem such small, mean things to attain such an object as ours."

Towards the end of July, Edith and Freddy arranged another assignation. Edith had invented a dental appointment to get off work early and went to meet Freddy at Victoria Station. After a couple of glasses of port in the buffet bar they left the station by a side entrance and traversed several mean side-streets, before ending up outside a seedy boarding house named, rather grandiosely, The Balmoral.

The place had such a disreputable look about it that Edith was initially reluctant to step over the threshold. But, after being reassured by Freddy, she allowed herself to be led into a dark hallway that smelt strongly of cats. Finding nobody in attendance behind the reception desk, Freddy rang the bell on the counter.

'How e*ver* did you come to know about this place?' Edith asked, lowering her voice.

'My shipmate, Dan, told me about it. "Rooms available and no questions asked",' Freddy laughed, 'he calls it the *"Immoral"*!'

Edith did not share his amusement. It offended her sensibilities even to be *seen* in such a place, let alone making use of its sleazy services. She was about to ask Freddy how he had found it so easily, when the arrival of the concierge curtailed any further conversation.

She was a stooped, elderly woman with an incredibly wrinkled face dressed entirely in black. 'Yes?' she croaked.

'Mr Horniman.' Freddy was businesslike. 'I telephoned earlier.'

As the old lady turned away to unhook a key from a numbered board behind her, Freddy winked at Edith.

'Seven and six.' The concierge held out a claw-like hand into which Freddy dropped three half crowns. 'Number 10, first floor, turn left at the top of the stairs,' she said, handing over the key before shuffling off.

When they let themselves into the room Edith's heart sank. The floor was covered in a dark green linoleum and the only furniture was a wash stand, a hard-backed chair and a bedstead with a small well worn rug by the side.

In spite of the dismal surroundings, the lovemaking was joyous and unrestrained. Once again Edith was transported, helped in part by another of Freddy's 'funny fags', after which she was susceptible to suggestion and more inclined to experiment.

It was almost 5.30 when they left The Balmoral, shielding their eyes as they walked out of the gloom into the dazzling late-afternoon sunshine. For Edith it was exactly the same experience as coming out of a matinée, emerging from the semi-darkness of a theatre into the stark light of reality with the sudden realization that the real world had been out there all the time, unheard, unseen and, for a short while, unimportant.

Outside Victoria station, Freddy saw her onto the omnibus that would take her to Liverpool Street, from where she could catch her train back to Ilford.

As the bus drove up Victoria Street she saw Freddy wandering off in the direction of Hyde Park and wondered where he would be spending the evening.

He always arrived back at number 41 late at night; usually long after Edith had fallen asleep and she had often speculated on where he had been and with whom. As the train to Ilford pulled out of the platform, her thoughts turned to her husband.

Percy was becoming more and more insistent on his conjugal rights, his 'home comforts' as he called them, and she was uncertain how much longer she could go on denying him before he became suspicious. In fact Percy had already confided in Norman Vellender about his matrimonial problems when they had met up for a drink one evening where, after a couple of pints, he had unburdened himself.

Norman could offer no explanation other than it was a well known fact that women were sometimes subject to inexplicable mood changes and that, with a little more patience on Percy's part, he was sure normal service would be resumed before too long.

Percy was not so certain. A suspicion had begun to permeate his mind, and that suspicion was focussed on Freddy. Not that he suspected anything untoward was going on, he assured Norman, but Freddy's presence in his house was somehow having an unsettling effect on his married life. 'And I'll tell you this, Norman,' he said resolutely, 'I'm going to do something about it.'

The opportunity was to arrive somewhat sooner than he had anticipated.

It was August Bank Holiday Monday, 1921 and the *ménage à trois* was sitting in the back garden enjoying the afternoon sun.

Edith and Percy were sitting together on a wicker seat. Edith was doing some sewing and Percy was glancing through the *Sunday Pictorial* while Freddy was sprawled out on the lawn reading a book.

Percy was not in the best of humours.

Earlier on, as Edith and Freddy had walked around the garden looking at the various plants and floribunda, Freddy had plucked a flower and presented it to her with a bow to which she had responded with a 'little-girl' curtsey, putting her index finger under her chin.

This incident had irritated Percy beyond measure. 'How *dare* this young whippersnapper, a lodger in *his* house, presume such an intimacy with *his* wife?'

He was still seething when Freddy spoke up.

'You were right about this book, Edith,' he said. 'Rattling good yarn. Have you read it, Percy?' He held up *'The Garden of Allah'* by Robert Hichens.

'Percy doesn't read books. Do you, dear?' Edith said, rather unkindly.

'Not that sort of trash I don't,' Percy responded without looking up from his newspaper.

'You should read a book before condemning it, Percy,' Freddy reasoned. 'You never know, you might even enjoy it.'

Percy lowered his paper. 'Let me tell you this, young fellow. You and my wife may enjoy reading about the exploits of idiotic people in unbelievable situations, but I have something better to do with my time.'

There was silence for a moment as Edith looked in her needlework basket.

'Oh, I need a pin! Percy, be a dear and fetch my pin cushion would you? I've left it upstairs on my dressing table.'

'Why don't you ask Freddy?' said Percy, not looking up from his paper.

Edith frowned. 'Because I'm asking *you*,' she said pointedly.

Percy made no reply, and there was a moment of tension broken by Freddy getting to his feet.

'On your dressing table, did you say?'

'Yes. Thank you, Freddy.' Edith was tight lipped. 'It's nice to know there is *one* gentleman in this house.'

As soon as Freddy had left on his errand, Edith turned to Percy. 'What an ill-mannered man you are,' she said icily.

'Not like your little lackey, eh?' Percy was vituperative. 'Your little lap-dog? You like to have someone tacked onto you to run all your little errands and obey all your little requests don't you? Well you'd better make the most of it my girl because he may not be around for much longer.' Percy allowed himself a grim smile of satisfaction.

Edith was incensed. 'Do *not*,' she said through gritted teeth, 'address me as 'my girl'. I am *not* your *girl*, I'm your *wife*!'

'Then it's about time you started behaving like my wife.'

Tempers were fraying.

'What do you mean by that?' Edith demanded.

The arrival of Freddy with the pin-cushion precluded any further discussion.

'Thank you, Freddy,' Edith said over-graciously.

Percy snorted. 'Aren't you going to throw him a biscuit?' There was another moment of tension, again broken by Freddy.

'I think I'll take a stroll to the park before tea,' he said diplomatically. 'Be about twenty minutes.'

Edith waited to hear the front door slam before rounding on Percy.

'Good heavens, man,' she fumed, 'have you no sense of propriety?'

'I could ask exactly the same of you,' he retorted. 'Do you think I haven't noticed you making eyes at that little whelp? Eh? How you always agree with everything he says and deride everything *I* say?'

Edith stood up. 'I am not going to listen to this nonsense any longer,' she said, and stamped off into the morning room where she began noisily to lay the table for tea.

Percy appeared in the doorway behind her. 'I'm not a fool, Edith. Although I know you take me for one.'

'Just what do you mean by that?' She turned to face him. 'I think you must be taking leave of your senses?' she said icily

'On the contrary, Edith.' Percy spoke quietly. 'I'm just coming to them. And I'll tell you this. When Bywaters comes back I'm giving him his marching orders.'

Valentines Park was thronged with people for the Bank Holiday afternoon: parents with young children, all in their Sunday best, young lovers hand in hand and spotty-faced youths ogling the laughing girls who strolled up and down the broadwalk in their bright summer frocks. Around the park, cricket matches were in progress, while the younger children found other ways to amuse themselves; the girls bowling hoops and the boys sailing their model boats on the lake.

Freddy stopped briefly by the lake to watch some small children feeding the ducks from the lapping water's edge, almost overbalancing as they threw pieces of bread out to the squabbling birds.

Hearing a church clock strike, Freddy looked at his watch. 4.30. Time for tea.

As he let himself into the house, he surprised Mrs Lester listening outside the morning room door.

So engrossed had she become in the row going on inside, that she had not heard the key in the lock but, although slightly flustered at having been caught eavesdropping, was not unduly fazed.

'Oh, it's you, Mr Bywaters,' she said, walking towards him.

'Yes, Mrs Lester.'

'I was just thinkin' of getting Mr Lester his tea, but I'll leave it now for a bit. She opened the door to her living room. 'Mr and Mrs Thompson are having words,' she said, confidentially before going inside and closing the door.

Freddy stood for a while outside the morning room door, uncertain what to do.

Inside, the argument had expanded, as domestic rows often do, to include their respective families. Behind the door he could hear Edith berating Percy on the shortcomings of his.

'At least *my* family know how to enjoy themselves,' she ranted. 'Sometimes it's as much as your people can do to crack a smile. Miserable bunch of so-and-sos.'

Percy's voice became hoarse with rage. 'How dare you? he shouted. 'My family have been very good to us, and I will not have you doing them down.' The veins were standing out on Percy's temples. 'Now I forbid you to say anything more against them. Do your hear?'

'I'll say what I damn well please,' Edith screamed back at him.

Percy's voice was breaking with rage. 'I'm warning you...' he roared.

Freddy's hand was already on the doorknob.

'Don't touch me,' Edith shrieked as Percy moved towards her. 'Argh!'

Hearing the sound of a chair overturning and the thud of a body hitting the floor, Freddy burst into the room to find Edith lying on the floor holding her arm and crying, with Percy staring at her in shock.

'You've broken my arm, you brute,' she wailed.

At this, Freddy grabbed Percy and swung him round. 'You swine!' he shouted. 'What kind of man are you, hitting a woman?'

Percy was aghast. 'I never touched her,' he protested. 'She fell over the...'

Before he could finish, Freddy grabbed him by his lapels, slammed him up against the wall, and confronted him eye to eye. 'If you ever lay hands on Edith again,' he hissed, 'I'll give you the biggest hiding of your life. You hear?'

Percy was now incandescent with rage. 'Get out, Bywaters,' he bellowed. 'This is nothing to do with you.'

As the two men lurched round the room struggling with each other, Edith became hysterical.

'Stop it! Stop it, both of you,' she cried. 'For God's sake *stop* it!'

The men relinquished their hold and stood glowering at one another. Percy, scarlet faced and breathing heavily, struggled to control himself.

'Alright, Bywaters,' he panted with as much composure as he could muster, 'go upstairs, pack your bags and get out of my house *now*! I will not have you spending another night under my roof.'

Freddy drew himself up.

'If I go, I shall take Edith with me,' he said, truculently. 'I'm not leaving her here to be abused by you.'

Percy regarded Freddy with undisguised contempt.

'My wife,' he said with heavy emphasis, 'will not be going anywhere with a guttersnipe like you.'

'That decision,' Freddy said coolly, 'is not yours to make. It is Edith's.'

Percy turned to Edith who was sitting in a chair nursing her arm.

'Did you hear what this upstart just said? he asked incredulously.

Edith looked up for a moment then lowered her head.

'I see,' he said grimly. 'The choice *does* seem to be yours. Very well, here it is. You leave, right now, with this...*person*, or stay here with me and try to resolve our differences. Which is it to be?'

'I'm not...' she began. 'I can't make...Oh God! It's all such a mess.' She broke down weeping.

Freddy went over and knelt beside her. 'Come with me, Edith,' he pleaded. 'I'll look after you.'

Percy gave a snort of derision. 'On what?' he demanded scornfully. 'Your wages as a cabin boy on a tramp steamer?'

Freddy stood up. 'I am *not* a cabin boy,' he protested. 'I'm a ship's...'

Percy shouted him down. 'Because that's all you'll have to live on,' he said threateningly, 'once Mr Carlton and Miss Prior get to hear about this, and they *will* get to hear about it, I can assure you of that.'

Edith turned away, distraught.

'Don't let him bully you,' Freddy said desperately.

'And where would you live, Edith?' Percy continued, beginning to sense victory. 'With his mother and the rest of the litter in Norwood? In a house with no bathroom and an outside lavatory? Is that what you want?'

Edith remained silent.

'It's up to you, Edith.' Percy's voice took on a harder edge. 'But I must warn you. If you walk out of that door you will never be allowed back - ever! On the other hand, if you decide to stay, things will have to be a very different from what they have been of late. Now then, which is it to be?'

Both men looked at Edith who was sitting, shoulders hunched, staring at the floor. Percy now felt more in command of the situation.

'Well?' he said sternly. 'I'm waiting.'

When Edith finally spoke, her voice was no more than a whisper.

'I want to stay,' she said, without looking up.

Freddy gasped.

Percy, relishing his moment of triumph, leaned towards Edith and cupped his hand to his ear.

'What was that?' he said, obliging her to repeat herself.

'I want to stay,' she said flatly, head bowed.

Percy, his face flushed with success, straightened up and turned to the crestfallen Freddy.

'You heard what my wife said, Bywaters,' he spat. 'Now get out of my house. If you haven't gone within ten minutes I shall fetch the police and have you removed.'

Freddy gave one last despairing glance at Edith, then turned on his heel and left the room

A few moments later Edith followed and made her way up to her bedroom where she locked the door behind her.

The shouting that had occurred during the fracas had enabled Mrs Lester, with her door slightly ajar, to follow the dramatics line by line. Now she watched, wide-eyed, as a grim faced Freddy stormed out of the morning room and bounded up the stairs to his bedroom.

''e's slung 'im out,' she whispered to her husband who was sitting up in his chair awaiting the next bulletin. 'And not before time if you ask me,' she continued. 'I knew that young shaver was trouble the minute I clapped eyes on 'im.'

Her lips pursed in disapproval. 'Nice goings-on, I must say. I don't know what the neighbours must think, I'm sure.'

Her ear still cocked for any further developments, Mrs Lester heard the morning room door being closed and, realizing that the curtain had been lowered on the drama, quietly closed her own door.

Upstairs, Edith was sitting on the side of the bed still nursing her arm and thinking about the disturbing turn of events.

During the fracas certain emotions had surfaced which she would have preferred to have stayed hidden, and words better left unsaid had been spoken. She blamed herself for over-reacting. Percy had not assaulted her - he hadn't even pushed her - she had stumbled over a chair and sustained nothing worse than a badly bruised elbow. However, it didn't do any harm to let Freddy think Percy was a violent man; it might make him more anxious to protect her. Now Freddy, in his hot-headed way, had let the cat out of the bag, but perhaps this too was no bad thing. It was bound to happen at some time - now it was sooner rather than later.

As for the future...she would have to wait and see.

Alone in the morning room, Percy was wracked by conflicting emotions as he struggled to come to terms with the fact that something had been going on between his wife and Bywaters behind his back - in his own house! Something serious enough for Bywaters to threaten to take Edith away from him. His only consolation was that she had declined to go. A small consolation, but an important one because it meant Edith had chosen the *status quo* in preference to an uncertain future.

He could not bring himself to believe that anything of a sexual nature had taken place between them. Edith had never been interested in the physical side of their marriage and he came to the conclusion that, being a romantic sort of woman, Edith had had her head turned by the attentions of a younger man and a mild flirtation had ensued which had somehow got out of hand.

Although still shaken by the upheaval that had taken place, he felt he had acquitted himself rather well in the circumstances. He had stood up to Bywaters and sent him packing, given Edith an ultimatum, and re-asserted his authority as master in his own house. The next few weeks would be difficult but he was sure he would win back the affection of his wife and show her the error of her ways.

Heartened by this uplifting thought, he resumed laying the table for tea.

Meanwhile Mrs Lester had positioned herself at her front room window determined not to miss the final act of the drama - Freddy Bywaters's exit.

She had not long to wait. A pounding of footsteps down the stairs followed by a loud slamming of the front door announced Freddy's departure.

She watched in grim satisfaction as he stamped up the pathway carrying a suitcase and a sailor's kit bag, turned left at the garden gate and marched off.

'Good riddance to bad rubbish!' was her final comment on the events of the afternoon. Then, rearranging the lace curtains, she turned to her slightly bewildered husband. 'The winkle man's down the road. Shall I nip out and get us a pint for our tea?'

Chapter 7

"Mine is a real live cage with a keeper as well...
to whom I have to account to every day, every hour,
every minute."

His sudden departure from number 41 left Freddy no alternative but to return to Westow Hill.

Upon reflection he regretted his outburst and the distress it had caused Edith, but life would not be all that different. He and Edith could still meet as they had been doing. His biggest regret was that, once again, he had allowed his temper to get the better of him - a failing that had landed him in trouble on more than one occasion.

Meanwhile, in order to allay any suspicions Percy might be harbouring, Edith had effected a reconciliation of a sort with him. To his delight, she began to allow him his 'home comforts' from time to time, even though the whole business of sexual relations with him had become increasingly repugnant to her.

As for Percy, he had good reason to be pleased with himself. Bywaters had been banished, his wife had come to her senses, and at work, he'd received a rise of seven shillings and sixpence. It didn't make up the loss of Freddy's rent money but it helped. And he did have his wife back.

It was to celebrate this increase to his weekly wage packet that he met up with three of his colleagues after work one evening for a drink.

Jack Reed and Bert Nuttall worked in despatch, while Miss Tucknott worked in the accounts department.

Like so many women of her generation, the carnage of the Great War had all but ruined any chance of marriage and at the age of 29, Alice Tucknott still lived with her widowed mother in Leytonstone.

With a couple of drinks already taken, Percy was in expansive mood as he regaled the company with an edited version of the events of the Bank Holiday.

'Get out or I'll throw you out, I told him.' Percy paused for effect. 'And I would have done, too. Heart trouble or no heart trouble.'

'You did right, Percy,' said Bert earnestly. The other two nodded in agreement.

'Oh yes,' Percy continued, 'I'm an easy going sort of chap as you know, but once my dander's up...'

Miss Tucknott spoke up. 'Beware the wrath of a patient man,' she said.

Percy raised his index finger in agreement.

'Exactly, Miss Tucknott,' he said. 'Right, time for another round I think.' Percy stood up. 'Same again, lads?' The two men nodded and drained their glasses. 'What about you, Miss Tucknott?' Percy turned to his lady colleague. 'Can I tempt you to another port and lemon?'

Miss Tucknott looked up coyly. 'Oh, Mr Thompson,' she cooed. 'You'll have me tiddly.'

Percy leaned towards her. 'Well you know what Marie Lloyd says,' he winked at the two men, 'a little of what you fancy does you good!'

Miss Tucknott slapped him playfully on his arm.

'Oh go on then,' she giggled, 'you've twisted my arm.'

'That's the ticket,' said Percy and weaved his way over to the bar.

After Freddy had left Ilford, Edith began writing to him on a regular basis, using her distinctive lilac-coloured notepaper with matching envelopes.

As a precaution against prying eyes at Westow Hill, Edith addressed her letters care of his ship the *SS Morea* and, as an added precaution, always referred to herself as 'Peidi' and signed them the same way.

For Edith, letters were a form of escape from her workaday life. In them, she could conjure up a romantic dream-world in which she could explore and pursue daring and outrageous flights of fancy impossible to experience in real life.

Freddy picked up the first of these letters when he went down to the P&O office at Tilbury to sign on for his next voyage. Recognizing the handwriting, he put it in his pocket, waiting until he got back home before reading it.

Finding the house empty, he went into the small back parlour, sat down at the table and opened the envelope.

Darlingest boy I know,

Your Peidi is very upset, as I am sure you are. Darlint, I couldn't face up to him on Monday. Everything happened so quickly - too quickly. I couldn't come with you although I wanted to with every bone in my body. It was horrible, but you were so brave standing up to that bully. Now you see what I see so often. One day, my love, we will have our own tumble-down nook somewhere, and instead of 'One Little Hour', we will have a lifetime of...

He broke off as Mrs Bywaters entered the room carrying a tea tray, and hastily stuffed the letter into his inside pocket.

His mother placed the tray on the table, sat down and began to pour the tea.

'From a lady friend?' she enquired.

'What?' Freddy feigned innocence.

'That letter you stuffed in your pocket when I came in the room,' she said, passing him a cup of tea.

Freddy smiled. 'What makes you think it was from a woman?'

'Men don't usually write to each other on lilac note paper,' she said, blowing on her tea before sipping it.

Freddy's smile broadened. 'No flies on you mum, are there?'

'No,' she said emphatically. 'And it didn't come through *our* letter box either. Who's it from?'

'A lady of great beauty, charm and intelligence who thinks I am the cat's whiskers.' Freddy smoothed back his hair and smiled smugly at his mother.

'Oh, *listen* to him!' Mrs Bywaters was dismissive. 'Proper little Rudolph Valentino. I *don't* think!'

The lovers last assignation before Freddy sailed was to be at the Regent Palace Hotel near Piccadilly Circus.

Once again Edith had managed to get time off work and had arranged to meet Freddy in the foyer at 3.30. The plan was that Freddy would arrive with a suitcase around midday, and book a double room, informing reception that his 'wife' would be arriving later.

Unknown to Edith, the Regent Palace had a reputation as a haunt for prostitutes. Not the over-made-up, 'Lookin' for a naughty gel, duckie?' type, but soberly dressed, discreet ladies, to whom the hotel staff were wont to turn a blind eye.

Blissfully unaware of the teeming demi-monde ebbing and flowing around her, Edith, having arrived a little early, sat alone in the foyer waiting for Freddy to arrive.

After a few minutes a middle aged, well dressed man sidled up and sat down opposite her.

'I haven't seen you here before,' he said quietly. 'How much do you charge?'

Edith was completely nonplussed. 'I beg your pardon?' she said, furrowing her brow.

'Ten bob for half an hour, how's that?'

Edith stared at the man uncomprehendingly before the penny dropped. 'How *dare* you?' she hissed. 'I'm a respectable woman.'

The man sprang to his feet. 'Sorry,' he said, and quickly made himself scarce.

Edith was still hot with embarrassment and indignation when Freddy arrived smelling slightly of drink. To her surprise and annoyance, instead of being outraged by what had happened, he seemed to find the whole episode rather amusing.

Her ruffled feelings were assuaged somewhat when she saw the room. It boasted a large double bed, carpet on the floor, a wash basin with hot and cold water and two spotless white towels. After the bleak austerity of the Balmoral, room 247 was positively palatial.

Once again their lovemaking was ecstatic.

For Edith, each time they met like this, all accepted standards of behaviour: respectability, restraint, modesty and morality were cast off, along with her clothes. Gradually sadomasochism was becoming more established in their relationship as the correlation between pain and pleasure added a new dimension to Edith's sexual voyage of discovery.

As she stepped out of the hotel foyer into the glare and clamour of Piccadilly Circus, Edith once again experienced that same sense of detachment from the throng surging around her - a feeling of unreality.

On the tram taking her to Liverpool Street Station, she was thinking of Freddy and how her life had completely changed in a few short weeks.

She was now totally besotted and could not begin to imagine her life without him. But there were problems ahead. Percy would never give her a divorce, of that she was certain. Would Freddy wait for her, or become impatient and find someone else, someone younger?

The difference in their ages troubled her. On Christmas Day she would be twenty-eight while he would still be in his teens.

Turning away from such disturbing thoughts, she turned her mind to their next meeting.

Freddy was due to leave for his next trip on December 11 and she wanted to make the best of the short time left. But getting any more time off in the afternoons would be difficult without imposing on the generosity of her employers and arousing their displeasure. No, if they were to meet again before he left, it would have to be one evening after she finished work. This would prove difficult but not impossible.

What she needed was an accomplice, an ally, a confidante. By the time the tram was swaying up the Strand towards Fleet Street, Edith had decided to enlist the aid of Lily Vellender.

Hurrying, heads down, in the blustery, snow-flecked wind on their way to Fuller's tearooms, the two friends were immersed in their own thoughts - Edith wondering how Lily would react to the bombshell she was about to drop, and Lily consumed with curiosity about what it could possibly be.

Fuller's, with its steamed-up windows and comforting aroma of coffee and toasted tea cakes, was an oasis of warmth and cheer in the gloom of that late November evening. They found a corner table, sat down and looked at each other for a while without speaking. Finally, Lily could bear the suspense no longer.

'Well?' she said, arching her eyebrows inquisitively. 'What was so hush-hush that we couldn't talk about in the showroom?'

Edith hesitated for a moment before replying.

'First of all,' she said solemnly, 'I want you to *swear* you won't tell a living soul.'

Lily stared at her friend, mouth slightly agape, and nodded.

'*Swear*!' Edith was insistent.

'Cross my heart and hope to die.' Lily was agog.

Edith chose her words carefully. 'I'm having a...romance,' she said quietly.

Lily's jaw almost hit the table. 'Edith!' she gasped. 'You mean..?'

Any further discussion was halted by the arrival of a waitress.

'Yes, ladies. What can I get you?'

'Pot of tea for two please.' Edith looked at the stunned Lily. 'Would you like a cake?'

Lily shook her head.

'Just the tea then.'

'Very good, madam.' The waitress wrote it down on her pad, tore off the top copy, placed it on the table and departed.

Lily, who had now recovered from the shock, leaned over, arms resting the table.

'When did you..?' she began, then changed tack. 'Who is it?' she asked bluntly.

Edith paused for a moment before answering.

'Hold onto your hat, Lily,' she warned, 'it's Freddy Bywaters.'

'*What*?' Lily's voice rose a full octave.

Edith put her finger to her lips and puckered her mouth into a soundless 'sshh'.

When Lily spoke again, her voice had returned to its normal pitch but was urgent with concern.

'Edie!' she said disbelievingly. 'What on earth can you be thinking about? Apart from anything else he's ten years younger than you.'

'Eight actually.'

Lily shook her head. 'Eight, ten, what's the difference? He's just a boy.'

'No he's not.' Edith was quiet but emphatic. 'He's a mature, intelligent young man and fun to be with,' she added meaningfully.

Lily sat back in her seat, folded her arms and looked at Edith in bemused disbelief.

'Oh, Lily,' Edith leaned across the table earnestly, 'it's just a mild flirtation, that's all. A dalliance. Where's the harm in that?'

'You mean you haven't actually..?' Lily left the last part of the question unsaid but the implication was clear.

'Of course not!' Edith managed to sound both shocked and amused at such a suggestion. 'We meet for lunch occasionally, that's all. Go for a walk, hold hands, then go our own ways.'

Edith was surprised how easy she found it to lie when it had anything to do with her and Freddy.

Lily's feelings were somewhat mixed. On the one hand, she was very fond of Edith, but on the other she liked and respected Percy and was a little saddened that

Edith was deceiving him. Of course, knowing what she knew now went some way to explaining Freddy's abrupt departure from Kensington Gardens on Bank Holiday Monday. Could it be, she wondered, that Percy had begun to suspect something and sent Freddy packing?

'I'm beginning to wish...' Lily began, but the arrival of the waitress with their tea stopped her in mid sentence. She waited until the girl had gone before continuing. 'I'm beginning to wish you hadn't told me,' she said, pouring milk into her tea cup.

Edith reached over and grasped Lily's hand. 'I had to tell someone,' she said earnestly, 'and you're my best friend. If I can't tell you, who *can* I tell?'

Edith had her own reasons for taking Lily into her confidence. A plan had been forming in her mind that would necessitate her friend providing her with an alibi.

After the seediness of the Balmoral and the distasteful incident at the Regent Palace, Edith had been trying to find somewhere a little more genteel for she and Freddy to retire to for their *liaisons d'amour.*

Then, quite by chance, she had bumped into Harry Renton an old friend who, it turned out, had a vacant, luxury flat in Bayswater to let. The rent was a guinea a week and initially, Edith had been keen for Freddy to take it on. The idea of their own little love-nest in a well appointed, self-contained flat was something she longed for. However, with Freddy away at sea for more than nine months of the year, she realized it was not a financially viable proposition. However, Edith had another idea up her sleeve.

Since moving to Ilford, Thursday nights had become the time she and Percy went their separate ways. Edith would meet up with a girl friend for a drink at the latest 'in' place, then perhaps go for a meal. Percy usually joined his cronies at the White Horse for a pint or two and a game of dominoes or darts. It was an arrangement that worked well, giving each of them a break from the other and the normal routine - which they both agreed was a sensible thing for a married couple to do. Although he didn't like the idea of Edith 'gadding the town', as he put it, Percy quite enjoyed his evening in masculine company and, for Edith, it now presented an opportunity to be with her lover.

She had already approached Harry Renton for the key to his apartment, telling him she knew of a prospective tenant who could only view the flat after six o'clock in the evening. Knowing her as well as he did, Harry had no qualms about entrusting her with the key. The first hurdle had been cleared; all she needed now was to get Lily to agree to cover for her. It would entail more lies of course, but by now Edith was becoming adept in the art of deception.

At first, Lily was extremely reluctant to become involved in the conspiracy but Edith was at her most persuasive. She swore that she and Freddy were only having a last meal together before he went back to sea. 'Please, *please* do this for me,

Lily,' she had begged, 'and I will never ask you again. *Ever*. I promise.'

Eventually Lily capitulated and, against her better judgement, agreed that if the subject ever came up in Percy's presence, she would say Edith had spent the evening with her.

Moscow Court was an imposing block of mansion flats situated in a quiet square off Bayswater Road. In their eagerness to save precious time, Edith and Freddy had taken a taxi from Aldersgate arriving at the flats just before six o'clock.

The flat was everything Edith had expected: nice furniture, good quality carpets and curtains, a splendid bathroom and, joy of joys, central heating. In the living room, the open grate had been boarded up and a modern gas fire installed.

As Freddy put a match to the burners, Edith drew the curtains and turned off the lights. Within ten minutes of arriving, they were making love on a hearth-rug, in the glow of a softly hissing gas fire.

During one of the brief interludes in their lovemaking, Freddy got up, went into the kitchen and reappeared carrying a pair of scissors. Edith smiled up at him.

'What are those for?'

'I want a lock of your hair to keep,' he said, kneeling down beside her.

'Oh, darlint.' Edith was touched. 'What a sweet thought.' She separated a strand of her dark auburn hair and offered it to Freddy.

'No,' he said, shaking his head, 'not from there, from here.' Then taking a lock of her pubic hair between his fingers, snipped it off. 'To remind me of you when we are parted,' he said.

Edith took Freddy's face between her hands. 'Darlingest boy,' she whispered, her eyes luminous with love, 'one day there will be no more separations.'

When they left Moscow Court it was snowing and the snow was already an inch deep on the railings and trees in the square, highlighting their stark outlines like a giant lino-cut print.

As they walked down Bayswater Road towards Marble Arch, Freddy scooped up a double handful of snow and threw it over Edith.

'Oh, you beast,' she spluttered, before scooping up a fistful of snow herself.

Within seconds, the two of them were engaged in a joyous snowball fight, laughing and shrieking like a couple of children as the snowballs flew thick and fast, back and forth.

Breathless and hungry after their exertions, Freddy dragged a protesting Edith over to a coffee stall on the opposite side of the road and ordered them each a hot meat pie and a steaming cup of Bovril.

After Freddy's boat had sailed on the 11th December, Edith's life settled back into the humdrum routine from which she now longed to escape. The constant need to invent new excuses to avoid Percy's insistence on his 'home comforts' had become a burden she found difficult to bear. Apart from the fact that she found sex with her husband repugnant, she was terrified of becoming pregnant by him - a calamity that sent an ice-cold stab of fear into her heart every time she thought about it.

One way to relieve the tedium was for her and Avis to take themselves off to the 'flicks' from time to time.

The Regal was a new picture palace in Ilford High Road where, attracted by the lurid publicity, they went to see a much talked about film called *'The Sheik'* starring Rudolph Valentino.

Sitting enrapt in the conspiring darkness of the cinema, Edith yearned to be, as Agnes Ayers was in the film, swept up into the arms of a dashing young man on a white stallion, and carried off to a tent in the desert for endless nights of love under star-sequined skies.

After the show and back in the real world, Edith knew that her only hope of an escape of that kind lay with Freddy. Not to a tent in the desert of course, but a place of their own somewhere; the 'tumble-down nook' or the flat in Chelsea they had talked about so often. The problem was that Freddy was not around. *With* him, she could keep the dream alive - nothing was beyond their reach - but thousands of miles apart, it was almost impossible.

She determined to do everything in her power to make her dreams a reality. While Freddy was away, she would write to him as often as possible, reassuring him of her undying love and planning their future together. A future that would of necessity entail the discarding of Percy somewhere along the way.

Freddy received the first of these letters when his ship docked at Marseilles, recognizing the lilac-coloured envelope as soon as he entered the P&O office on the dockside.

Over the next six weeks or so, he received five more - all written on the same coloured notepaper in the same flowery style.

When replying to her letters he always addressed them care of Carlton & Prior. As Edith was invariably the first to arrive in the morning, it was she who gathered up and sorted the early post, tucking his letters into her handbag with a heart-lifting thrill of anticipation. Then after carrying them around with her all day, reading and re-reading them, she would tear them into little pieces on her walk to Aldersgate station and scatter them like confetti in her wake.

With Christmas 1921 approaching, Edith busied herself with preparations for the coming festive season; there were presents to be bought and wrapped, provisions to lay in and cards to be sent.

Edith was looking forward to an old-fashioned Christmas with her family who were all coming to number 41: Mr and Mrs Graydon, Newenham, Harry and Billie and, of course, Avis.

It was also a busy time at Carlton & Prior and Edith was kept at full stretch. Not that she minded. Being fully occupied took her mind off Freddy for a while and helped to dull the pain of separation.

A few days before Christmas, Edith was opening the morning post at the breakfast table when she recognized Freddy's handwriting on an envelope bearing an Indian stamp and carrying a Bombay postmark. It was addressed to Mr and Mrs Percy Thompson.

'Good heavens!' Edith managed to sound surprised. 'We've got a card from Freddy Bywaters.'

'What?' Percy looked up sharply from his *Daily Sketch*.

Edith studied the envelope. 'From Bombay,' she said. 'Fancy that.'

'He's got some neck,' Percy growled.

Edith read the card out loud:

Dear Edie,

Do you remember last Xmas you wrote to me wishing me all the best.

I never wrote you, so this year I'm going to make sure of it. I want to wish you all that you can wish yourself. I know all those wishes of yours will run into a deuce of a lot of money. Such items as fur coats, cars and champagne, will be prominent on the list - anyhow, good health and I hope you get it. Have a very real good time, the best that is possible. I shall be about 2 days this side of Suez. Never mind I will have a drink with you. Once more the very, very best at Xmas and always.

Yours very Sincerely,

Freddy.

'Cheeky young pup.' Percy rustled his newspaper irritably. 'Throw it on the fire.'

'Percy, don't be so unkind. Whatever happened to the Christmas spirit and good will to all men? I shall put it up with the others,' she said walking over to the fireplace.

As she placed the card on the mantelshelf she was secretly elated, knowing that Freddy had found a way of sending her a birthday card without arousing any suspicion.

'There,' she said, turning to face Percy. 'Let us accept it in the spirit in which it was sent.'

Percy grunted and took a spoonful of porridge.

As Edith had hoped, Christmas at 41 turned out to be most enjoyable. Having her family around her on her birthday created a congenial atmosphere and, in true Graydon tradition, everyone played their part in the celebrations. Edith was so delighted that the first family Christmas at her new home had been a success that, on Christmas night, her resolve weakened by an excess of alcohol, she and

Percy made love. Edith did not respond, she just let it happen - a non-participation Percy either did not notice or chose to overlook in his eagerness to restore the *status quo ante* to his married life.

Chapter 8

*"...something awful happened, darlint. I don't
know for certain what it was but I can
guess. Can you?"*

In the second week of January 1922, something happened that sent Edith's life into a tail-spin - she missed the start of her period.

Although 'that time of the month' had always been troublesome for her she had *never* been late before, and she was frantic with anxiety. A pregnancy now would ruin everything. If the child were Percy's she did not want it. If it were Freddy's baby (and she was convinced it was), Percy would believe it to be his. No - the only answer was a termination, and the sooner the better before her condition became too obvious. Speed now being of the essence, she dashed off a letter to Freddy.

Darlingest Boy,

I write in haste and trepidation. Since our last meeting in Moscow(?) something hasn't happened that should have happened. Do you understand, darlint?

I desperately need your help. What shall I do? Write back soon
Forever. Peidi.XXX

The letter caught up with Freddy a week later when his ship docked at the port of Aden.

In spite of his debonair image, this was a situation he had never encountered before. Uncertain how to proceed, he decided to consult his cabin-mate, Dan. Although Dan was only a couple of years older than Freddy, he seemed to have acquired a vast experience of life and the ways of the world. If anyone knew what to do it would be him.

'Quinine!' Dan had no hesitation when the question was put to to him. 'Three teaspoonfuls a day for five days, then half a bottle of gin and a boiling hot bath. That should do the trick.'

'Quinine?' Freddy had been prescribed it once for malaria, but that was all he knew about it.

Dan nodded. 'We've got plenty in the sick-bay. I'll swipe a bottle for you if you want.'

Freddy put his hand on Dan's shoulder. 'Thanks, Dan. You're a pal.'

'S'alright.' Dan grinned at Freddy. 'You *do* get yourself into some scrapes with the ladies, don't you?'

It was another week before the package arrived at Carlton & Prior. Edith had been monitoring the morning mail every day but, to her chagrin, it arrived with an afternoon post.

She was sitting in her tiny office when Rose Jacobs brought it to her. 'This has arrived addressed to you,' she said, consumed with curiosity.

'Oh, how nice.' Edith glanced at it briefly before popping it into her handbag. 'Thank you, Rose,' she said dismissively.

Rose loitered for a moment as though expecting some sort of explanation. 'Shut the door, there's a dear,' Edith said, hunching her shoulders, 'it's jolly draughty in here.'

Although Rose got on well enough with Edith, she had always harboured a niggling resentment against her because of her position in the company and the obvious high regard in which she was held.

Why, she wondered, was someone writing to Edith care of Carlton & Prior? And not for the first time either. She could remember at least two other occasions when it had happened and she also recalled a young man had left a letter with Jim the doorman to pass on. She was thinking it all a bit odd when a ringing telephone summoned her back to her duties.

Edith waited until she was on the train home before opening the packet.

Inside was a small bottle labelled, 'Tincture of Quinine: Use as directed'. She put the bottle in her bag, opened the accompanying letter and began to read.

Darling Peidi Mia,

I have managed to snatch a moment alone at last, and who should be in my thoughts but my darlingest Peidi.

Dan and I have been pushed to blazes since Marseilles and I have had little time to myself, even to write to my own sweet girl.

I must say your news left me astounded and very worried about the consequences, Oh, if only I were there by your side. Sometimes I wonder if things would be better for you if we were pals only, and you were able to make the best of life with P.

Meanwhile you must act quickly to avoid any further complications. A teaspoonful three times a day for a week, then a really hot bath should have the desired effect. It's enough for an elephant actually but you may have to persevere with it for a while.

Love.

Freddy.XXX

Edith lowered the letter and stared unseeingly out of the carriage window. What did he mean by, *"Sometimes I wonder if things would be better for you if we were to be pals only?"* Was Freddy having second thoughts? A sudden chill of fear caused her to shudder momentarily. Was this the thin edge of a wedge that would eventually split them apart?

As Edith agonized over the possible implication of those lines, she gradually became aware of her reflection in the window. The harsh, overhead lighting in the carriage and the blackness of the night outside lending her face a pale, almost wraith-like quality.

She turned away from the window and looked again at the letter. She didn't *want* to make the best of her life with Percy! In fact she wanted him out of her life altogether. Somehow she had to convince Freddy she was actively doing something positive to achieve that end. As the train clattered its way to Ilford, Edith realized she had to convince Freddy she was taking steps to get rid of her husband.

Subterfuge would be necessary because, in truth, there was nothing much she *could* do except, when the time was right, to ask Percy for a divorce and she did not hold out much hope of *that* being successful.

As she left Ilford station she carefully tore the letter up into tiny pieces and allowed them to trickle out of her fingers to be snatched up by the swirling east wind.

That night, in the bathroom before going to bed, she took the first dose of quinine and almost brought it straight up again, the bitter taste leaving her with eyes watering, lips puckered into a moue of disgust, and a determination to have some sugar lumps standing by in future.

Towards the end of the week the bottle of quinine was almost empty and Edith was beginning to feel unwell, experiencing odd shooting pains in her abdomen and occasional bouts of nausea. On the morning of Thursday 24th of January she was looking so off-colour that even Percy, not the most perceptive of men, commented upon it. Mrs Lester had already observed that Edith was looking 'peaky' but, when she declined her morning bowl of porridge, Percy suggested she should take the day off work. But Edith was made of sterner stuff and soldiered on.

It was a decision she came to regret when, around midday, with the pains in her stomach occurring more frequently, she was on her way to the lavatory when she fainted. When she came round she was lying on the floor in Miss Prior's office with a cushion under her head being tended by an elderly doctor.

As soon as she became aware of what had happened, her immediate thought was to avoid any further medical examination. By way of an explanation she told the doctor she was having a particularly difficult period which seemed to satisfy him.

After writing out a prescription for some pain-killing tablets he left, promising to return a little later.

In the interim, her anxious employers did everything they could to make her comfortable. Mr Carlton fetched her a blanket from his car, and Miss Prior provided a hot water bottle to hold against her stomach.

When the doctor called back, her condition had not improved so Mr Carlton insisted that she be taken home in his car by Jim the doorman with strict instructions for her not to return until she had fully recovered.

It was Mrs Lester's custom to make a pot of tea for herself and her invalid husband at around four o'clock in the afternoon. With a couple of Rich Tea biscuits in the saucer, she would position herself on a chair by the front room window to cast a beady eye over the comings and goings of Kensington Gardens.

She was just about to dunk her first biscuit into her tea when Mr Carlton's car drew up outside the house. She rose slowly to her feet and watched as Edith, supported by Jim, made her way slowly up the path to the front door.

Although on the wrong side of fifty, Mrs Lester could move swiftly when the occasion demanded and she had already opened the door while Edith was still fumbling in her handbag for the key.

'Oh, my goodness, Mrs Thompson!' Mrs Lester's face was a picture of concern. 'Whatever's the matter?'

'Miss Graydon collapsed at work,' Jim volunteered, as Mrs Lester stood aside to let them in.

'Oh, dear. Shall I get the doctor?'

'It's alright, Mrs Lester,' Edith was breathing heavily. 'I've seen a doctor. I just need to get to bed now.'

Mrs Lester nodded gravely. 'Yes, that's right, best place.'

Edith and Jim had reached the foot of the stairs.

'I can manage now, Jim,' she said smiling weakly.

'You sure, Miss Graydon?' Jim was reluctant to leave Edith on her own.

'Yes, thank you. You've been most kind,' she said, and slowly began to mount the stairs.

'There's a cup of tea in the pot. Would you like one, dear?' Mrs Lester called after her.

'No, thank you, I'll just...'

Edith rounded the bend in the stairs and was lost to view. Jim waited until he heard the bedroom door close before making his way to the door with Mrs Lester close behind him.

'What did the doctor say?' Mrs Lester was eager to glean as much information as she could.

'Some sort of stomach upset, I believe.'

'Would you like a cup of tea before you go, Mr..?'

'Denton. Jim Denton. No thank you, madam. Better be getting back.'

Mrs Lester opened the door and Jim stepped outside. 'Cheerio then,' he said, and raised his cap before walking down the path to the car.

Mrs Lester closed the front door. 'Well, I never,' she mused as she opened the door to her sitting room, eager to appraise Mr Lester of the latest drama.

Edith had dropped off into a fitful sleep for about an hour when a searing pain suddenly wracked her body, forcing her into an upright position clutching her stomach.

She became aware that she was bathed in perspiration, her flannelette nightgown clinging to her like a wet towel. Then another shaft of pain went through her stomach like a sword thrust.

'Oh, my God!' She switched on the bedside lamp, dragged herself out of bed and over to the door. Outside in the hallway, the smell of cooking coming from the kitchen almost made her retch. Once inside the bathroom, she just managed to lock the door before sinking to the floor. In great pain, she managed to lift herself onto the lavatory seat where she sat, both arms wrapped round her stomach, with tears running down her face. Suddenly she experienced a pain so excruciating that, in spite of herself, she cried out in agony.

Downstairs in the kitchen, Mrs Lester was preparing her evening meal when she heard Edith's cry of pain.

'Good Lord!' she said to herself. 'What on earth..?'

In the bathroom Edith had pulled herself up and was looking down in anguish at the toilet bowl. Then, with her hand shaking, she pulled the chain and flushed the tiny foetus down the lavatory.

She was at the wash basin splashing cold water on her face, trying to erase the horror of what had happened from her mind, when there was a knock on the bathroom door.

'Are you alright in there, Mrs Thompson?'

It was Mrs Lester with her ear against the bathroom door.

Edith closed her eyes in despair for a moment.

'Yes!' she called back, trying to sound as normal as possible.

'Can I get you anything, dear?'

Edith took a deep breath before replying. 'No thank you. Just...leave me alone. I'll be alright.'

Edith waited until she heard Mrs Lester descending the stairs before resuming her ablutions. As she towelled herself down, she caught sight of her face in the bathroom mirror. It was deathly pale with dark circles under her eyes, reminding her of a death mask she had once seen on a trip to Madame Tussaud's.

Back in the bedroom, she changed her nightgown, brushed her hair, climbed back into bed, and with a huge sigh of relief, fell instantly into a deep, restorative sleep.

By the time Percy arrived home about an hour later there was a cooked meal awaiting him in the kitchen and a blazing fire in the morning room. Mrs Lester had come up trumps. However, her motives had not been entirely altruistic. There had been no more talk recently about them having to leave number 41, but she felt it didn't do any harm to remind the Thompsons now and again how useful it was to have someone as dependable as herself ready to step into the breach should an emergency arise.

Like most men of his generation, the gynaecological workings of a woman's body were a closed book to Percy, and he was more than happy to accept his wife's explanation of 'female troubles' as the cause of her collapse.

With her robust constitution, Edith was soon back on her feet again and, after the trauma of the last few days, seriously considering a visit to the newly-opened Marie Stopes Birth Control Clinic to discuss some form of contraception.

Chapter 9

"P.S. Have you studied bichloride of mercury?"

As soon as she was able, Edith wrote to Freddy. The letter caught up with him when his ship stopped off at Alexandria for a few days.

He was sitting outside a dockside café with a glass of beer in front of him when he opened the envelope. The first part of the letter, which he read with a mixture of relief and regret, chronicled her collapse at work and the subsequent miscarriage. But it was the next part that caused him to sit up.

"Why aren't you sending me something? I wanted you to - you never do what I ask you darlint - you still have your own way always. If I don't mind the risk why should you?"

Freddy took a gulp of beer before continuing.

"I was buoyed up with the hope of the light bulb and I used a lot - big pieces too - not powdered, but it had no effect. I quite expected to be able to send you the cable, but no, nothing has happened from it.

"Wouldn't the stuff make small pills coated together with wax and dropped in licorice? Try while you're away.

"You tell me not to leave finger marks on the box. Do you know I did not think of the box but I did think of the glass or cup, whatever was used. Do experiment with pills while you're away - please darlint.

"I do always love you and think of you.
Peidi."

This was followed by a disturbing postscript.

"Have you studied bichloride of mercury?"

Freddy put down the letter, a look of bemused disbelief on his face.

'Bichloride of mercury?' he said to himself. 'What in Heaven's name is she playing at?'

He knew well enough her penchant for over-dramatization, but this was ridiculous. How could she possibly put lumps of glass in Percy's food without his noticing? And what did she mean by 'why haven't you sent me something like I asked you to?' Sent her what? He had heard that women sometimes go a bit doolally when they've just lost a baby, but this was just plain barmy.

As he walked back to his ship Freddy was beginning to have slightly ambivalent feelings towards Edith.

On the one hand she was a vivacious, witty, charming companion, and their love making transcended anything he had ever experienced. On the other, he had to admit there were problems. Obviously there was the age difference - not so important now, but might be in later years. Also, she appeared to be totally dependent on him, which was a responsibility he could well do without at the age of nineteen.

Much as he loved her, he just could not come to terms with her tendency to blur the dividing line between reality and fantasy and confuse fact with fiction.

It was fun role-playing with her when they were together, but Edith kept up the pretence even when they were apart, imagining their love affair as a stage play with herself in the leading role as the tortured young wife torn between loyalty and love.

When he got back to his cabin on the *Morea*, his shipmate, Dan, was lying on his bunk reading a book.

'The quinine worked,' said Freddy said.

Dan looked up from his book. 'Oh, good,' he said. 'Everything alright?

'Seems to be.' Freddy lay on his bunk and lit a cigarette. 'Thanks, Dan.'

''S'alright.' Dan grinned. 'Teach you to be more careful next time.'

Freddy blew a smoke ring and watched it curl upwards to the ceiling.

'Know anything about bichloride of mercury?' he asked, casually.

'Well, mercury's a poison, I know that,' said Dan. 'So bichloride of mercury must be one too, only more so I should think. Why?'

'Oh, I came across it in a book, that's all,' Freddy said, as he blew another smoke ring.

Despite his misgivings, when his ship docked at Tilbury a few weeks later, Freddy could hardly wait to see Edith again.

Being in funds and eager to push the boat out, so to speak, he reserved a table for two at the Holborn Restaurant in Kingsway.

It was a Thursday night, Edith's 'night off', and she had once again dragooned a reluctant Lily Vellender to cover for her.

When she arrived at the restaurant, Freddy was waiting for her at a table next to the orchestra, looking tanned and handsome as he rose to greet her.

After a short, passionate embrace, they sat down, held hands under the table and looking adoringly into each others eyes as the Don Cross Quintet played *Roses of Picardy* in a slow fox-trot tempo.

Edith looked around. 'I say. It's rather grand here, isn't it,' she said, squeezing Freddy's hand.

'Only the best for my best girl,' he said.

'Shall we order?' she asked.

Freddy shook his head. 'There's something we have to do first,' he said, enigmatically.

A smattering of applause signalled the end of the fox-trot. Up on the bandstand the pianist was strapping on a piano accordion.

'Well, what is it?' Edith's eyes were bright with expectation.

Freddy held up his index finger and adopted a listening pose. As if on cue the band began to play '*One Little Hour*' in tango time.

Edith looked at Freddy in astonished delight. 'They're playing our song.'

Freddy raised his eyebrows. 'Good Heavens!' he said affectedly. 'So they are. Fancy that.'

Edith's eyes misted over. 'Oh, you darling boy,' she whispered, 'thank you.'

Freddy rose to his feet. 'Tu vas danser avec moi, madame?' he said with a bow.

Edith stood up and offered him her hand, 'Enchanté, monsieur.'

Freddy led her out onto the floor and they began to dance, their bodies moving in rhythm to the music and in perfect harmony with each other.

As they whirled and swooped around the floor they became aware that some of the other couples had stopped to watch, which spurred them on to essay some of the more flamboyant movements of the tango which they carried off with panache and elegance.

When the dance ended, Edith was convinced that the applause that followed was directed as much towards her and Freddy as to the orchestra.

As they waited on the platform at Liverpool Street station Edith's head was still in a whirl of excitement. It had been a wonderful evening and even the bleak atmosphere of a grimy suburban branch line could not dispel the feeling of euphoria she felt.

When the train pulled in, Edith made to board the nearest carriage but was pulled back by Freddy.

'No, not that one,' he said, taking her by the arm and leading her to the front of the train. 'I saw a better one up here,' and so saying, opened he door to an empty carriage.

As soon as the train had started off on its journey, Freddy pulled down the blinds on all the windows and turned to a bemused Edith.

'Now then,' he said taking off his overcoat, 'we have exactly seven and a half minutes before the first stop, so there's no time to lose.'

Edith's eyes widened.

'You mean *now*?' she gasped. 'In *here*?'

Freddy laughed out loud at her astonishment.

'Why not?' he said. 'It's much warmer than Valentines Park.'

Although quite shocked, Edith was experiencing a pulse-quickening frisson of excitement at the thought of such an outrageous idea.

Freddy looked at his watch.

'We only have *six* and a half minutes now,' he said.

'Come along then, you'd better step lively young man, or the next station will be arriving before you do!'

Chapter 10

"Things are all going smoothly with me - I am giving
all and accepting everything. I think I am looked on as a
dutiful wife whose spirit is at last bent to the will of her husband."

During the Spring and Summer of 1922 Edith led a curious double life.

She and Percy attended social functions together, took part in whist drives, visited relatives, entertained guests, went to dances and the theatre - all without anyone suspecting anything untoward in their relationship or their marriage.

Edith had decided that the best way to achieve her ends was to keep Percy sweet. In order to do this she had to appear to acquiesce to all his ideas of how a 'proper wife' should behave. Percy wanted a stable home life and a wife who respected his needs. Distasteful as it was to her, Edith was now obliged to submit to his demands in the bedroom, all the time writing copious letters to Freddy pledging her eternal love, and bemoaning the life of Hell she was leading.

Although not the most observant of men, Percy was nevertheless no fool and guessed that Edith and Freddy were still seeing each other on a fairly regular basis. As a shipping clerk he was aware of the comings and goings of the *Morea* and of Edith's noticeable high spirits when the ship was docked at Tilbury. Still unable to believe there was anything of substance between them, he was prepared, for the moment, to leave things as they were. He wasn't entirely happy with the situation but but he clung to the belief that, given time, Edith would come to her senses and her infatuation would begin to pall.

He was buoyed up in this by the knowledge that on October 6th the *SS Morea* was leaving England bound for China and the far East on a voyage of some six months duration. With Bywaters out of the way for that length of time, he saw it as an opportunity to rekindle the love they once shared and put an end to this nonsense once and for all. To achieve this end he now played his trump card.

Edith, with her aspirations to middle class respectability, had always wanted to engage a live-in housemaid.

Percy had always resisted the idea, primarily on the grounds of cost, but he had now changed his mind. He was convinced that what Edith now needed most in her life was stability. Having a child would provide that.

Accordingly, he had given the Lesters formal notice to quit, and had invited Ethel Vernon up to London on October 4th, all expenses paid, to discuss her employment as a housekeeper.

Ethel Vernon was a young woman now living in Truro who had once worked for Percy's sister, Lillian Chambers..

Knowing nothing of her husband's ulterior motives, Edith was delighted at the prospect.

The only person in the house not overjoyed at the turn of events was Mrs Lester. After years of failing health, Mr Lester had died in the summer of 1922. Now, when she could at last think about making some sort of life for herself - This!

'Disgraceful I call it,' she complained to Mrs Kettle when they met in Mr Jenkinson's butcher shop. 'Poor Mr Lester would turn in his grave if he knew the shabby way they're treatin' us.' Mrs Kettle made sympathetic noises. 'After all I've done for that man over the years, too. Fetchin' and carryin' till all hours, and *this* is the thanks you get.' Mrs Lester's lips pursed in a grimace of disapproval. 'It's that toffee-nosed wife of his that's behind it, you mark my words,' she said grimly. 'Solicitor's letters, if you please! Whatever next?'

She was interrupted by Mr Jenkinson.

'Yes, Mrs Lester,' he said, wiping his hands on his apron. 'What can I do for you today?'

'Half a pound of best end of neck, please.'

As the *Morea* steamed slowly up the Thames estuary, Freddy was grappling with a problem which had beset him for some time now.

He was very much in love with Edith but the question he kept asking himself was, did he *really* want to settle down with her - as they had so often planned - when he was only just out of his teens?

In all probability he would have to give up his job as a seaman and find something else. But try as he might, he could never see himself holding down a humdrum job in an office or factory for very long.

At times he was completely certain about what he wanted, at others plagued by doubt and apprehension. Of one thing he was sure - a decision would have to be made before he left on his next trip to the Far East.

Freddy's ship docked at Tilbury around 3pm and he began what would be his last home shore leave for six months. During the next week, Edith and he met almost every day at lunch time and after work, but there was no more lovemaking. Apart from the fact that Edith had several social commitments to fulfil that month, there was nowhere for them to go. They had to make do with meetings in tearooms or public houses where they could do no more than hold hands and gaze adoringly at one another.

On Saturday 30th of September Percy assumed Edith had gone to work. She had set off at the usual time, but had met Freddy at Ilford station where they took a bus to Wanstead Park arriving just after 8am.

Freddy has chosen this particular park because its thick clumps of bushes and shrubs were ideal for the sort of romantic tryst he had in mind. With a long absence in the offing he was determined to make the best use of the few days leave that remained.

As they walked arm-in-arm, through the deserted park kicking up piles of brittle brown leaves, the early morning mist was thinning out and a pale October sun was trying to make itself felt.

Edith loved the tawny oranges, russet browns, faded yellows and sepia tints of Autumn and today in Wanstead Park, as the sunlight filtered through the trees, she thought those colours were as vibrant as she had ever seen them.

Almost as soon as they had entered a secluded bower, Freddy was unbuttoning Edith's clothes. Within minutes they had begun a frenzy of lovemaking that was to surpass anything that had gone before. A series of what felt like low voltage electric shocks began to pulsate through Edith's body, culminating in the first orgasm she had ever experienced; a climax so overwhelming in its intensity that she swooned momentarily.

Later, when they were lying on the grass in an awed silence, Freddy finally made up his mind. Still looking up at the sky he said: 'Peidi, you must ask Percy for a divorce.'

Edith turned her head towards him. 'He'd never agree,' she said sadly. 'He's told me he's determined not to make things easy for us and he won't. You know how much he hates you.'

Freddy sat up. 'Then we'll run away together,' he said. 'Go and live abroad: Australia, New Zealand, somewhere far away. Just the two of us.'

Edith sighed. 'Do you really mean that?'

Freddy nodded. 'We'll find that tumble-down nook we've always talked about and spend the rest of our lives together.'

Edith rested her head on his lap. 'Till death us do part?' she asked, smiling up at him.

'Yes,' he said resolutely. 'We'll give him an ultimatum. Either he agrees to a divorce on the grounds of your adultery with me or we'll run away together - simple as that. When he's had time to consider the implications, he'll realize that a divorce with him as the injured party will be far less humiliating than the role of a cuckold whose wife has deserted him for a younger man.'

Edith sat up. 'You could be right,' she said.

'Will you do it then?'

Edith paused for a moment then nodded her head vigorously. 'Yes,' she said firmly. 'What have we got to lose?'

Freddy put both his hands on her shoulders. 'Neck or nothing?' he said, gripping her tightly.

Edith nodded. 'The hope for all, or the finish of all,' she said. 'Without you my life isn't worth living anyway.'

Freddy took her face in his hands and kissed her tenderly.

'This is going to be my last voyage' he said. 'When I come back, come what may, we will be together and all this will be behind us. But we must act before I leave on Friday. Why don't you ask him tonight?'

Edith shook her head. 'I think the best time will be Tuesday night. We're going to the theatre which should put him in a good mood. I'll bring it up as soon as we get home. How's that?'

Freddy nodded. 'Perhaps I ought to be with you,' he said.

'No!' Edith's voice rose sharply. 'No, darlint,' she said, softening her tone. 'He's much more likely to agree if it's just me. Having *you* there would just get his back up. He probably wouldn't even let you in the door.'

Freddy was unconvinced. 'But what if he gets violent?'

'*Please*, darlint, leave it to me. I won't let you down, I promise.'

Freddy stood up and helped Edith to her feet. 'Come on, Peidi,' he said. 'I'm gasping for a cup of tea.'

On the morning of Tuesday the 3rd of October 1922, Percy Thompson went off to work a happy man. He was wearing his best blue suit and bowler hat in readiness for the evening theatre trip but, in spite of a noticeable chill in the air, had declined to take an overcoat. Edith had also put on her finery, and as the two of them walked to Ilford station together, Percy had, he felt, good reason to be pleased with himself. Bywaters, that perpetual thorn in his side, would be out of the way until next March, Ethel Vernon was coming to London the next day and, just lately, he had detected a change in Edith's attitude. She seemed to be more amenable towards him, more content with life.

Yes. On the whole, everything appeared to be be coming up roses.

Chapter 11

"Yes, darlint, be jealous, so much
that you will do something desperate."

Freddy met Edith briefly at lunchtime and again when she finished work just after 5pm; walking with her to Aldersgate station for the first part of her journey to the West End.

Before they parted Edith arranged for them to meet again on the following day to review the outcome of her conversation with Percy. At 5pm on the next day she was due to meet Ethel Vernon at Paddington station and escort her to Ilford. It was an odd situation in view of the fact that she intended to leave her husband but she consoled herself with the thought that àt least there would be someone in the house to look after him when she had gone.

As they took their farewells, Edith asked Freddy what he was going to do that evening.

'Kick my heels all night, I expect - wondering what's happening.'

Edith looked at him thoughtfully for a moment. 'Why don't you take Avis out?'

Freddy was slightly taken aback. He was on good terms with Avis, and always visited the Graydons when on leave, bringing small presents for the family and spending time with them, but Edith's suggestion seemed odd to say the least.

'Well it will save me wasting the evening, I suppose.'

Avis was a cheerful, sensible girl and jolly good company; just what he needed tonight. 'I'll pop over to Manor Park now and catch Avis when she comes home from work,' he said.

Edith met Percy at Aldersgate and they made their way to Piccadilly Circus.

They had booked tickets for the Criterion Theatre to see a new farce by Ben Travers called *The Dippers* starring Cyril Maude and Binnie Hale. In the foyer they met up with Edith's uncle and aunt Jack and Lily Laxton and had dinner in the Criterion Hotel restaurant before entering the theatre for curtain up at 8.40.

It was about this time that Freddy and Avis arrived at the Avenue Hotel in Church Road, just round the corner from 231.

Mr and Mrs Graydon had always been fond of Freddy and, harbouring the expectation that eventually he and Avis would become romantically attached, were pleased when he arrived to take her out.

Avis herself had never made any secret of the fact that she was smitten with the handsome young seaman. Like many other young woman of her generation, her sweetheart had been killed in the war, and at the age of twenty-five she was clinging to the hope that one day Freddy might ask her to marry him.

Meanwhile, the theatre party enjoyed a meal together. Edith was in great form; laughing and joking at Percy's expense. As usual he was the butt of her humour but gladly endured it in his pleasure at sharing a happy moment with the wife he loved so much and who now was apparently back to her old self.

Back in Manor Park in the saloon bar of the Avenue Hotel, Avis was becoming a little concerned about Freddy's drinking. In the past hour he had drunk six pints of Bass and was about to return to the bar for more.

'Going to have another?' Freddy said, getting to his feet.

'No thanks. And neither should you. 'You've had enough,' she added.

Freddy snorted derisively. 'Don't you believe it,' he said, and made his way unsteadily over to the bar.

It was 10.45 when the Thompsons and the Laxtons left the Criterion and entered Piccadilly Circus station; the Laxtons to return to Stamford Hill and Edith and Percy en route to Liverpool Street to catch the 'theatre' train back to Ilford.

As they bid their farewells, uncle Jack commented on the fact that Percy wasn't wearing a topcoat.

'Oh, he's too mean to buy one,' said Edith laughing. 'I've offered to buy him one myself but he says it's a waste of money because he's already got one.'

'And so it is,' said Percy. 'I'm not prepared to splash out hard-earned cash on something I've already got.'

'It's a bit parky out there tonight, Percy,' uncle Jack said jovially. 'You could catch your death walking home from the station.'

Before Freddy left Avis outside her house at around 11pm, he asked her to accompany him to the cinema the following night - an invitation she readily accepted.

Avis watched him walk off in the direction of East Ham station with a look of concern on her face. He had drunk eight pints of beer in less than two hours, followed by a double brandy, and his usual outgoing, cheerful nature had changed to one of withdrawal and moroseness as the drink had taken hold.

Just before the bend in the crescent, which would have obscured him from view, Freddy stopped briefly, turned and waved, then was gone. Avis stood at the front door for a few moments thinking about him, then, as the chill night air began to make its presence felt, went inside.

Freddy reached East Ham station at around 11.15. On the way there he had been thinking constantly about Edith and what a fool he had been not to insist on being with her when she put her ultimatum to Percy. What sort of man, he asked himself, would leave his sweetheart to face a brute like Percy Thompson on her own?

On an impulse he pulled up the collar of his overcoat, turned on his heel and left the station.

He had no clear idea in his mind of what he intended to do. All he knew was that he had to make sure Edith was alright and keep an eye on Percy in case he tried any funny business.

Still with no definite plan of action in mind, he made his way through the deserted streets of Manor Park towards Ilford.

As he walked, his hands were thrust into his overcoat pockets fingering the seaman's knife he had put in his coat just before coming out that night. He had bought it a year previously for use on the *Morea* and like many seamen, he often carried it with him when ashore, particularly abroad.

As the 11.30 from Liverpool Street station snaked its way past the back yards, rear gardens and cul-de-sacs of east London, Freddy was standing in York Road behind Ilford station not quite knowing what he was going to do next - other than to perhaps confront Percy there and then.

When the train eventually steamed in and jerked to a halt he watched some half a dozen people, including Edith and Percy, alight and make their way to the footbridge that crossed the railway line and led out onto York Road.

As the group came over the bridge, he could see a man and a woman in front, then Edith and Percy, followed by two middle-aged ladies and a man.

From where he was standing in the shadows he could see that Edith was holding Percy's arm, and that they were laughing. In his slightly befuddled state this perplexed him. What was Edith doing hanging on to Percy's arm like that? This was the night she was supposed to be telling him their marriage was over! Had she changed her mind?

Kensington Gardens was about half a mile from the station and, at the steady pace they were walking along Belgrave Road, it would take them the best part of twenty minutes.

Freddy moved quickly. He ran swiftly along Wanstead Park Road which ran parallel to Belgrave Road, then turned right down Endsleigh Gardens and stood on the corner where it joined Belgrave Road and looked back. The other people from the train seemed to have disappeared, but he could see Edith and Percy in the distance. Looking around he saw a clump of bushes in the front garden of the corner house, pushed his way through and stood breathing heavily, waiting.

As they approached, Edith appeared to be in high spirits. It had been an enjoyable evening, and she found herself in such a happy frame of mind that she was having second thoughts about the confrontation with Percy.

To shatter his hopes so abruptly after such a grand night out suddenly seemed a rather cruel thing to do.

Freddy would be away for six months. Why stir up something now? she thought. Surely she could find a more opportune and less hurtful time to broach the subject.

She was also thinking of the repercussions. What about her job? What would her family think? She realized that, in her eagerness to convince Freddy of her love, she'd failed to think things through properly.

For his part, Percy was happier than he had been for many a day, convinced that the tide was at last beginning to turn in his favour. Tonight, Edith had been like her old self, vivacious, funny and affectionate. She had even agreed to go to a dance with him at the weekend! Yes, the future looked decidedly rosy.

His happy thoughts were abruptly ended as they crossed over Endsleigh Gardens, when a figure stepped out of the shadows and stood in front of them, barring their way. To her horror Edith realized who it was.

'Oh, my God, Freddy. No!' she wailed. 'You've ruined everything.'

Percy was unable to comprehend what was happening. 'Bywaters?' he said, disbelievingly. 'What on earth..?'

Incensed by Edith's affectionate attitude towards Percy, and fired by alcohol, Freddy moved forward, grabbed him by the lapels of his jacket and shoved him violently up the street.

'You've got to give Edith a divorce, Thompson,' he shouted into his face. 'She doesn't love you, she loves *me*.'

Edith tried to come between them.

'Freddy, for God's sake, stop this!' she screamed.

With the blood now pounding in his head, Freddy was deaf to all entreaties and pushed Edith aside with such force that she fell and hit her head on the pavement where she lay stunned for a moment.

The sight of Edith lying on the ground finally galvanized Percy into action.

'You guttersnipe!' he roared, 'how *dare* you strike my wife?' and lunged at Freddy trying to grab him by the throat.

As he did so, Freddy lashed out at him several times with his knife. Percy gave a cry of pain, stopped and looked down in disbelief at the blood dripping from a wound on his forearm. To his horror, he realized that he was badly cut about the arms, chest and face.

As Percy stumbled towards his attacker, and grasped him round the waist to stop himself falling, Freddy struck again while he was doubled over, sinking the knife deep into the nape of his neck.

Somehow Percy got to his feet and staggered into the darkness further up Belgrave Road. Suddenly, he could go no further and collapsed against the brick wall skirting the road.

By now, Edith had come to and scrambled to her feet. As Freddy moved towards

Percy she cried out: 'Don't! Don't!' she pleaded. 'Oh, *don't!*'

Freddy stopped and, with one last look at Edith, ran off into the darkness.

By the time Edith got to him, Percy had managed to drag himself up to a semi sitting position, slumped against the wall. She knelt beside him and cradled his head in her arms. As she did so blood welled up in his mouth and spilled out over her hands and down the front of her coat.

'Oh, God! Oh, God!. she cried.

Percy was trying to speak. 'Edie,' he gasped. 'Why did he..?'

With a great effort Edith managed to control the panic in her voice.

'Lie still, dear,' she said. 'I must go and fetch help.'

'No.' Percy grasped her weakly by the wrists. 'Don't leave me, Edie,' he whispered. 'I...'

Edith gently disengaged herself, stood up and looked around frantically. As if in answer to her prayers, coming towards her were a man and a woman who had been walking behind them when they entered Belgrave Road.

Edith dashed back towards them. 'Oh, my God, help me,' she cried. 'It's my husband. He's bleeding badly. Please get a doctor.'

Startled out of their wits at being accosted in the early hours of the morning by a frantic woman covered in blood, the couple nevertheless agreed to help.

The woman, Miss Pittard, immediately set off for Doctor Maudsley's surgery at 32 Endsleigh Gardens. Edith and the woman's companion, Mr Clevely, followed.

When they reached the surgery, Edith began hammering on the knocker. When a light came on behind the glass-panelled front door, Edith turned to go.

'I must get back to my husband. Tell the doctor to come quickly,' she called as she ran back down the road.

Edith's mind was in turmoil as she desperately tried to come to terms with what had happened. The most important thing was to get Percy to a hospital as soon as possible, and after that..? As she tried to concentrate her mind a man appeared out of the darkness.

Mr Webber, a salesman, had been preparing for bed in his house in de Vere Gardens, some distance away from where the fight had taken place when he had heard Edith's pitiful cry quite clearly and decided to investigate.

Miss Pittard came running towards them to announce, breathlessly, that the doctor was on his way. 'Oh, thank God!' Edith said, fervently. Then turning to Percy. 'Won't be long now, dear. Everything's going to be alright.'

For the first time Miss Pittard saw Percy lying on he floor.

'What happened?' she asked, unable to see anything other than a crumpled figure on the pavement.

Even in her traumatized state, Edith's first instinct was to protect Freddy. 'I don't know,' she said. 'Somebody flew past, and when I turned to speak to him, blood was pouring out of his mouth.'

Five interminable minutes later, Doctor Maudsley arrived accompanied by Mr Clevely who was carrying his medical bag.

The part of the street in which Percy was lying was in semi darkness and Dr Maudsley had to strike a match to get a look at his patient. In the brief flare, he could see that blood was still seeping from Percy's mouth. Kneeling down beside him, he first felt for a pulse, then opened Percy's shirt front and listened to his heart through a stethoscope. After making one last attempt to find a pulse, he got to his feet and removed the stethoscope from his ears. 'I'm afraid there's nothing I can do,' he said gravely. 'I'm sorry, madam, your husband is dead.'

Edith let out a cry of anguish. 'No! No!' she wailed. 'Why did you not come *sooner* and save him?'

As Miss Pittard put a consoling arm round Edith's shoulders, Doctor Maudsley went back to his house to telephone for an ambulance and to notify the police. From his cursory examination under difficult conditions, he concluded that Percy had died as the result of an internal haemorrhage.

Meanwhile Freddy, his mind racing and unsure of the outcome of his encounter with Percy, was breathlessly making his way back to his home in Norwood.

After the fight, he had run further up Belgrave Road, then down Seymour Gardens where he disposed of the knife by dropping it down a drain. He then carried on down Highlands Gardens and through Wanstead Flats where he slowed down to a walking pace, heading in the direction of Stratford.

As he passed through the sleeping streets of Leytonstone, the combination of physical exertion and the cold night air had cleared his head sufficiently for him to realize the enormity of what had happened, and he realized that if the police became involved, he would have a lot of difficult questions to answer. Perhaps it mightn't come to that. Edith would cover up for him, so he would just have to wait and see what transpired.

Back at the scene of the crime, a police ambulance had arrived, driven by PC Harry Palmer, closely followed by two colleagues, constables George Pearcey and Cyril Geal on bicycles. They were joined a little later by Sergeant Walter Mew who now took command of the situation.

It all seemed fairly straightforward to Mew. Some poor devil had collapsed and died in the street from what the doctor who attended the man had said was an internal haemorrhage. He ordered Geal to go to the mortuary with Palmer while he and Pearcey escorted the distressed Mrs Thompson back to her house. On the way Edith suddenly said: 'They will blame *me* for this.' At the time Mew thought it an odd thing to say, but assumed it was due to her distraught condition and thought nothing more of it.

It was 1.15 when they arrived at number 41 where Edith opened the door and switched on the hall light.

Lying half awake in her upstairs bedroom, Mrs Lester heard unaccustomed, gruff voices coming from below and ventured out on to the landing in dressing gown and hair curlers to investigate.

The sight of two burly police officers and a dishevelled, distraught Edith caused her to catch her breath

'Good gracious me, Mrs Thompson,' she called. 'Whatever's happened?'

For perhaps the first time, Edith was actually glad to see Mrs Lester. The stocky little figure descending the stairs with a look of baffled concern on her face was the embodiment of normality in a world that was collapsing about her. She reached out a hand to her. 'There's been a terrible accident, Mrs Lester,' she said, her voice shaking. 'Mr Thompson has been taken to hospital.'

Now that Mrs Lester was closer to her she could see Edith's blood-soaked clothing. 'Lord help us!' she exclaimed. 'You're all covered in blood. What in Heaven's name has happened?'

Sergeant Mew interjected. 'Is there somewhere we could..?'

Mrs Lester quickly collected herself. 'Oh, yes, of course,' she said hastily. 'This way, if you please,' and led them down the hallway to the morning room.

As soon as Edith had been made comfortable Mrs Lester suggested she should make everyone a 'nice cup of tea'. Hot, sweet tea was always the best thing for shock in Mrs Lester's view, and she felt she needed something of the sort herself after all that had happened. She was joined in the kitchen a few moments later by Sergeant Mew.

'Can I have a word, Mrs...Lester, is it?' he said, sitting down at the kitchen table and producing his note book.

Mrs Lester nodded. 'Yes, that's right, Sergeant,' she said. 'Fanny Lester.'

'And how long have you lived here, Mrs Lester?'

'About ten years now,' she said, laying out the tea tray. 'Long before the Thompsons bought the place.'

'Get on alright with them do you?' he asked.

'Well, we don't mix socially, nothing of that sort,' she said, 'but we get on well enough, yes.'

'Cordial without being over-friendly then?' the sergeant said, smiling.

'Yes, that's right.' Mrs Lester couldn't help but notice what a fine figure of a man the sergeant was and began to regret not taking the curlers out of her hair before coming downstairs.

'Which hospital did they take Mr Thompson to?' asked Mrs Lester as she filled the milk jug.

'They didn't take him to a hospital, they took him straight to the mortuary.'

Mrs Lester almost dropped the tea pot in her surprise. 'But...Mrs Thompson said...'

'I'm afraid Mrs Thompson is in a state of shock.' Sergeant Mew had experience of this sort of thing. 'She's been told her husband is dead, but she can't, or won't, accept it.'

'Oh, my good Gawd!' Mrs Lester's legs suddenly gave way and she was forced to sit down. 'Whatever happened?' she asked, in a state of shock almost as profound as Edith's.

'Some sort of seizure, I believe. Doctor said it was a haemorrhage of some kind.'

There was silence for a moment as Mrs Lester digested the information. She shook her head. 'It don't seem possible,' she said. 'Why, I saw him only this morning; right as rain he was. "Be back late tonight, Mrs Lester," he said, "we're off to the theatre". I don't know, I really don't. Makes you think, don't it?'

Mew stood up. 'Shall I take the tray in or you, Mrs Lester?'

'Thank you, Sergeant.' Mrs Lester gave him a wan smile. 'Much obliged.'

When Freddy reached Stratford, he hailed a passing taxi

As the cab drove through the early morning streets of Mile End and Whitechapel, his mind was still working feverishly.

He desperately needed to speak to Edith to find out how Percy was. Perhaps she would telephone him at his mother's house? Anyway, he would be off to the Far East in 48 hours; that would give him a bit of breathing space. He guessed Percy had been badly hurt and that the police would be involved, but if things got really bad, he could always jump ship somewhere and lie low. For the moment he would just have to sit tight and await developments.

Meanwhile, back at Ilford Percy's Thompson's body had been taken to the police mortuary at St. Mary's church on the High Road where Palmer and Geal, began to undress and wash the body in readiness for the pathologist's examination.

First they emptied his pockets, and made a note of the contents, but it wasn't until they removed Percy's blood-soaked shirt that the stab wounds to the body were revealed.

It took the two policemen a few moments to realize the importance of their discovery. Palmer was the first to speak.

'This is no accident, Cyril,' he said tersely. 'Best get on to the station right away.' Geal nodded and headed off in the direction of the telephone.

Palmer looked down at the pale, lacerated body lying on the mortuary slab. 'You poor bugger,' he said, as he pulled the sheet up over Percy's head.

Sergeant Mew had just finished taking a statement from Edith when a constable arrived from Ilford police station. Taking the sergeant aside, he informed him of the latest developments. Almost certainly, it was now a murder inquiry.

Mew immediately cycled over to the mortuary and, with Palmer and Geal in attendance, examined the body of Percy Thompson. When the inspection was over there was no doubt in his mind that Edith Thompson must know more than she was letting on.

As he cycled back to Ilford police station he recalled the remark she had made after the 'accident'. 'They will blame *me* for this', she had said. Perhaps it hadn't been, as he had thought at the time, the remark of a distraught woman, but that of a *guilty* one!

After joining up with Sergeant Walter Grimes and acquainting him with the latest developments, they both returned to the scene of the crime to search for the murder weapon. Finding nothing, they began to walk the short distance back to Kensington Gardens.

They walked in silence for a while, each lost in his own thoughts. Grimes was the first to speak.

'Do you think *she* could have done it?'

Mew shook his head. 'No,' he said, 'but a pound to a penny she knows who did.'

It was just after 3am when Freddy arrived back at Westow Street and quietly let himself into the house.

As he moved towards the stairs, his mother's voice called from above. 'That you, Freddy?'

'Yes, mum,' he called back.

'What time do you call this?' she said. Receiving no answer, she closed her bedroom door.

As Freddy was lying awake in his bed in Norwood, Mrs Lester was ushering Mew and Grimes into the morning room where Edith was sitting still in her bloodstained clothes.

After thanking Mrs Lester for her assistance and suggesting she might now be better off in her bed, Mew got straight to the point. 'Mrs Thompson,' he said, 'did your husband carry a knife?'

Edith frowned. 'Good Heavens, no!'

'Do you have any objection to my examining your handbag?' he asked.

'Whatever for?'

Mew glanced briefly up at Grimes before continuing. 'New evidence has come to light regarding your husband's death,' he said, weighing his words carefully. 'He sustained...certain wounds to his body which *could* indicate something other than an accident.'

Edith's face was expressionless as she handed over her bag.

After rummaging through it briefly, Mew passed it back to her and stood up.

'Thank you, Mrs Thompson,' he said, picking up his helmet. 'I'm afraid there are going to be a lot more questions with regard to this matter. If I were you I'd try to get a good night's sleep.'

After the policemen had left, Mrs Lester came into the morning room. 'Come along, dear,' she said gently. 'I'll help you up to your room.'

Edith looked up at Mrs Lester, her face haggard . 'Oh, Mrs Lester,' she said with great sadness, 'what am I going to do?'

Outside in the street, the two policemen stopped briefly to compare notes.

'What do you think, Walter?' Mew asked, adjusting the front lamp on his bicycle.

Grimes looked pensive. 'She's covering up for someone, no doubt about that,' he said. 'Question is, why?'

Mew shrugged. 'It's out of our hands now,' he said, mounting his bicycle. 'The CID will have to sort that lot out.'

As the two guardians of the law cycled off together down Kensington Gardens the only house with a light still burning was number 41.

When Edith entered her bedroom, she saw that Mrs Lester had very kindly lit a fire for her and switched on one of the bedside lamps.

It was as she closed the door that Edith noticed Percy's blue Melton overcoat hanging from a hook on the bedroom door. Lifting it off, she laid down on the bed, switched out the light and pulled the coat up under her chin.

Lying there alone in the bedroom she had shared with her husband, watching the leaping shadows thrown up onto the ceiling by the flickering fire, Edith became aware of the aroma of Percy's pipe tobacco emanating from his overcoat and was suddenly engulfed by an overwhelming sense of loss and desolation. Percy was dead. His life cut short and her life devastated. That wasn't how it was supposed to be. *This* love story was meant to have a happy ending.

The bright and beckoning future Edith had dreamed of was suddenly dark and forbidding, and the present, overcast with remorse and anxiety.

Chapter 12

'Fate ordained our lot to be hard.'

By 11am the following day the area around Belgrave Road and Kensington Gardens was thronged with people as news of the murder spread quickly among the local populace. The *Ilford Recorder* and the *East Ham Echo* had already despatched reporters to the scene where, in due course, they were soon to be joined by members of the national press.

On the opposite side of the road to number 41, a small group of onlookers who had gathered to watch the comings and goings were rewarded when a taxi pulled up outside the house and Inspector Richard Sellars of Limehouse CID alighted.

Asking the cabby to wait he knocked on the front door, announced himself to Mrs Lester and was shown into the front parlour where Edith was being comforted by her mother.

After being told the dreadful news, Mrs Graydon had arrived in the early hours of the morning prepared to stay for as long as she was needed.

Having been appraised of all the known facts, Sellars was convinced that Edith was lying, and was determined to get to the truth.

'Mrs Thompson,' he began. 'This morning I have seen a police surgeon's report which concludes that your husband was stabbed to death last night.'

There was a gasp from Mrs Graydon and a moan of anguish from Edith as she buried her head in her hands.

Mrs Graydon was aghast. 'Surely not, Inspector?' she said, her voice heavy with disbelief.

'I'm afraid so, madam.' Sellars was in no mood to beat around the bush. 'Mrs Thompson,' he said pointedly, 'as you were the only other person present when that assault took place, would you care to make a statement?'

Mrs Graydon interrupted. 'Is this absolutely necessary, Inspector?' she pleaded, 'my daughter is mentally and physically exhausted.'

Sellars was unmoved. 'I'm afraid so, madam,' he said coldly. 'A man was brutally murdered last night and it is my duty to investigate that crime and bring the perpetrator to justice.' He turned his attention to Edith. 'I will ask you again, Mrs Thompson, would you like to make another statement?'

With an effort Edith composed herself. 'I have nothing to add to what I told Sergeant Mew last night,' she said defiantly.

Having lain awake most of the night, Freddy was hollow-eyed and listless the next morning.

'What were you doing out till all hours last night?'

Mrs Bywaters had come in from the shop to put the kettle on.

'Fell asleep on the train,' Freddy lied. 'Had to walk all the way back from Norwood Junction.'

'Serves you right.' Mrs Bywaters had no time for stop-outs. 'You couldn't have been up to any good at that time of morning anyway,' she added, tartly, as she went back into the shop.

By now, Freddy had decided the best thing to do was to behave as normally as possible until he knew exactly what was happening. He would go about his activities just like any other day. He would go to London with his mother, call in at the P&O office and then take Avis to the pictures just as if nothing had happened.

In the front parlour of 41 Kensington Gardens Inspector Sellars was looking at a copy of Edith's statement to Sergeant Mew.

'I'll just remind you of that statement, Mrs Thompson,' he said, and began to read: *'"We were coming along Belgrave Road and just passed the corner of Endsleigh Gardens, when I heard him call out 'Oh-er', and he fell up against me. I put out my arms to save him, and found blood, which I thought was coming from his mouth. I tried to help him out. He staggered for several yards towards Kensington Gardens, and then fell against the wall and slid down; he did not speak to me. I cannot say if I spoke to him. I felt him, and found his clothing wet with blood. He never moved after he fell. We had no quarrel on the way; we were quite happy together."'.*

Sellars looked up from the sheet of paper making no attempt to conceal the look of scepticism on his face. 'In the light of what I have now told you,' he said slowly, 'I would strongly advise you to make a fuller statement.'

Edith shook her head. 'I have nothing more to say.'

Sellars shrugged. 'Then I'm afraid I will have to ask you to accompany me to Ilford police station,' he said, getting to his feet.

Edith was in despair. 'Oh, no!' she said, clasping her hands. 'Why?'

'Because,' Sellars said heavily, 'I need to question you further on this matter in the presence of another police officer.'

Edith looked at her mother imploringly.

'Don't you think my daughter's already been through enough, Inspector?' Mrs Graydon said.

'We won't detain her any longer than necessary,' said sellers. Then, turning to Edith: 'Would you get your things, Mrs Thompson. I have a taxi waiting outside. The sooner we get this sorted out the sooner you will get back home.'

On her way out Edith knocked on Mrs Lester's door.

'I shan't be long, Mrs Lester,' she said. 'I have to go to the police station for a little while.

As the taxi drove off Mrs Lester watched from the doorway then went in and closed the door. 'Well, I never!' she said to herself. 'Mrs Thompson carted off to the cop shop. Fine goings-on I *must* say!'

When Freddy arrived with his mother at St Paul's station the first thing he did was to buy a midday newspaper. Finding no mention of anything untoward, he left his mother and made his way to the P&O offices where he had some things to do concerning the Far East trip.

It was around 11.40 when Edith, accompanied by her mother, arrived at the police station where she was shown into a cheerless room containing just a table and four wooden chairs. Inspector Sellars immediately reported to his divisional detective inspector, Francis Hall who, as senior officer, now took over. After considering the possible implications, Hall came to the conclusion he would need the help of an experienced senior detective. Picking up the phone on his desk, he dialled Whitehall 1212.

Detective Chief Superintendent Frederick Wensley was one of the Yard's 'Big Four' top detectives with a string of successful investigations to his name. A combination of dogged persistence coupled with a shrewd, analytical mind had helped him rise swiftly through the ranks to the senior position he now held with such distinction.

He was sitting at his desk debating whether to have an early lunch in the canteen or nip out for a sandwich and a pint at the pub, when the telephone rang.

'Wensley.'

'Good morning, sir. Inspector Hall here, Ilford CID.'

'Yes, Inspector, what can I do for you?'

Wensley listened intently as Hall outlined the details of the previous night's murder and his suspicions regarding the victim's wife.

Even before Hall had finished speaking, Wensley had made up his mind. 'I'll be over directly,' he said, hanging up the phone.

As he was driving to Ilford through pouring rain, Wensley mulled over the case he had been asked to handle.

There was nothing like a good murder to get his pulse racing and the adrenaline flowing, but his last big success had been back in March when he had brought young Harry Jacoby to justice for the murder of Lady White.

At 57 years of age, and with retirement beckoning, wouldn't it be nice, he mused, to bow out with another big 'un to his credit. If the wife *was* shielding someone, as Hall had suggested, then that someone was almost certainly a man. A lover perhaps? When he finally pulled up at his destination the scent of the hunt was already strong in his nostrils.

After a short but detailed briefing from Inspector Hall, Wensley immediately put in a telephone call to Chadwell Heath police station requesting the assistance of a female police officer. Then, accompanied by Hall, he went into the interview room.

As they entered, Edith was pacing up and down in an agitated manner.

'Mrs Thompson?' I'm Superintendent Wensley, and I...'

Edith rounded on him. 'Why are you doing this to me?' she demanded tearfully. 'Haven't I been through enough with my husband dying in my arms, and now being treated like this...' Unable to control herself, Edith burst into tears. As Mrs Graydon moved to comfort her daughter, Wensley intervened.

'Would you mind stepping outside for a moment, madam?' he said gently. 'I'm sure the desk sergeant will provide you with a cup of tea.'

Mrs Graydon took one last look at Edith, and was ushered out of the room by Hall.

'Please sit down, Mrs Thompson.' Wensley's tone was soft and conciliatory.

Wensley sat down opposite her and offered her his breast pocket handkerchief to dry her eyes. He waited patiently until Edith had recovered her composure before continuing.

'You know that is has been established beyond doubt that your husband died as a result of stab wounds?'

Edith nodded, wiping her eyes. 'Yes. It's horrible.'

'It *is* horrible,' Wensley said, 'and *puzzling*; because, you see, we cannot understand how he came by those injuries. Now please, Mrs Thompson, think back to last night. Is there anything you may have forgotten in all the alarm and confusion? Anything at all that might be of help to us?'

Although Edith was still not thinking clearly she had enough sense to realize that the time had come to change her story.

'Wait a minute,' she said, her brow wrinkling with concentration. 'Yes there was something. I remember now. Someone flew past. Yes, that's right. Percy said 'Oh-er', and when I turned to look at him there was blood coming from his mouth.'

'I see.' Wensley sat back in his chair and placed his fingertips together. 'Was this someone a man?'

'I suppose it must have been,' Edith said. 'It was very dark. I couldn't really see.'

'Which means you can't give us a description of him?'

'No,' Edith replied. 'As I said, it was very dark.'

Wensley studied her for a moment, then leaned forward, his arms resting on the table.

'Mrs Thompson,' he said earnestly, 'if you are - how shall I put it - *shielding*

FREDDY, PERCY AND EDITH IN THE BACK GARDEN OF 41 KENSINGTON GARDENS.
THIS PICTURE WOULD HAVE BEEN TAKEN IN JUNE OR JULY 1921.

EDITH AND PERCY IN ILFRACOMBE, AUGUST 1914. THERE IS A MARKED
DIFFERENCE BETWEEN THE HAPPY, CONFIDENT COUPLE HERE AND THE
STRAINED AND DISTANT THOMPSONS IN THEIR LAST PICTURE TOGETHER
TAKEN IN THEIR GARDEN IN SEPTEMBER 1922 (see front cover).

EDITH WITH FAMILY FRIEND, REG AKAM.

EDITH THOMPSON,
STUDIO PORTRAIT c1918.

FREDDY BYWATERS, STUDIO PORTRAIT c1919.

SOUTHSEA BEACH, 11 JUNE 1921. TAKEN BY AVIS WHILE THEY WERE WAITING TO BOARD THE FERRY FOR SHANKLIN. IT APPEARS THAT THERE WAS ALREADY AN INTIMACY BETWEEN FREDDY AND EDITH THAT PERCY WAS NOT YET AWARE OF.

THE OSBORNE HOUSE HOTEL, SHANKLIN PROMENADE c1920
(first building to the right of the clock), WHERE EDITH AND PERCY OCCUPIED
ONE OF THE ROOMS FACING THE SEA.

IN THE GARDEN OF 41 KENSINGTON GARDENS. PERCY WAS
ALREADY BECOMING RESENTFUL OF FREDDY'S OMNIPRESENCE.

D.I. FRANCIS HALL (left) AND
CHIEF INSPECTOR FREDERICK
WENSLEY LEAVING THE
AUTOPSY ON PERCY THOMPSON,
2 NOVEMBER 1922.

SERGEANT LILIAN WYLES.

MONTAGUE SHEARMAN K.C.
WHO PRESIDED OVER THE TRIAL.

THOMAS INSKIP,
THE SOLICITOR GENERAL.

SIR EDWARD MARSHALL-HALL K.C. (left)
WITH SIR HENRY CURTIS-BENNETT K.C.

CECIL WHITELEY K.C.

41 KENSINGTON GARDENS, ILFORD 1922.

15 WESTOW HILL, SOUTH NORWOOD 1922.

somebody, I strongly urge you to tell me now.'

'That's absurd,' she said. 'Why should I possibly want to shield anyone who attacked my husband?'

'Oh, a sense of loyalty perhaps - or love.'

There was a silence for a moment as they regarded each other.

'You see,' Wensley continued, 'if you *do* know who did this, and don't tell me, that makes you an accessory to murder.'

Edith straightened her back. 'There is nothing more I can tell you,' she said. 'May I go home now?'

'Not for the moment, I'm afraid.'

'This is *outrageous!*' Edith's voice was trembling. 'You are treating me like some...common criminal.'

Wensley crossed to the door

'We'll move you into the matron's room for the time being,' he said. 'It'll be more comfortable for you in there,' and went out, closing the door behind him.

Inspector Hall was waiting outside in the corridor smoking a cigarette.

'Any joy?' he asked.

Wensley shook his head. 'Not much. You're right about her covering up for someone though. Question is who, and why?'

'Mr Richard Thompson, the dead man's brother, is here, sir. I asked him to come in and talk to us.'

'Where is he?'

'In the CID office with Inspector Sellars.'

'Right, let's go and have a chat with him.'

As they walked to the office, Wensley said: 'The thing is, if Mrs Thompson sticks to her story, and no further evidence comes to light...we're up a gum tree.'

When they entered the CID room, Richard Thompson was standing looking out of the window.

'Mr Thompson?'

'Yes.'

'I'm Superintendent Wensley and this is Inspector Hall. Please sit down.'

Wensley and Thompson sat down while the two police officers remained standing.

'Thank you for coming in to see us, Mr Thompson. Especially at such a sad time for you and your family. As you know this is now a murder enquiry.'

Richard nodded. 'Yes. What a dreadful business,' he said sadly. 'Poor Edith. It must have been awful for her.'

'Yes. Tell me. How well do you know your sister-in-law?'

Richard shrugged. 'Fairly well, I'd say. I was best man at their wedding.'

'Was it a happy marriage, would you say?'

'As far as I could tell.' He paused. 'Well, apart from that bit of unpleasantness with their lodger that time.'

Wensley, who had been doodling on a note pad, suddenly looked up. 'Unpleasantness?'

'Yes. Young chap called Bywaters. From what I could gather my brother thought he was mooning around Edith a bit too much, and chucked him out. I could never understand why he put up with him in the first place.'

Wensley and Hall exchanged glances.

Wensley wrote 'Bywaters' in capital letters on his note pad.

'Do you know his first name?'

'Freddy. He's a seaman. Works for the P&O line.'

'Do you know his whereabouts now?'

'He lives over in south London, Norwood I think. But he's away at sea at the moment, I believe.'

'Thank you, Mr Thompson,' he said. 'You've been most helpful.'

Richard was a little surprised at the abrupt termination of the interview. 'Oh,' he said. 'Right you are. I'll...um, be off then. I hope you catch the swine who did this. Percy was a good man. Not an enemy in the world,' he said as he headed for the door.

'We'll do our best,' Hall said, opening the door for him.

As soon as Richard Thompson had left, Wensley picked up the telephone. 'Get me the head office of the P&O line, would you?' he asked the operator, then leaning back in his chair, put his hands behind his head and looked thoughtfully up at the ceiling. 'I wonder?' he said quietly.

The desk sergeant knocked and entered. 'Sergeant Wyles is here, Sir.'

'Oh good. Show her in.'

Lilian Wyles entered in a bedraggled state, her uniform soaked.

'Good grief!' Wensley said jovially. 'You look like a drowned rat. You didn't *swim* over from Chadwell Heath, did you?'

No. Sir,' she said, smiling nervously. Superintendent Wensley was a legend, and meeting him face to face was quite unnerving even for a police sergeant of Wyles's experience. 'I was driven over in the sidecar of a motorcycle.'

'Right, well get dried off, get yourself something to eat, then I want you to sit with a Mrs Thompson who is helping us with our enquiries into a murder. Don't get into conversation with her, just try to confine your answers to yes and no if you can but make a mental note of whatever she says. Could be important. She's in a bit of an emotional state at the moment so handle her carefully.'

As Wyles left to commence her duties the telephone rang. Sellars picked it up. 'Sellars.'

He held the phone to Wensley.

'P&O head office, sir.'

The matron's room was carpeted and comfortable, with an upholstered easy chair and a fire burning in the hearth but Edith was very ill at ease. While she was being detained there were things that needed attending to. Her employers would be wondering how long it would be before she was back at her desk at Carlton & Prior and someone would have to meet Ethel Vernon at Paddington Station. More importantly, there were certain personal items relating to Freddy in her desk drawer at Carlton & Prior that had to be removed.

Mrs Graydon did her best to placate her daughter but, as time went by, she was becoming more and more agitated.

Back in Inspector Hall's office, Wensley read over the notes he had made during the telephone call before reading them to Sellars.

'Frederick Edward Francis Bywaters. Born 1902. Ship's Writer with P&O since 1917. Lives at 15 Westow Hill, South Norwood. Right! Send two men over there with a search warrant. If he's there, tell them to bring him in.'

'So he's not at sea then?' said Hall, sensing a breakthrough.

'No,' Wensley said with grim satisfaction. 'His ship doesn't leave until midday Thursday.'

'I'll get on to it straight away.'

Wensley's pulse was beginning to quicken. 'And I'll go and have another chat to Mrs Thompson I think.'

Edith was sitting in the armchair with her eyes closed when Wensley entered.

'Would you mind stepping outside for a moment, Mrs Graydon?' he said.

'How much longer is this going to go on, Superintendent?' Mrs Graydon was almost as exasperated as her daughter.

'Not much longer now,' he said, reassuringly.

When Mrs Graydon had gone Wensley sat down opposite Edith.

'What now?' she said wearily.

'Mrs Thompson,' he said, casually, 'do you know Freddy Bywaters?'

Edith managed to retain her composure at this bombshell but although her face betrayed nothing, her mind was in a whirl.

Aware that he might have touched on a raw spot, Wensley was watching her closely.

'Yes,' Edith said calmly. 'He's a friend. A family friend.'

'Nothing more?'

'How do you mean?'

'Wasn't he a lodger in your house at one time?'

'A paying guest. Yes.' Edith was still apparently unfazed. 'He left in August of last year.'

'Under a cloud, I believe?'

'There was a difference of opinion between him and my husband. Yes.'

'When did you last see him?'

Edith thought for a moment. 'I'm not sure,' she said. 'He calls in on my family every so often. He's very friendly with my sister Avis, you see.'

'You haven't seen him recently then?'

'No.' Edith said nervously pushing a stray strand of hair behind her ear. 'What does Freddy Bywaters have to do with all this?' she asked.

Wensley shrugged. 'I was rather hoping *you* might tell me?'

Edith shook her head. 'I have already told you everything I know.'

Wensley stood up. 'I will arrange for your mother to pick up some clean clothes and toilet articles for you,' he said coldly. 'I am detaining you overnight.'

Edith's pent-up emotions suddenly spilled over and she burst into tears. 'This is monstrous,' she sobbed. 'I demand a solicitor...'

But Wensley had gone.

While Freddy wandered aimlessly around St Paul's Churchyard, Detective Constables Pike and Edwards were knocking on the door of his mother's house in Norwood.

When Mrs Bywaters opened the door to be confronted by two police officers enquiring after the whereabouts of her son, her first reaction was one of concern. Plain clothes policemen didn't come knocking on your door for pinching apples.

After establishing that her son was not at home, Pike produced a search warrant and Mrs Bywaters reluctantly admitted them into the house.

As they climbed the stairs to Freddy's bedroom, Edwards asked Mrs Bywaters if she knew where her son might be.

'Not now I don't,' she said, 'but I know where he'll be round about six o'clock time. 231 Shakespeare Crescent, over Manor Park way. He's taking a lady friend to the pictures.'

As she opened the door to Freddy's bedroom she asked, 'What do you want to see my Freddy for? He hasn't done nothing wrong, has he?'

'No, no,' Pike reassured her. 'Just want to ask him a few questions, that's all.'

Mrs Bywaters stood by the door watching as the two police officers methodically searched her son's room.

After going through the pockets of Freddy's clothes, they began to search the room. Underneath the bed, Edwards found a suitcase containing some clothes and a small bundle of letters written on lilac-coloured stationery. While he was sorting through them Mrs Bywaters spoke.

'They're from another lady friend of his. Writes to him all the time, she does.'

Edwards looked at the letters in his hand for a moment, then came to a decision. 'I'll take these with me, I think.'

Mrs Bywaters sniffed. 'I can't think why,' she said dismissively. 'Just a load of soppy love talk, that's all they'll be.'

Superintendent Wensley was having his long delayed lunch in a pub near the station when Hall burst through the door cock-a-hoop. 'Edwards and Pike have just got back from Norwood, Sir. They've found some letters from Mrs Thompson in his bedroom. I think you'd better come and read them.'

Mrs Graydon returned home in some distress and informed her husband about Edith's overnight detention at Ilford police station.

Mr Graydon was stunned by the news. 'What reason did they give?' he asked incredulously.

'To help them with their enquiries, that's all they would say.'

Mr Graydon shook his head. 'They can't think Edith had anything to do with it, surely?'

For the first time Mrs Graydon's resolve began to falter. She took out a handkerchief and dabbed her eyes. 'I don't know what to think, Will,' she said sadly. 'Edith wants me to go and see Avis to ask her to meet Ethel Vernon at Paddington Station. Then she wants her to go over to Carlton & Prior and remove some 'personal items' - they were the words she used - from the drawer in her desk. 'Most important', she said. And to ask Rose Jacobs to look after them for her.' She looked up at her husband, her face clouded with doubt. 'What does it all mean, Will?' she asked tearfully.

Mr Graydon put his arm around her. 'Come on, old girl,' he said gently, 'bear up.'

Mrs Graydon dried her eyes and got to her feet. 'I've got to get some toilet articles and a change of clothes for Edith,' she said. 'I don't know what time I'll be back. Will you be alright?'

Mr Graydon kissed his wife. 'Don't you worry about me,' he said tenderly. 'You go and look after Edith.'

It was almost six o'clock when Freddy arrived at St Paul's station to begin his journey to Manor Park and bought the *Evening News*.

There, tucked away on the inside front page was the news he had been dreading. It was a small article headlined. *"Shipping Clerk Murdered - Midnight Mystery at Ilford"*. It continued:

'Who is responsible for the mysterious death of Percy Thompson (33)?...It is stated that Mrs Thompson, who is about 27 years of age, has declared that she saw nobody attack her husband. She has shown great distress, and the police have found it difficult to obtain a coherent account of the affair from her...'

So the worst had happened, Percy was dead. After taking a few minutes to get over the initial shock, he read the article again.

No description of the assailant. No mention of a suspect. Good old Edith! She had covered up for him as he had hoped she would.

What now? Carry on as normal. Tomorrow he'd be off on a six month trip. Right now, he'd go to see the Graydons and offer his condolences.

With renewed optimism he put the newspaper in his overcoat pocket and bought a ticket to Manor Park station.

By the time he had finished reading the last of the letters, Wensley was a happy man. 'This puts a whole new complexion on everything,' he said, settling back in his chair.

'One, Mrs Thompson and Bywaters were lovers. Two, there was bad blood between Bywaters and Mr Thompson. Three, some of the these letters indicate a strong desire to do away with her husband.' He turned to Hall. 'Not a bad day's work I'd say. What do *you* think?'

Hall nodded.

'All we have to do now is place Bywaters at the scene of the murder and the game is up - for both of them.'

When Mr Graydon opened the door Freddy was the first to speak.

'I've just read about Percy in the evening paper,' he said in shocked tones. 'What a terrible thing.'

Mr Graydon nodded. 'Dreadful business. Come in, son.'

They walked through to the kitchen Freddy said: 'I could hardly believe it. Still can't. How is Edith taking it?'

'At the end of her tether by now I should think. They've had her down the police station since eleven o' clock this morning.'

Freddy was disturbed by this news. What were the police up to? he wondered.

'I've just made a pot of tea,' Mr Graydon said. 'Would you like a cup?'

While waiting for Ethel Vernon at Paddington station, Avis was trying to make some kind of sense out of what was happening.

She had already been to Carlton & Prior, removed the 'personal items' from Edith's desk and given them to Rose Jacobs for safe keeping, as requested. It was what those items *were* that had set her thinking.

What on earth was her sister doing with photographs of Freddy, and a picture of his ship, the *SS Morea*?

The more she thought about it the more troubled she became. However, her peace of mind would have been even more disturbed had she known that as soon as she had left Carlton & Prior, Rose Jacobs had picked up the phone and rung the police.

When Ethel Vernon arrived, they took a taxi to Kensington Gardens where, in view of all the confusion and uncertainty, Avis decided to leave her for the time being to await further developments.

As Avis arrived back home, Pike and Edwards were about to unlatch the front gate.

'Can I help you?' Avis asked, paying the cabby.

'We're police officers, Miss,' Edwards said.

'Oh dear. What now?' The bewildering events of the last eighteen hours had left Avis apprehensive.

'We're looking for a Frederick Bywaters. We were told he might be here.'

'Freddy?' Avis was confused. 'Yes, he er...What do your want him for?'

'Can we talk about it inside?' Edwards said, nodding in the direction of the front door.

Freddy was sitting at the kitchen table drinking his tea when Avis entered, closely followed by Pike and Edwards.

'These two gentlemen are police officers,' Avis said to Freddy, 'they want to talk to you.'

'Are you Frederick Bywaters?' Pike asked.

Although taken by surprise, Freddy remained calm. 'I am.'

'Then we must ask you to accompany us to Ilford police station,' said Pike.

'What for?' Freddy wanted to know.

'We'd like to ask you a few questions.'

'About what?'

The two policemen exchanged looks.

'It's to do with the murder of Mr Thompson last night.'

'Why me?' asked Freddy, sipping his tea.

'I understand you knew him.'

'We all did,' Freddy said, indicating Mr Graydon and Avis.

'Yes, but it's *you* they want to talk to, Mr Bywaters. So if you'd just get your coat...'

'I'd like to finish my cup of tea first, if you don't mind.'

The two policemen were becoming irritated by Freddy's cockiness, but Pike decided to let it pass.

'Of course,' he said, amiably. 'No hurry.'

In the CID room at Ilford police station, Wensley was issuing orders on the telephone.

'...I want you to search the cabin of Frederick Bywaters...that's right, and bring back anything you find, anything at all...the SS *Morea,* spelt M.O.R.E.A...Yes, Tilbury Docks. Thank you.'

After hanging up the phone, he placed the letters prominently on the desk in front of him and nodded to Hall who opened the door to admit Edith.

'Would you like to come in, Mrs Thompson?' he said.

Edith was ushered in by Sergeant Wyles, who then withdrew.

'Do sit down!' Wensley indicated the chair opposite him.

As Edith moved towards the desk her eyes fell upon the letters. Knowing both men would be watching her closely she fought to control her emotions, but the blood had already drained from her face and her knees gave way momentarily.

Hall took her arm and helped her into the chair.

Wensley studied her for a moment before speaking. 'Do you recognize these letters?' he asked.

Edith nodded.

'They're signed 'Peidi'. Is that you?'

'Yes,' she said quietly. 'I wrote those letters.'

'Would you agree with me,' Wensley continued, 'that they are couched in very passionate terms?'

'Affectionate,' Edith corrected.

'Oh, more than that I would say.' Wensley put on his spectacles, picked up one of the letters and read it out loud.

"Yes, darlint, you are jealous of him - but I want you to be - he has the right by law to all you have the right to by nature and love - yes, darlint - be jealous, so much so that you will do something desperate."'

Wensley looked at Edith over the top of his glasses. 'Just how desperate did you want him to be, Mrs Thompson? Desperate enough to commit murder?'

By now, Edith had managed to regain some of her composure and was thinking a little clearer. So they know about her love affair with Freddy - but that was not a crime. They still had nothing to link him with Percy's death.

'Of course not,' she said, dismissively.

Wensley picked up another letter.

'What about this then?' he said.

' *"Don't forget what we talked in the tearoom. I'll risk it and try if you will."* This letter is dated the day before your husband was murdered.' He paused for a moment. 'What was it you were prepared to risk, Mrs Thompson?'

'My husband's anger when I asked him for a divorce.'

They looked at each other in silence for a few moments.

'Is there anything all at you want to say to me?' he asked with the air of a man who already knew the answer.

Edith shook her head emphatically.

Wensley sighed. 'Very well,' he said, heavily.

Hall opened the door and Edith made her exit, back erect and head held high.

'What do you think, sir?' said Hall, closing the door.

Wensley put his hands together as if in prayer and placed them in front of his mouth. 'I think,' he said, 'that they were in it together. I think they planned it together, and carried it out together. Early hours of the morning, badly lit street, no one about, no witnesses - perfect. Trouble is, if she sticks to her story and we can't budge her, we're up the creek without a paddle.'

The telephone on the desk rang. Hall picked it up.

'CID...Right, thank you.' He put the phone down and turned to Wensley. 'They've just brought Bywaters in, Sir.'

In her room, Edith was pacing up and down wringing her hands, watched by her concerned mother and an impassive Sergeant Wyles.

'Do sit down, dear,' Mrs Graydon pleaded. 'It doesn't do any good getting all worked up like this.'

Edith stopped by the window and looked out across the station yard to the back of the police station and the door to the CID office.

'Oh, God!' she cried vehemently, throwing her head back. '*When* is this nightmare going to end?' She turned away from the window. 'How long are they going to keep me here?'

While Edith was standing with her back to the window, Freddy, escorted by two uniformed policemen, came out of the door of the main building, walked across the yard and went towards the door leading to the C.I.D. office.

If he had glanced to his right he would have recognized Edith immediately, even with her back turned towards him. If Edith had turned around at that moment she would have seen her lover under police escort. If Mrs Graydon had been standing up she would almost certainly have seen Freddy.

The only person who *did* see him was the one person in the room who had no idea, at that time, who he was - Sergeant Wyles.

From the moment Freddy entered the CID room he was on the offensive. 'What's all this about? Why have you brought me here?' he demanded to know.

'Please sit down, Mr Bywaters.' Wensley indicated the chair opposite his own.

'Here, let me take your coat,' said Hall.

He helped Freddy off with his overcoat and hung it on the hat stand. Freddy sat down and looked around the room while Hall remained standing.

'I'm Superintendent Wensley and this is Inspector Hall,' Wensley began.

'What do you want with *me*?' Freddy demanded.

'We are investigating the murder of Mr Percy Thompson,' Wensley said, 'and you are here to help us with our enquiries. Would you tell us about your movements last night. Mr Bywaters?'

'Certainly,' Freddy said. 'I arrived at Mr and Mrs Graydon's house at around seven o'clock, sat around chatting for an hour, then I took Avis Graydon out for a drink at the Avenue Hotel where we stayed until closing time. After that, I saw Avis home, left her about eleven o'clock and walked to East Ham underground station where I caught a train to Victoria. When I got there, I found I'd missed the last train to Gypsy Hill so I decided to walk home. I finally got back at about three o'clock in the morning.'

'You didn't go anywhere near Ilford?'

Freddy smiled. 'Why would I want to do that?' he said. 'It's in the opposite direction.'

Wensley was beginning to find Freddy's attitude irksome, but pressed on.

'Do you carry a knife, Mr Bywaters?' he asked.

'Freddy snorted derisively. 'Good Lord, no.'

'Lot of seaman do,' Wensley reasoned.

'Not this one,' Freddy said, holding up his two fists. 'Not while I can use these.'

By now Wensley decided he had had just about enough of this young whippersnapper's impertinence and decided it was time to take him down a peg or two. Opening a drawer, he took out the bundle of letters and placed them on the desk.

The effect was not quite as dramatic as Wensley had hoped. Freddy was surprised, certainly, but his face betrayed no other emotion.

'Do you recognize those letters?' Wensley asked.

'Since they are all addressed to me, of course I do,' Freddy said irritably.'

'From Mrs Thompson?'

'Yes.'

'Were you and she lovers.'

'You must have read the letters. I would have thought that was obvious.'

Again, Wensley had to restrain himself from putting this cheeky young pup well and truly in his place.

'Can you explain,' he said civilly. 'The references in those letters to what appears to be attempts by Mrs Thompson to rid herself of her husband?'

'Yes I can,' Freddy said airily. 'Edith, Mrs Thompson, is - how shall I put it? She lives in a fantasy world a lot of the time. By writing those sort of letters she was trying to prove to me that she was doing something positive to remove her husband so that we could be together. In reality, she was doing nothing of the sort. It was all pure invention.'

During the interrogation, Hall had been standing by the door near the hat stand, and had become interested in some stains on the arm of Freddy's overcoat.

'Excuse me, sir,' he said to Wensley, who was considering Freddy's last remark. He turned to Freddy. 'Were you wearing this coat last night, Mr Bywaters?'

Freddy hesitated for a moment, but realizing it was something that could easily be checked, replied in the affirmative.

'Would you come and have a look at this, sir,' said Hall.

Wensley got up and went over to where Hall was standing holding the coat sleeve.

Lowering his voice Hall said, 'these stains look like blood to me, sir.'

Wensley put on his glasses, looked closely at the sleeve for a few seconds then straightened up. 'Well I know a quick way to find out,' he said.

Taking the *Evening News* from the pocket of the coat he said to Freddy, 'Mind if I use a piece of your newspaper?' Without waiting for a reply, Wensley tore off a strip of paper and folded it over into a wad. Then, using a little water from a jug on the desk, he dampened it.

'I saw a police doctor do this once,' he said to a mystified Hall. 'It's a bit rough and ready, but...'

Taking the dampened wad of paper he pressed it gently on the stain, then lifted it off. 'Hey presto!' he said, triumphantly. There, staining the wad of paper, were several small red blotches.

Wensley turned to Freddy. 'We shall be retaining your overcoat for forensic examination, Mr Bywaters.'

Freddy jumped to his feet. 'You can't do that,' he said hotly. 'I shall be needing it.'

'Not tonight, sonny.' Wensley was savouring this moment. 'You will be staying here.'

Freddy was indignant. 'Are you arresting me?'

'No, lad.' Wensley began to fill his pipe from a tobacco pouch. 'Just detaining you overnight for further questioning, that's all.'

He nodded to Hall, who opened the door and beckoned to the waiting police escort.

'Mr Bywaters will be staying the night with us,' he said with heavy irony. 'Make up a bed for him in the library would you. Oh! And make sure he's well looked after.'

As Freddy was led away still protesting vigorously, Hall allowed himself a wry grin. 'Cocky little bugger, isn't he?' he said.

Wensley lit his pipe.

'He's like a lot of young people nowadays,' he said between puffs. 'No respect for their elders. But,' he went on, 'he's no fool. He knows we can't hold him for very long before...'

The telephone on the desk rang. Hall picked it up.

'CID...Yes...Good. Bring them all back here.'

Hall replaced the receiver. 'They've found another bundle of letters in Bywaters's cabin on his ship, sir. Fifty or more they reckon. All written on the same lilac-coloured notepaper.'

Wensley sat back in his chair and puffed on his pipe . 'I think it's all beginning to knit together rather nicely,' he said from behind a swirl of tobacco smoke.

'Don't you?'

In makeshift beds, under the same roof, less than twenty feet apart, Edith and Freddy both lay awake in the darkness of an unaccustomed room, each unaware of the other's presence and close proximity.

Freddy, though worried, was still optimistic and thinking clearly.

He had assumed that Edith had been released long since and wondered how she was coping. From what had transpired it was obvious that she had not told the police anything; otherwise they would have charged him by now. Edith was still covering up for him, thank God!

And even if the stains on his coat sleeve *did* turn out to be the same type of blood as Percy's, what did that prove? There must be millions of people with the same blood group - including himself, more than likely.

The discovery of the letters had been a bit of a facer, and he cursed himself for not destroying them as Edith had always advised him to do. But they didn't prove anything either - except the existence of a love affair between them.

No, if Edith kept her head and stuck resolutely to her story, there was not one shred of positive evidence linking him with the crime.

His knowledge of the law was fairly sketchy but he did know that after a certain time they either had to charge him or release him, something like that anyway. It was not beyond the realms of possibility that they would let him go in time to board his ship before she sailed on the midday tide. With something approaching confidence occupying his mind, Freddy turned over and settled down to sleep.

In contrast to Freddy's optimism Edith was deeply despondent. She had fully expected to be at home in her own bed this night, not lying on an uncomfortable camp-bed in a police station.

Although utterly exhausted, Edith knew that sleep would be impossible. She got out of bed, went over to the window, and looked over the deserted station yard. It had been raining, and in the reflection from several still-lighted windows around the quadrangle, the asphalted surface looked like a pool of ink-black water. A distant church clock struck three. The melancholy that Edith always associated with church bells, turned her mind once again to Percy, lying cold and lifeless in a bleak mortuary somewhere.

Suddenly, overcome with grief and remorse, she started to cry, her body wracked by huge, gulping sobs.

Back in the CID room it was almost midnight by the time Superintendent Wensley had finished reading the last of the letters found in the *Morea*.

He leaned back in his chair, took off his glasses and rubbed his eyes. 'Getting too old for these late-night jobs,' he said, yawning.

'It's been a long day, sir.' Hall was feeling pretty tired himself.

'But a very productive one, I'd say.' Wensley lit up his pipe. 'Let's just go through what we've got so far. It's all beginning to fit together like a jigsaw,' he said, contentedly. 'It's all in these letters. They're the key, in that they provide us with the most important ingredient - motive.

'It's all here: adulterous, scheming wife, jealous lover, unwanted husband. As for opportunity - we only have Bywaters's account of his whereabouts at the time of the murder. He says he left Manor Park at 11 o'clock and arrived home at *three in the morning*! Which, in my book, gave him ample time to get himself over to Ilford, do his dirty work, and get back to Norwood.

'Which brings us to the weapon. Bywaters denies ever owning a knife but he's a sailor. They all carry knives.' Wensley paused to fill his pipe.

'It was cleverly planned, I'll give them that. She goes off to the theatre with her husband knowing full well that it'll be past midnight by he time they get back to Ilford. Then, in a dimly-lit street, with no one about, Bywaters creeps up behind the unfortunate Mr Thompson and stabs him in the back. After he makes good his escape - and not before - Mrs Thompson calls for help. Since when, she has done her utmost to keep the truth from us and protect her fancy man. But she won't succeed. They will both be brought to justice, you can be sure of that. And it's these letters that will do for them.'

Wensley consulted his pocket watch and rose to his feet. 'Time I was getting off home,' he said crossing to the hatstand.

'Far to go, sir?' Hall said, helping him on with his overcoat.

'Palmer's Green.'

'Nice up that way.'

'Yes, very pleasant. Oh, by the way, I have to be at the Yard tomorrow so I'll be in some time late afternoon.'

'Thanks for all your help, sir,' Hall said sincerely. 'It's been quite an education.'

'Work on the *woman*,' Wensley said as he walked to the door. 'I think she's about ready to crack.'

After midday on Thursday 5th October, Freddy found himself still under lock and key and Edith's mental state was becoming more volatile as the day wore on with no indication as to when she would be free to go.

In the CID room, Hall had been joined by his colleague, Inspector Sellars and, over a cup of tea, they were assessing the situation and discussing their next move.

Sellars was all in favour of the well-tried 'nice copper, nasty copper' approach with each taking it in turns to question, one aggressively, one kindly. But Hall had another idea.

Knowing that Edith had no inkling of Freddy's presence at the station, he saw an opportunity to shock her into an admission of guilt.

'What if Mrs Thompson were suddenly confronted by the sight of lover-boy being restrained by two big, uniformed coppers, as if under arrest?'

'She'd think the game was up and break down and confess. Is that what you're thinking?' Sellars was dubious.

'It's a possibility, Dick. She's in a very delicate emotional state at the moment. I think seeing Bywaters for the first time since the night of the murder, apparently under arrest, might just take her over the edge.'

Sellars shook his head. 'I don't know. It's all highly irregular. Wensley would never sanction a thing like that.'

'Wensley doesn't need to know, does he,' Hall said.

There was a moment of silence while Sellars examined his conscience.

'As far as I'm concerned,' Hall went on, 'in this instance, the end justifies the means, and if using a bit of skulduggery helps bring these two bastards to justice, I for one will not be losing any sleep over it, I can tell you that.'

Sellars was finally won over. 'Alright,' he said, 'how shall we go about it?'

Wensley was not due back until 5 or 6 so they decided to wait until late afternoon to spring their trap.

At 4.30 Sellars went into the library, ostensibly to talk to Freddy, and stationed himself by the window overlooking the courtyard.

Meanwhile, Hall went to the matron's room and asked Edith to accompany him to the CID office, along with Sergeant Wyles.

As they crossed the yard and entered the main building, Sellars was waiting.

Timing it to perfection, he flung open the library door just as they were passing to reveal Freddy, flanked by two policemen.

The effect on Edith was far greater than either of the two conspirators had imagined.

Before Freddy could utter a word Edith reacted. 'Oh God! Oh God! she cried. What can I do? Why did he do it? I didn't *want* him to do it.'

The dam had finally burst.

Freddy started to say something but was immediately bundled away, and the library door slammed shut.

In the corridor, Edith, ashen-faced and trembling, was being supported by Sergeant Wyles.

'Mrs Thompson,' Hall said gravely. 'In view of what you have just said - in front of witnesses - I would strongly advise you to make a statement at this time.'

Still numb from shock, Edith just shook her head.

Hall was becoming impatient. Having come so close to a confession he was in no mood to be thwarted. Now, eager to seize the moment, he decided to lie. 'It's no use your saying Bywaters didn't do it,' he said grimly, 'because he's already told us he *did*.'

For Edith this was the final straw.

'Yes,' she said, her voice trembling. 'I must tell the truth. I know that now.'

'Yes, that's the best thing.' Hall was reassuring. 'Make a clean breast of it, then you can put this whole ghastly affair behind you.'

In the library, Freddy's supreme self-assurance had all but deserted him.

He was slumped in a chair, his chin on his chest, desperately trying to think of a way out of the perilous situation in which he now found himself. In his heart, however, he knew the game was up. Edith's fragile resistance had finally crumbled. From now on it would be a battle for survival.

A young constable entered with a message for Sellars.

'Inspector Hall's compliments, sir,' he said. 'Would you join him in the CID room, soon as you can.'

As Sellars crossed to the door, Freddy lifted his head. 'What's going to happen to Mrs Thompson? he asked.

'You'll find out soon enough,' Sellars replied curtly, closing the door firmly behind him.

From the look of triumph on Hall's face, Sellars knew immediately that their plan had succeeded. A constable had just finished typing out Edith's statement which Hall was checking through with a look of of grim satisfaction.

Edith, a picture of utter dejection, was sitting with her hands clasped tightly together, staring at the floor.

'Mrs Thompson.' Hall said briskly. 'In the presence of Inspector Sellars and Sergeant Wyles, I am now going to read you the statement you have just made to me.

'"*When we got near Endsleigh Gardens, a man rushed out of the gardens and knocked me away and pushed me away from my husband. I was dazed for a moment. When I recovered, I saw my husband scuffling with a man. The man whom I know as Freddy Bywaters was running away. He was wearing a blue overcoat and a grey hat. I knew it was him, although I did not see his face.*"'

Hall looked up. 'Is that correct?' he asked.

'Yes,' Edith replied in a whisper.

'Then would you be good enough to sign it at the bottom for me?'

Edith signed her name followed by Sellars, Sergeant Wyles and finally Hall himself.

When all the formalities had been completed, Hall carefully blotted the signatures, and stood up. Then, turning to Wyles he said, 'Take Mrs Thompson back to the matron's room, would you, Sergeant?'

Edith was bewildered. 'But...you said I would be free to go after this.'

'I said no such thing.' Hall was dismissive. 'You may be an accessory to a murder and as such, you will remain in custody till we reach a decision about whether to charge you. Take her away, Sergeant.'

Wyles took Edith by the arm and led her away. As they reached the door, Edith turned to Hall. 'This is monstrous,' she said, her voice breaking with emotion. 'You led me to believe...'

But Hall had already turned away.

It was almost 6pm when Freddy was eventually taken to the CID room.

Hall had decided to let him 'sweat' for a bit; a ploy he often used to soften up a suspect before interrogation.

In Freddy's case, however, it had given him time to think and to decide what he was going to do. He realized that for him there was no escape, but he was determined to clear Edith and extricate her from the ghastly mess in which he had landed her.

Hall waited for Freddy to sit before speaking.

Holding up Edith's confession he said: 'Mr Bywaters, I intend to charge you *and* Mrs Thompson with the wilful murder of Percy Thompson.'

Freddy leapt to his feet.

'Why her?' he demanded angrily. 'Mrs Thompson was not aware of my movements that night.'

Hall motioned to Freddy to sit down.

Realizing he had touched a raw nerve Hall again decided to resort to subterfuge.

'Tell you what I'll do,' he said. 'You give me a full confession and I'll do my best to get Mrs Thompson back home by tonight.'

Freddy nodded. It was the only thing he could do now. 'I wish to make a statement:

'Mrs Edith Thompson was not aware of my movements on Tuesday 3rd October. I left Manor Park at 11pm and proceeded to Ilford. I waited for Mrs Thompson and her husband. When near Endsleigh Gardens I pushed her to one side, also pushing him further up the street. I said to him, 'You have got to separate from your wife', He said, 'No'. I took my knife from my pocket and we fought and he got the worst of it.

'Mrs Thompson must have been spellbound for I saw nothing of her during the fight. I ran away down Endsleigh Gardens, through Wanstead, Leytonstone, Stratford; got a taxi at Stratford to Aldgate, walked from there to Fenchurch Street, got another taxi to Thornton Heath, then walked to Upper Norwood, arriving home about 3pm.

'The reason I fought with Thompson was because he never acted like a man to his wife. He always seemed several degrees lower than a snake. I loved her and I couldn't go on seeing her leading that life. I did not intend to kill him. I only meant to injure him. I gave him an opportunity of standing up to me as a man but he wouldn't. I have had a knife some time; it was a sheath knife. I threw it down a

drain when I was running through Endsleigh Gardens.'

Leaving Freddy sitting at the desk, Hall crossed over the corridor and went into the matron's room where Edith was pacing anxiously up and down.

'I would like to talk to you again, Mrs Thompson. Would you come with me?'

Edith glanced up at the clock. It was just after 8pm. Perhaps they were going to let her go home.

As Edith arrived , she and Freddy exchanged glances and wan, rueful smiles, but did not speak.

Also in the room were Hall, Sellars, two uniformed policemen, Sergeant Wyles and Superintendent Wensley who had joined them during Hall's absence.

Wensley was delighted by the speed with which the investigation had been brought to such a successful conclusion - so much so that he chose not to enquire too closely into the methods used to achieve that end. As he saw it, two murderers had been brought to book, and if a few rules had been bent in the process, then so be it.

Hall, who had been sitting at his desk, rose to his feet.

'Frederick Edward Francis Bywaters. Edith Jessie Thompson,' he said. 'You are jointly charged with the wilful murder of Percy Thompson...'

At this there was a gasp of disbelief from Edith.

'It is wrong! It is wrong!' Freddy protested vehemently.

Hall carried on regardless. 'You will remain here overnight and appear at Stratford Magistrates Court tomorrow morning. You don't have to say anything, but anything you do say will be taken down and may be used in evidence against you. Take them down to the cells.'

Edith was stunned. She had fully expected to be released now that Freddy had confessed.

'No...no...' she stammered. 'I am innocent.'

As Freddy was led away, he cast an anguished glance back over his shoulder at Edith, but it went unnoticed.

Left alone in a dismal, bare prison cell Edith was sitting motionless on the bunk bed, her legs drawn up under her chin, staring into space, utterly unable to come to terms with the devastating turn of events.

Not ten yards away, Freddy was lying on his bunk planning his next moves. He had done his best for Edith, now he had to look after himself. First he would co-operate fully with the police, that would go well for him in court. At twenty years of age he was still a minor in the eyes of the Law - that was in his favour too. Perhaps the court would accept a plea of manslaughter. He could claim provocation, even self-defence. No, Freddy Bywaters wasn't finished yet, not by a long chalk.

At 231 Shakespeare Crescent the mood was one of stunned disbelief.

Mrs Graydon had arrived home in some distress at having to leave her daughter at the police station for another night, only to learn of Freddy's arrest in connection with Percy's murder.

As she, Mr Graydon, Newenham and Avis sat together in the front parlour, each deep in thought, each desperately trying to make some kind of sense out of the baffling sequence of events, it was Avis who was beginning to think the unthinkable. Having seen the contents of Edith's desk she knew there was a strong connection between Edith and Freddy, and was beginning to realize that there was far more to this tragic affair than had first been apparent.

Mrs Graydon was the first to break the silence.

'They can't think young Freddy had anything to do with it, surely?' she asked looking at the others for support.

Newenham shook his head. 'There's no smoke without fire, mum,' he said solemnly.

Mrs Graydon heaved a deep sigh. 'I don't know what to make of it all, I really don't,' she said sadly.

'If only there was something we could *do*!' Mr Graydon had been racking his brains to come up with a solution.

Avis rose to her feet. 'I'll tell you exactly what we can do,' she said briskly. 'First thing tomorrow morning I'm going round to see Mr Stern.'

Chapter 13

*"The days pass - no they don't pass, they just drag
on and on and the end of all this misery and
unhappiness is no nearer in sight."*

F.W. Stern was the family solicitor, a portly man with a round face and receding hair. But to Edith on the morning of 6th October he was nothing less than a knight in shining armour, galloping to her rescue astride a fiery white stallion. Indeed, she was so overcome with relief at seeing him that she threw her arms around his neck and had to be restrained by Sergeant Wyles.

He had hastened to the police station as soon as Avis had contacted him and discovered, to his dismay, that his client had already been charged with murder and was due to appear at Stratford Magistrates Court that very morning.

Left alone with Edith in an interview room, Mr Stern immediately set about putting her mind at rest, and assuring her that the charge of murder laid against her was preposterous and would never stand up in court.

Edith leaned across the table and grasped Mr Stern's arm tightly. 'Then why are they doing this to me?' she pleaded.

'As I understand it,' he said slowly, 'they are alleging collusion between you and Mr Bywaters in your husband's murder.'

Edith shook her head in disbelief. 'I don't understand.'

'There are some letters I believe, letters I haven't had time to read yet, which the police say implicate you in the crime.'

'That's absurd,' she said, her eyes brimming with tears.

'Of course it is.' Stern's manner was reassuring. 'And I'm sure the court will think so, too. It's quite possible,' he went on, 'that you might even be sleeping in your own bed tonight.'

Edith looked up, a glimmer of hope in her eyes. 'Oh, Mr Stern, do you really think so?' she said, wiping away the tears with the back of her hand.

'Shouldn't be at all surprised,' he said, smiling confidently.

In the huge surge of relief and gratitude that engulfed her, Edith was tempted to throw her arms around Mr Stern's neck again, but contented herself with squeezing his hand. 'Thank you, Mr Stern,' she said emotionally.

Stern placed his other hand on hers. 'I'll be there by your side,' he said. 'We'll soon sort this mess out, don't worry.'

Edith's and Freddy's appearance at Stratford Petty Sessions that morning coincided with the opening of the inquest at into the death of Percy Thompson at Ilford Town hall where, after hearing formal evidence of identification by Mr Graydon, there was an adjournment until Thursday 19th October. The body was then removed from the mortuary and, by arrangement, taken to the Graydon family home at 231 Shakespeare Crescent.

As the Thompsons had no 'head of family', (Percy's father having died some years previously), Mr Graydon offered to undertake the distressing legal necessity of identifying Percy's body. Not only that, he also offered to have Percy's remains laid out in the front room of 231 and take care of all the funeral arrangements.

It was a generous gesture from a kindly man and one that was gratefully accepted by the dead man's family.

Outside Stratford Magistrate's Court a sizeable crowd had gathered, spurred on by the prominence given to the case by the popular press who, suspecting a possible sensation, had despatched their top crime reporters to cover the committal proceedings.

Freddy was the first to arrive accompanied by an Inspector Leonard Williams carrying the exhibits to be used in evidence.

Later, in the cells beneath the court, as Freddy watched the inspector labelling his personal effects, he realized that the police had not yet found the murder weapon.

After thinking about it for a moment, he decided to make his first move in co-operating with the police.

'Have you not found the knife yet?' he asked.

Williams shook his head. 'Searched every drain in Endsleigh Gardens.'

Freddy frowned. 'Did I say Endsleigh Gardens?'

'That's what's in your statement.'

'Now I come to think about it, Freddy said, 'it wasn't Endsleigh Gardens, it was *Seymour* Gardens. Yes. Last drain on the left before Belgrave Road.'

Williams looked up sharply.

Without the murder weapon, the police case was not a particularly strong one. A good barrister might argue that Freddy's statement could have been made under duress and although the bloodstain on his overcoat *was* the same type as the murdered man's, it was also the same as the accused - hardly conclusive evidence. But the *murder weapon*; Now that was something else entirely. Fingerprints on the handle, bloodstains on the blade...

He looked at Freddy, wondering what had possessed him to volunteer information that could, quite possibly, send him to the gallows.

'Thank you, Mr Bywaters,' he said. 'Your co-operation will be noted.'

'Glad to be of help,' Freddy said and smiled, unaware of the perilous position in which he had just placed himself.

On entering the court, Edith smiled at her family seated in the public gallery before taking her place in he dock.

After the charges had been read out Inspector Hall went into the witness box and read the statements made by the two accused.

Five minutes later, with the brief formalities completed, Mr Stern rose to make an application for bail which, to his dismay, was denied. 'But Your Honour,' he protested, 'Mrs Thompson is a woman of substance and impeccable character, with her own home and a supportive family. Surely an order for bail is appropriate in her case?'

The presiding magistrate was having none of it. 'Mr Stern.' he said dryly,' your client is facing a charge of wilful murder. I hardly think it right or proper to allow her freedom of movement and contact. Application denied.'

Stern looked across at Edith, but she was sitting with her head bowed. She would not, after all, be sleeping in her own bed that night and her disappointment was intense.

After being allowed a few moments with her mother, Edith was taken by taxi to Holloway Prison in north London, while Freddy was sent to Brixton.

When Edith arrived at the courtyard at Holloway, the unrelieved grimness of the building made her shudder. But there was worse to come. All her personal belongings were confiscated, recorded and placed in a draw-string bag. Then, she was told to remove her clothes and take a bath; all under the stony stare of a grim-faced wardress.

She was given flannelette prison issue underwear and a shapeless, coarse-textured smock. Finally, she was issued with a pair of heavy shoes that were at least two sizes too big for her.

By the time she had been medically examined by a male doctor and had her hair searched for lice, she was praying for the humiliation to be over. There was, however, one final indignity to be visited upon her. As a first-time prisoner, assessed as 'at risk', Edith was put on suicide watch; which meant constant observation, day and night - even when using the lavatory!

To a woman of Edith's delicate sensibilities, the very thought of being observed whilst engaged in her bodily functions was appalling, but the demands of nature were such that eventually she was forced to ask permission to go to the toilet.

None of the cubicles had doors and several were occupied as Edith made her way past looking for a vacant one.

Once she was settled, the wardress positioned herself directly in front of her and watched impassively as Edith relieved herself. As Edith emerged from her cubicle another prisoner came out, hitching up her clothes. 'First time's always the worst, dearie,' she said, not unkindly. 'You'll soon get used to it.'

That night Edith found great difficulty in getting off to sleep. With the overhead light burning continuously and the unrelenting clamour of a large prison, she had tossed and fretted in her unyielding bed until the early hours before dropping off.

She was wakened from a fitful sleep by a wailing female voice. A shrill, mournful ululation that echoed around the high-vaulted building like the cry of a banshee.

It was followed, a few minutes later, by the sound of heavy footsteps ringing on a cast iron walkway, the slam of a cell door that resounded like a gunshot - then silence.

As she turned over on her side seeking solace in sleep, the immediate future was almost too painful to contemplate: the rigour and indignity of prison life, the ever-present, all-pervading smell of urine and faeces, the loss of any sense of worth or identity. As she began to drift off, she was thinking that anything must be preferable to a long prison sentence, even death itself.

Being a seaman and more used to hardship, prisoner number 8606. Bywaters. F. had quickly adjusted to prison routine, even managing to get a reasonable night's sleep.

Next morning, after a breakfast of porridge, bread and margarine and a mug of brackish, strong tea, the door of his cell was unlocked by a warder and an old lag 'trusty' entered carrying a bucket and mop.

He was a small, wiry old man with bright blue, darting eyes and a mouth full of bad teeth.

As Freddy sat on his bunk watching him sluice the stone-flagged floor, the trusty spoke.

'What you up for, mate?'

Freddy hesitated for a moment.

'Murder.'

'Blimey!'

The old man stopped mopping and looked at Freddy with renewed interest.

'It'll be the high-jump for you then,' he said cheerfully.

'Don't you believe it.' Freddy swung his feet over the side of the bunk. 'I'll get it reduced to manslaughter. You see if I don't.'

The old man shook his head. 'I wouldn't bank on it if I was you,' he said. 'I was cleanin' out the governor's office yesterday and I 'eard 'im orderin' a brand new rope for our scaffold.'

For a moment Freddy was taken aback, causing the old man to convulse into a paroxysm of chesty laughter.

'I'm pullin' your leg, you chump!' he cackled, slapping his thigh. 'Why, we ain't even *got* a scaffold in Brixton. They'll have to cart you over to Wandsworth or up to Pentonville to string you up.' Then picking up his bucket he shuffled off, still wheezing with laughter.

After he had gone and the warder had re-locked the door, Freddy lay back on his bunk, his hands clasped behind his head, thinking.

So they'd already written him off, had they? Well, he would show them. He had never backed down from a fight in his life and he certainly wouldn't now it was his *life* he would be fighting for. Yes! He'd give them a run for their money alright.

On the rain-swept morning of Monday 9th October, the murder weapon was eventually recovered from the drain in Seymour Gardens, exactly where Freddy had indicated.

When it was delivered to Inspector Hall at Ilford police station he carefully unwrapped the cellophane paper in which it had been placed and stood looking at it for several minutes before speaking. It was a wooden handled sheath knife with a six inch blade sharpened on both sides, and although it had lain at the bottom of a drain for six days, there were still smears of blood visible on the blade.

'Wait till the jury get a look at *that*!' Hall said with grim satisfaction. 'That little toe-rag won't stand a dog's chance.'

Tuesday the 20th of October was the day of Percy Thompson's funeral. It was 11.30am when a Daimler car and the hearse, garlanded with floral tributes, arrived outside number 231.

Sitting in the Daimler with their sons Newenham and Billie as it followed the hearse slowly around Shakespeare Crescent and across Browning Bridge, Mr and Mrs Graydon felt a great sense of sadness regarding the funeral arrangements, quite apart from the loss of a much loved son-in-law.

Ever since Edith had been charged with Percy's murder, the Thompson family had cut off all contact with the Graydons. So wide was the gulf separating the two families that even upon this, the saddest of occasions, the Thompsons could not bring themselves to cross the threshold of number 231, opting instead to join up with the cortège when it reached the Carnegie Library.

As the car carrying the Thompsons fell into line behind them, Mrs Graydon turned from looking out of the back window.

'It's such a shame,' she said sadly. 'Our two families should be united at a time like this, not at loggerheads.'

Mr Graydon put his arm around his wife's shoulders. 'We've offered them the hand of friendship, Ethel,' he said, hugging her. 'We can do no more.'

In the Nonconformists chapel at the City of London cemetery the two families sat at opposite sides of the aisle as the Reverend Charles Noakes conducted the funeral service, and stood apart and remote at the Graydon family plot where the body was to be interred.

The rain, which had threatened all morning had held off, but the sky was overcast and the wind biting as Percy Thompson's earthly remains were lowered into the ground.

After the grave had been temporarily covered over, a small group of people stayed behind to view the floral tributes laid out on the grass nearby. Among them was a wreath of lilies, white carnations and roses from Edith.

Another was signed. *'With love. Your mother and dad. (Graydon)'*.

There was a tribute from Percy's employers, Messrs O.J. Parker, and a small bunch of red roses from his work colleague, Miss Tucknott - who had for many years secretly harboured an unrequited affection for Percy - and a small wreath inscribed, *'Rest in Peace. Mrs and Miss Lester'*.

Mrs Lester did not attend the funeral.

Not being family, or what you might call 'friends', she felt it wasn't her place.

However, there was another reason for her non-attendance. She had been 'cut to the quick' by the abrupt and insensitive way Percy had served notice to quit so soon after her husband had passed away. Nevertheless, she had been shocked and saddened by the dreadful circumstances of his violent death.

As for *Mrs* Thompson - who would have thought she would end up like this? Accused of murdering her husband! Her picture in all the papers!

To say Mrs Lester had been flabbergasted by the momentous events of the past week would be to seriously understate the effect upon her as each sensational development unfolded. 'Whatever next?' was the question she kept asking herself.

As if in answer, the following day she received a letter calling upon her to present herself at Stratford Magistrate's Court on Wednesday 25th October as a witness for the prosecution.

Such was the publicity now afforded the case in the popular press, that a crowd of some two thousand people were milling around outside the court on Wednesday the 11th of October, all hoping to catch a glimpse of the two accused.

When a taxi drew up and Edith alighted, dressed in black, the crowd surged forward hoping to get a look at the 'scarlet woman' whose face was now on the front of almost every newspaper.

Inside the court she and Freddy were once again together in the dock while the prosecution outlined the case for the committal.

After approximately an hour the court was adjourned and the two accused were again remanded in custody, this time until Tuesday 17th of October when she and Freddy were once again back in the same courtroom. By now both of them had begun to look forward to their court appearances as it relieved the tedium of prison life and afforded them the opportunity of seeing one another.

For Edith, it had the added benefit of wearing her own clothes - if only for a few brief hours.

Monday October 23rd marked the last day of the inquest on Percy Thompson at

Ilford Town Hall, while at Stratford, Edith's former employer, Mr Carlton, had been summoned to identify the handwriting on sixteen of the letters. Seeing Mr Carlton again under such distressing circumstances affected Edith deeply.

When their eyes met briefly, and she saw the look of sad disbelief on his kindly face, she was forced to look away.

After identifying the handwriting on the letters as that of Edith Thompson Mr Carlton's place in the witness box was taken by Edith's work colleague, Rose Jacobs.

In a halting voice, and highly embarrassed, Miss Jacobs told the court that upon hearing of Miss Graydon's arrest, she had searched the desk in her office and found three letters from Bywaters, a photograph of him, a photograph of the *SS Morea*, a 'where is it' book and several souvenirs, all of which she handed over to the police.

It was an act of malice Edith found difficult to understand from someone she had always got on well with.

When Miss Jacobs had finished her evidence, Mr Stern rose to plead for the letters - which he had only just finished reading - to be deemed inadmissible as evidence, on the grounds that Bywaters had already assumed full responsibility for the crime.

Accepting his point, the magistrate told the jury that the question of the letters would be dealt with in another court, and that their verdict should only concern the cause of death and the guilt, or otherwise, of the accused.

After only eight minutes deliberation, the jury returned a verdict of 'wilful murder' against Frederick Bywaters. No mention was made of Mrs Thompson.

The next day, Freddy and Edith were again back in the dock when, Mr Stern's dismay, the prosecution announced their intention of reading out the letters.

In spite of Stern's strenuous objections it was ruled that, in view of the latest batch of letters recovered from the *Morea*, there *was* now a *prima facie* case against Mrs Thompson, and that the letters *could* therefore be submitted as evidence.

Edith Thompson's *Via Dolorosa* was about to begin.

As Mr Hancock for the prosecution began to read out selected excerpts from the letters, all Edith's innermost thoughts, passions, yearnings, dreams, hopes and despairs were relayed in a flat, unemotional manner to a hushed court, her self-control began to fall apart. Her great love for Freddy was being made to appear cheap and sordid - her sentiments trite and foolish.

With the most intimate details of her private life cruelly exposed, she became more and more distressed and, during a passage which seemed to indicate a plot to murder her husband, Edith fainted. At which point the court was adjourned until after lunch in order to give Edith time to recover. When the hearing resumed

Edith's mental state was still unstable and when the references to putting pieces of light bulb in her husband's porridge were read out, Edith again collapsed.

The court matron was summoned and, with water and smelling salts to hand, the hearing continued.

It was almost 5pm before Edith's ordeal came to an end with the defendants being remanded until the following morning.

Even before the last member of the Bench had left the courtroom, the gentlemen of the press were involved in an unseemly scramble to get to the few available public telephones and be the first to inform their editors of the sensational new development.

When the court resumed, the three main witnesses were Mr Graydon, Mrs Bywaters and Mrs Lester.

Overnight, Edith had managed to regain some of her composure and was listening intently to the evidence. When Mrs Lester said that Mr and Mrs Thompson quite often 'had high words', she even managed a faint smile.

It was not until her beloved father entered the witness box that her resolve began to falter.

For a man of Mr Graydon's standing, rectitude and respectability, the events of the past few weeks had affected him grievously. His modest terraced house was constantly besieged by reporters and photographers. He had been pointed out in the street, stared at - with curiosity by some and scorn by others - his privacy intruded upon, his good name sullied.

As he stood in the witness-box, stooping slightly and ill at ease, Edith was overcome with sorrow and remorse. And when he talked about his daughter's marriage and that no children had resulted from the union, she began to weep.

At the end of proceedings that day, the prosecution asked for a remand for another week. In granting the request the magistrate made it plain that he would not tolerate any more long delays because of the obvious distress it was causing Mrs Thompson.

Overnight, the first snow of winter began falling over London and Edith could see large flakes swirling past the barred window of her prison cell, invoking poignant memories of the snowball fight with Freddy in Bayswater Road after leaving Moscow Court - hardly more than a year ago now, but for Edith as remote as a childhood memory.

In spite of the magistrate's stricture on the subject, on Wednesday 1st November the prosecution once again asked for a further week's remand. The reason being the Crown had applied for, and had been granted, an exhumation order on the body of Percy Thompson. Bernard Spilsbury, the eminent pathologist, was to conduct the autopsy and prosecution hopes were high that enough incriminating evidence would be uncovered to convince a jury of Edith's culpability.

On the night of Thursday November 2nd, the remains of Percy Thompson were disinterred from their resting place and Spilsbury and his assistant, Webster, set to work.

For the Crown it was to prove a bitter disappointment.

In spite of exhaustive examinations of the stomach, gut, kidneys and liver, *no traces of poison were found,* and no indication of any previous attempts at poisoning. Also, and more significantly, *no glass, powdered or otherwise, was found in the intestines*! The many references to poison and glass in Edith's letters had now been exposed for what they were - pure invention!

When the results were made known, Edith's family were convinced that their daughter would be exonerated. Edith herself was overjoyed; surely now the jury must rule that there was no case for her to answer.

But the implacable forces arrayed against her were not about to allow something like a negative autopsy report to deflect them from their purpose, which was to see her standing in the dock of the Old Bailey, with her lover, charged with the wilful murder of her husband. Far from faltering in their endeavours, it spurred them on to increase their efforts to bring her to book.

Six days later, Edith and Freddy briefly appeared in he dock at Stratford and were remanded for another week; and again on Wednesday 15th. With so much time on their hands they were now writing to one another almost every day, recording the trivia and minutiae of their sequestered lives: books they were reading or recommending, endearments, remembrances, hopes and dreams. They never discussed the case, its implications or ramifications, knowing that if they did, it would be censored.

What they did not know was that all their letters were being withheld in the mistaken belief that they were using some sort of code in them in order to pervert the course of justice.

For the last time, Edith and Freddy were taken to Stratford Magistrate's Court on 24th November where it was ordered that they would both stand trial at the Old Bailey for the murder of Percy Thompson.

During the hubbub that followed, as Edith was being led away, her distraught mother rushed forward and clung on to her coat crying: 'My child! My child!' until she was restrained by court officials.

As for Edith, she seemed unable to grasp what was happening as, wide-eyed and uncomprehending, she was taken down to the cells to await her transfer back to Holloway.

Edith returned to her prison cell in the depths of despair. Grief-stricken for the family and bitterly disappointed with the verdict, she was at her lowest ebb.

But within a few days she began to discover fresh reserves of strength and resilience. In spite of everything, her belief in the essential fairness of British Justice was undiminished, and the certainty of her innocence, unshakable.

She was convinced that when the truth came out at the trial, when she was allowed to tell her story, no jury of twelve good men and true could possibly convict her.

Chapter 14

"If things should go badly with us, I shall always
have this past year to look back upon and feel that
'Then I lived'. I never did before and I never shall again."

With the trial at the Old Bailey looming, a welcome piece of news was conveyed to Edith via Mr Stern. Her defending counsel was to be the recently knighted, Sir Henry Curtis-Bennett who, with the possible exception of Marshall-Hall, was considered to be the finest advocate of his day. A man of imposing stature, magisterial bearing, and possessed of a deep, mellifluous speaking voice which, when combined with his considerable oratorical powers, had often wooed and won many an uncertain juror.

The date of the trial was set for Wednesday 6th December and Edith and Curtis-Bennett met up in a room at Holloway Prison on Monday 4th November.

Although greatly impressed by Curtis-Bennett's formidable presence and reputation, Edith was not overawed and conducted herself with dignity and confidence.

After outlining his thoughts on the conduct of the trial, Curtis-Bennett then touched on the thorny question of the letters.

In all some 62 had now come to light; providing the Crown with a veritable arsenal of heavy guns to use against his client, and Curtis-Bennett was determined to fight tooth and nail to have them declared inadmissible.

Having read them all, he knew how damning their contents could be made to look in the hands of a skilful advocate. However, should he fail to have them excluded, he assured Edith, he had an answer to every would-be incriminating passage contained within them.

'Thank you, Sir Henry,' Edith said, 'but after I have told the court *my* side of the story I shall having nothing to fear.'

Curtis-Bennett was taken aback.

'Mrs Thompson,' he said incredulously. 'You are surely not thinking of going into the witness-box?'

'Oh, yes. 'Edith replied firmly. 'I have been waiting a long time for the opportunity to have my say.'

Curtis-Bennett was horrified.

'Mrs Thompson,' he said sonorously,' I must, in the strongest possible terms, urge you to reconsider. With the greatest respect, you have absolutely no notion of how damaging these letters could be to your defence. Why, we have the Solicitor General himself leading for the Crown! He will be cross-examining. I beg you, let *me* answer for you!'

Edith was polite but firm.

'I'm sorry, Sir Henry,' she said, 'but my mind is made up. I intend to have my day, and my say, in court.'

Curtis-Bennett stood up and shook hands with Edith. 'We shall talk again before the trial,' he said solemnly.

'We shall, Sir Henry,' Edith replied, 'but I will not change my mind.'

The counsel appointed to defend Freddy was Cecil Whiteley. KC. Not quite as eminent and charismatic as Curtis-Bennett perhaps, but a diligent and respected barrister.

Their first meeting took place on the same day in a room set aside for the purpose at Brixton prison where, after introducing himself, Whiteley began to outline the general thrust of his defence strategy. He had not got very far when Freddy interrupted him.

'Excuse me, Mr Whiteley,' he said, 'I want to make it perfectly clear to you, there must be nothing used in *my* defence that would in any way reflect badly on Mrs Thompson, or undermine *her* case. She is completely innocent and I cannot allow you to jeopardize her chance of acquittal for my sake.'

Whiteley was nonplussed. 'But, Mr Bywaters,' he said concernedly, 'the prosecution case against you is a particularly strong one. To be frank, it is my opinion that the only real hope you have of avoiding the death penalty is for me to convince the jury that you were seduced by an older woman and beguiled by her to such a degree that you felt compelled to confront her husband.'

Freddy shook his head violently.

'No! No! You mustn't say that. If you do I shall deny it.'

The two men regarded one another across the table for a moment, before Whiteley spoke.

'Very well,' he said wearily. 'I will do my best. But I must tell you, I will be entering this fight with one arm tied behind my back.'

At 10.30am on Wednesday 6th December, in the Number One court at the Old Bailey before Mr Justice Shearman, the eagerly anticipated trial began.

As ever, the popular press had played their part in whipping up the fever of excitement that gripped the public; portraying Edith Thompson as a femme fatale, an older woman who had seduced a gullible young man and incited him to commit murder - the *Daily Mail* even going so far as to dub Edith "The Messalina of Suburbia".

It was in this climate of near-hysteria that, on the first day, tickets to the public gallery were changing hands outside the Law Courts for as much as two pounds each as the rich and famous jostled with the self-righteous and the prurient to witness what had already become a cause célèbre.

Edith was first to enter the dock. She had slept badly the previous night and the paleness of her face was accentuated by the mourning clothes she was wearing - a black musquash coat and a wide-brimmed black velvet hat.

As she reached the top of the stone staircase from the cells below into the dock, she was greeted by a buzz of excited anticipation from the public gallery and a murmur of interest from the assembled lawyers and judiciary in the courtroom.

'The Messalina of Suburbia' had come to judgement.

Looking around, Edith was immediately struck by the theatricality of the setting: The bewigged and black-gowned barristers and court officials with serious faces, the judge, on high, clad in scarlet, his face sphinx-like under a shoulder-length wig, and the jury - eleven men and one woman - all middle-class, solemn-faced and soberly dressed. In the well of the court were the witnesses, dressed in their Sunday best and, up in the gallery, the hoi polloi, craning their necks to get a better view of the drama about to unfold below them.

There was another buzz of excitement as Freddy entered the dock a few moments later, looking handsome and well groomed in a black jacket, grey trousers and spats.

Cecil Whiteley then rose to plead that the two accused should not be tried together as evidence produced against Edith (the letters), would be detrimental to his client's case, even though they in no way touched on the actual murder.

His plea was summarily dismissed. Curtis-Bennett then requested that the letters should be excluded from the case because, if they were produced as evidence against Edith to show her involvement in the murder as it happened, then the mentions of poisoning and other matters not related to that charge would be disastrously damaging to her defence of the charge of which she was now accused.

Once again Justice Shearman was intractable and Edith's last real hope was dashed when he ruled that the letters should be admitted.

The jurors were recalled and the Solicitor General, Thomas Inskip, rose to make his opening address for the prosecution.

With Freddy already having confessed to the murder, he concentrated his main attack on Edith.

After referring in a disparaging manner to Mrs Thompson's continuing to work even though a married woman, and her reluctance to have children, he then got down to the main thrust of his attack reading excerpts from some of the press cuttings Edith had sent to her lover with the letters.

"Poisoned chocolates for University Chief. Deadly powder posted to Oxford Chancellor."

"Ground glass in box."

"Chicken broth death. Rat poison kills woman."

These cuttings represented only a tiny section of the many Edith had sent with her letters. The majority referring to things like fashion, social events and gossip were, of course, ignored.

Having lost no time in creating a miasma of suspicion regarding Edith's motives, Inskip turned to the letters, again reading out specially selected excerpts.

All concerned passages with references to poison or powdered and broken glass and repeated urgings to her lover to 'do something' to deliver her from a loveless marriage and a husband she had come to despise.

"Darlint, you must do something this time -I'm not really impatient - but opportunities come and go..." "It would be so easy, darlint - if I had things - I do hope I shall." "I used the 'light bulb' three times, but the third time he found a piece - so I have given up - until you come home." "This year seems no further advanced. Why should you not send me something?...If I do not mind the risk why should you?"

Pausing only long enough to take in the effect all this was having on the jury, Inskip concluded by reading a passage from *'Bella Donna'*.

"It must be remembered that digitalin is a cumulative poison and that the same dose, harmless if taken once, yet frequently, becomes deadly."

With very little material evidence against her, Edith became aware that she was being judged not only by what she had written but what she had *read*.

Inskip put down the letters and regarded the jury for a moment before continuing.

'I suggest,' he said dryly, 'that, through this correspondence, it becomes clear that it was Mrs Thompson who was urging Bywaters on to commit the crime in some way or other in order to secure happiness upon which her passion was set.'

Then, while referring to the material evidence of the case, he mentioned the post mortem which he said 'showed there were *practically* no traces of any poison'.

Edith was aghast. There was no trace of *any* poison in Percy's body. She looked sharply over to her counsel but Curtis-Bennett was conferring with one of his juniors and appeared not have heard.

The moment had passed and Inskip had moved on.

'I suggest to you, members of the jury,' he intoned, 'that you will have to consider whether the hand that struck the blow was moved, was incited, to the crime by Mrs Thompson...There is undoubted evidence in the letters upon which you can find that there was a preconcerted meeting between Mrs Thompson and Bywaters at the scene of the murder.'

Again Edith sat up, astonished. There had been no such thing. Surely Sir Henry would challenge that outrageous assumption? But her counsel said nothing.

The Solicitor General finished his opening address by saying:

'...If you are satisfied that Mrs Thompson incited the murder and that, incited and directed by her controlling hand, Bywaters committed the murder, then it will be my duty to ask you, after hearing the evidence, to find she, who incited and proposed the murder, as guilty as Bywaters who committed it.'

It was just after midday when Inskip sat down and the prosecution began calling witnesses involved in the tragic events following the murder.

Edith's tenuous grip on her emotions held quite well until Dr Drought, the surgeon to the Ilford Police Division, began to describe Percy's injuries in graphic detail. As the knife used in the attack was passed across the court and Percy's bloodstained trousers held up to view, she broke down.

As the first day of the trial ended, Curtis-Bennett felt that the case against his client, as laid out by Inskip, was far from convincing. He was clearly relying solely on the letters to incriminate her.

What *he* had to do now was to show those letters up for what they were - the outpourings of a besotted, over imaginative, passionate woman.

Before taking leave of his client, Curtis-Bennett reassured Edith of his unshakable belief in her innocence, but once again urged her to seriously reconsider her decision to enter the witness-box.

At 4am the following morning a queue, consisting mainly of unemployed men, had begun to form on the frost-encrusted pavement outside the Central Criminal Court in Newgate Street, to obtain tickets for the public gallery - tickets they would sell later in the day for the equivalent, to them, of almost a week's wages.

After another poor night's sleep, Edith was pale and lethargic when she entered the dock just a few moments after Freddy had taken his place.

Freddy was bearing up far better, convinced that the worst he could expect was a custodial sentence for manslaughter, which would mean an acquittal for Edith.

After several police officers had given evidence, pathologists Spilsbury and Webber were called.

A murmur of surprise hummed around the court as Bernard Spilsbury stated quite categorically: 'I did not find *any* signs of poisoning, nor did I find *any* scars on the intestines. I also found no indication of the presence of glass, either in large pieces or in powdered form'. For the first time in the trial, Edith experienced a surge of hope. It was to be short-lived.

After informing the court that the case for the Crown was finished, Inskip produced the four typed sets of Edith's letters and passed them to the jury, one for each group of three. Then his assistant, Travers Humphreys, began reading them out in a dull, uninflected monotone.

As the intimate details of her private life were once again revealed to all and sundry, and her love letters stripped of any depth or meaning by the lacklustre delivery, Edith covered her face with her hands and wept.

As Travers Humphreys droned on through letter after letter, the judge mercifully intervened and requested the jury to read the remainder themselves. 'After all,' he added dismissively, 'it is mostly gush.'

With that, the case for the prosecution was complete.

Cecil Whiteley was first to speak for the defence and called Freddy Bywaters.

As Freddy walked across the court to the witness-box his step was sure, his bearing upright and his manner composed.

After being sworn in, he was handed a portfolio of copies of the letters - letters which Edith always assumed had been destroyed but had now returned to haunt them.

For the next ninety minutes Freddy gave a résumé of his life, family and occupation. He also told of his friendship with the Graydons, the Isle of Wight holiday, his overseas voyages, and his brief stay at Kensington Gardens. But when asked if he and Edith were already lovers by the summer of 1921, he denied it. It was a lie, but he strongly suspected that some members of the jury might not take kindly to the thought of an unfaithful wife, her lover and the cuckolded husband all living under the same roof.

Whiteley then turned to the references to suicide in some of the letters and read out the following extract:

' *"All I could think about last night was the compact we made. Shall we have to carry it thro? Don't let us, darlint."'*

'What was the compact? he asked pointedly.

'Suicide.'

'Who suggested that?'

'Mrs Thompson suggested it.'

'Did *you* ever make any agreement that you should commit suicide?'

Freddy hesitated briefly before answering.

'Well, I suggested it as a way of calming her down,' he said carefully, 'but I never intended to carry it out.'

Edith suddenly felt betrayed. As far as *she* was concerned their suicide pact had been a solemn, last resort agreement between two desperate lovers. Now Freddy seemed to be implying that the whole thing had been just a game on his part.

Whiteley then read out the next part of the same letter.

' *"I'd like to live and be happy - not for a little while but for all the while you love me. Death seemed horrible last night - when you think about it darlint it does seem a horrible thing to die when you have never been happy, really happy, for one little minute.'"*

Whiteley put down the letter and turned to Freddy.

'I am going to ask you at once, Bywaters,' he said gravely. 'At any time, was there any agreement between you and Mrs Thompson to poison her husband?'

'Never!' Freddy replied emphatically. 'There was never such an agreement.'

'Was there any agreement that *any* violence should be used against her husband?' Whiteley continued.

'No! The greatest violence was separation.'

Whiteley pressed home his point.

'As far as you could tell, reading these letters, did you ever believe in your own mind that she herself had ever given any poison to her husband?'

'No!' Freddy replied, again with heavy emphasis. 'It never entered my head at all,' then added. 'She had been reading books.'

Whiteley then turned to another passage in a letter he felt needed clarifying.

' *"Darlint - you must do something this time - I'm not really impatient - but opportunities come and go and I think and think and think - perhaps it will never come again."*

'*"You must do something"*,' Whiteley repeated the phrase. 'What was it she had been waiting for you to do?'

'To take her away,' Freddy answered.

Whiteley again pressed his point.

'It is suggested by the prosecution, that this means you were going to do something in connection with her husband. Is there anything in that?'

'No. It is entirely wrong.'

After more detailed questioning, Whiteley referred to the passage concerning the use of pieces of light bulb.

'Did you attach any importance to it at all?' he asked.

Freddy shook his head. 'No. I thought it was mere melodrama.'

Once again Edith was perplexed by Freddy's dismissive attitude. Did he *really* think of her in such a condescending way? Or did he have some ulterior motive for saying what he had?

Whiteley began winding up his examination by reading out one last quotation from the letters.

' *"Have you lost heart and given up hope? Tell me if you have, darlint?"'*

Turning to Freddy, Whiteley asked: 'Had there been *any* agreement that *any* act of violence should be done to her husband either by you or by her?'

'No,' Freddy said. 'Nothing at all.'

'In these letters that have been read, was there anything which incited you to do any act of violence to Mr Thompson?'

Freddy shook his head. 'Nothing whatsoever,' he said.

As he sat down, Cecil Whiteley was pleased with the way his examination had gone. His client had presented a clean-cut, personable figure in the witness-box, and had answered all the questions in an honest, straightforward manner.

From his adverse comments, it was obvious that the judge had taken a dislike to his client, referring to him as an 'adulterer', and interrupting his evidence in an effort to disconcert him, but young Bywaters, he felt, had created a good impression on the jury, and that was all that mattered.

After the court had adjourned for the day Curtis-Bennett met with Edith in one of the holding cells to discuss the day's events and to try once again to dissuade her from giving evidence.

He began by explaining to her the tactics of the prosecution.

'You see, Mrs Thompson,' he said, 'there were, in all, five other indictments laid against you: Conspiracy to murder. Soliciting to murder. Inciting to commit a misdemeanour, administering poison with intent to murder, and administering a destructive thing with intent to murder.'

He looked at her for a moment to ensure she had understood before continuing.

'In electing to proceed with the *capital charge,*' he went on, the Crown have, to coin a phrase, put all their eggs in one basket. Because if *that* charge is thrown out, as I am convinced it will be, they cannot then proceed with the lesser charges, and they will be dropped.' He smiled encouragingly at Edith.

'So you see, Mrs Thompson,' he said urbanely, 'there is really no need for you to go into the witness-box. Put yourself entirely in my hands, and let *me* answer for you. Bywaters has already paved the way for the letters to be discredited.'

Edith gave a rueful smile. 'But don't you see, Sir Henry,' she said quietly. 'If I do *not* give evidence on my own behalf, the jury might think I have something to hide. I am innocent, and the only way I can convince the jury of that is by going into the witness-box.'

Curtis-Bennett shook his head.

'If I had not thought you innocent, Mrs Thompson,' he said forcefully, 'I would never have accepted the brief. But you must allow *me* to decide what is the best course of action.'

But Edith was unshakable. 'I'm sorry, Sir Henry,' she said firmly, 'but I intend to have my day in court.'

Curtis-Bennett left the Old Bailey a troubled man. Thomas Inskip was not the most gifted of advocates, but his cross-examination skills had been well honed over the years, and in spite of all her apparent sophistication, Mrs Thompson would be completely out of her depth.

Cecil Whiteley had not fared a great deal better with *his* client.

It was while they were discussing their tactics for the following day, that Freddy dropped a bombshell by introducing something he had not mentioned before regarding his fatal encounter with Percy Thompson. 'I was only defending myself you know,' he said abruptly.

Whiteley sat up.

'*Defending* yourself? From what?

'Thompson said: "I've got a gun", and reached to his hip pocket. He said: "I'll shoot you". I had to stop him. It was him or me - so I struck out.'

Whiteley was flabbergasted.

'But why have you not mentioned this before?' he asked incredulously. 'If you *were* defending yourself and in fear of your life, you cannot be guilty of murder.'

'I've only just remembered it,' Freddy said lamely. 'Anyway, that's how it happened.'

Whiteley chose his words carefully. 'If I submit this as evidence, Mr Bywaters,' he said gravely, 'and the jury reject it, it could influence the jury's acceptance of anything you have said previously in evidence, and harm your case.'

Freddy considered his position for a moment before deciding it would be worth the risk. 'It's the truth, Mr Whiteley,' he said forcefully, 'and I want it to be heard.'

Whiteley nodded. 'Very well, Bywaters, so be it.' He gathered up the scattered papers from the table and thrust them into his briefcase. 'Let us hope,' he said with a wry smile, 'that the jury are less sceptical than I.'

In the bitter-chill, early hours of Friday 8th December, the queue for public gallery tickets was over a hundred strong, the first claimants having arrived before 2am to ensure their places. Some had even brought along camp stools and thermos flasks, lending it the air of a queue for the gallery of a theatre rather than a court of law.

When the doors of the public gallery were opened at 9.30am, a surging mass of men and women, some clutching tickets which had cost them £4 or more, jostled and shoved each other in an unseemly scramble to secure the best seats.

Freddy Bywaters entered the witness-box, perhaps not quite as confidently as he had on the previous day, and apprehensive about the forthcoming cross-examination from the Solicitor General.

But first it was Whiteley's turn. His client having already confessed, Whiteley suspected that candour would be the best strategy and hoped that Bywaters would at least impress the jury with his veracity and openness.

With this in mind, he reopened his examination by inviting Freddy to tell the court, in his own words, the events of the night of October 3rd.

As he recounted the story of the night in question, Freddy was again at pains to emphasise that Mrs Thompson had absolutely no pre-knowledge, or forewarning of his movements or his intentions.

Whilst Freddy was describing the sequence of events leading up to his pulling out the knife, Whiteley decided it was a suitable moment to introduce the new evidence.

'Did Mr Thompson do anything before you took the knife out?'

'Yes,' Freddy replied, 'he punched me with his left hand and said: "I'll shoot you!" going at the same time like this.' At this point Freddy showed the court how Percy Thompson had reached towards his hip pocket.

A concerted gasp of astonishment rippled through the court. The prosecution could scarcely believe their ears. On this, *the third day of the trial*, Bywaters's counsel was introducing a claim of self-defence?

Whiteley waited until silence had been more or less restored in court before resuming his questioning. 'Why did you draw your knife?' he asked.

'Because I thought I was going to be killed,' Freddy replied. 'After I put my knife in his arm there was a struggle - all the time struggling. I thought he was going to kill me. I thought he was going to shoot me if he had the opportunity, and I tried to stop him.'

There was a moment of silence in court during which a sense of incredulity was almost palpable.

Whiteley then asked: 'Have you any recollection at all as to how the wounds at the back of Mr Thompson's neck occurred?'

'Not any exact recollection,' Freddy said, shaking his head. 'All I can say is I had the knife in my left hand...they got there somehow.'

When Whiteley sat down at the end of his examination, he was well aware that his client's clumsy attempt to convince the jury he was acting in self-defence had not succeeded. Worse than that, and more damaging, it had raised doubts regarding Bywaters's probity.

When Inskip rose to begin his cross-examination, he was convinced that the very *idea* of a respectable, suburban shipping clerk carrying a pistol in his pocket on a night out to the theatre was so patently absurd that the jury would see it for what is was - a desperate attempt by the accused to save his neck.

Now, if he could catch Bywaters out in *other* untruths or evasions, he would be able to undermine his trustworthiness and destroy his credibility and, in so doing, call into question the oft-repeated assertion that Mrs Thompson had not been privy to, nor taken part in the murder of her husband.

'Was it on the holiday which you spent with her and her husband in Shanklin that you fell in love with Mrs Thompson?' he asked pointedly.

Freddy was taken unawares by this approach. He had expected to be questioned on the evidence he had just given.

'No,' he replied, slightly ruffled.

'Did she declare any particular affection for *you*?' Inskip asked.

'She did not.'

'Nor you for her?'

'No.'

'Are you sure of that?'

'I am positive.'

Inskip studied Freddy for a moment before continuing. 'When did you say you first felt, or declared, you love for her?' he asked casually.

'I first told her just before I went away in September 1921. That was *after* I had left her husband's house.'

'That was the *first* time you and she had declared yourselves to each other?'

'Yes,' Freddy said. 'As a mutual affection.'

Inskip held up one of the letters.

'This letter from Mrs Thompson is dated 11th of *August*, 1921,' he said. 'I shall read it to you.

' *"Darlingest, Will you please take these letters back now? I have nowhere to keep them except a small cash box I have just bought and I want that for my own letters only and I feel scared to death in case anybody else should read them. All the wishes I can possibly send for the very best of luck today, from Peidi."'*

Inskip paused for a moment for the court to digest what he had just read.

'Does that satisfy you,' he asked mildly, 'that your evidence is wrong as to the date you told her you loved her?'

Freddy realized he could not retract now. 'No,' he said.

Inskip raised a quizzical eyebrow before passing on to another letter.

'Here is another letter, dated August 20th,' he said and read out: ' *"Come and see me Monday lunchtime, please darlint. He suspects. Peidi."'*

Again he allowed a few moments to elapse before continuing. 'How do you explain that?' he asked.

Freddy hesitated. 'I cannot remember what it refers to,' he said lamely.

Having established that Freddy had misled the court over the date he and Edith had become lovers, Inskip moved on to another subject - the many references to suicide contained in the letters. He quoted from one date 18th November 1921.

' *"All I could think about was the compact we made. Shall we have to carry it thro?"'*

'Was that the pact of suicide abandoned after that letter?' Inskip asked.

'I never really took it seriously,' Freddy replied.

'Was the removal of her husband ever mentioned by her to you?'

'No.'

'Never?'

'Never.'

'Did you tell your learned counsel that you read her letters as 'melodrama'?'

'Some of them.'

'What was it you understood to be melodrama?' he asked pointedly.

'She had a vivid way of declaring herself,' said Freddy. 'She would read a book and imagine herself as the character in the book.'

After another hour of almost line-by-line questioning regarding the contents of the letters, Inskip came to the phrase: *"Yes darlint be jealous, so much so that you will do something desperate."* But I was not jealous, said Freddy.'

'She was appealing to you to *be* jealous and do something desperate,' Inskip said. 'What did she mean by 'desperate'?'

'By 'desperate', she meant to take her away.'

Inskip made sure the jury saw the look of amused disbelief on his face before continuing. 'Then why did you not take her away?'

'Financial reasons,' Freddy replied.

Inskip paused for a moment.

'Have you at any time, ever thought of marrying her?'

Freddy took a deep breath. 'No!' he said bluntly.

Edith, who had been listening intently to the evidence was taken aback. What did he mean? Was he still trying to protect her in some way? Was it that, by saying he had no intention of marrying her, he would undermine the motive advanced by the prosecution for her husband's murder - that of jealousy? Edith decided it had to be that.

The Crown now turned to the new evidence - that Thompson threatened to shoot him.

'Why,' he asked, 'did you not put into your statement of 5th October anything about the incident of the attack of which you have told us today? Had you forgotten so soon after the event?'

Freddy was prepared for this. 'No,' he said. 'When I saw Mrs Thompson, she was looking so ill I thought she was going to die, and I thought the sooner I got it down the quicker she would be released.'

'So you omitted that part of your story which was concerned with the threat to shoot you?'

Again Inskip made sure that the jury did not miss the scepticism in his voice.

'I did,' Freddy replied. 'That was my main object; I wanted to help her.'

Inskip feigned perplexity.

'Can you suggest how it helped her to omit that important fact?'

'She would have been released,' Freddy said doggedly. 'I did not trouble about details or anything like that.'

'Is this true in your second statement,' Inskip read: ' *"I only meant to injure him"*?'

'I meant to stop him from killing me.'

Inskip repeated the line again, with heavy emphasis. ' *"I only meant to injure him"*. Was that true? That you went there to injure him?'

'No, it is not.'

Inskip pressed on. ' *"I gave him the opportunity of standing up to me as a man, but he would not."* Was that true?'

'When I said that, it referred to a previous occasion.'

'Did you, on *this* occasion, give him the opportunity to stand up to you as a man?'

'No,' Freddy replied, 'I did not suggest any violence or fisticuffs at all.'

Inskip exhaled sharply. 'Do you mean to suggest,' he asked incredulously, ' that *he* made the first assault on *you*?'

There was no going back now.

'Yes, he did.'

'And that's when you drew your knife?'

'I did.'

Inskip fixed Freddy was a stern look. 'Is it a fact,' he said icily, 'that you never saw any revolver or indeed a gun at that moment?'

Freddy returned his stare unflinchingly. 'I never saw it, no,' he said.

Inskip cast a withering look at the prisoner in the dock, gathered up his papers and sat down.

Whiteley immediately rose to re-examine.

'Would you tell the court again.' he asked, 'what went through your mind when Mr Thompson shouted "I will shoot you."?'

Freddy nodded.

'Although I never saw a revolver I believed that he had one, otherwise I would never have drawn my knife. I was in fear of my life.'

'At any time,' Whiteley asked in ringing tones, 'have you had any intention to murder Mr Thompson?'

'I had not,' Freddy replied emphatically.

Whiteley looked up at the judge. 'That is our case, M'lud.'

When Freddy had returned to the dock, Curtis-Bennett got to his feet and called Edith Jessie Thompson to give evidence.

As Edith made her way to the witness-box many in the public gallery stood up to get a better view of the suburban housewife who was now more famous than the actress, Gladys Cooper and, as others in the gallery followed suit, a police sergeant on court duty was forced to remonstrate with them. 'Sit down please,' he called to them. 'Please sit down.'

When the hubbub had subsided, Edith accepted the judge's offer to sit for what she knew was to be the biggest challenge of her life - the fight to save it.

Dressed entirely in black, her pale face, eyes dark-ringed, Edith looked every inch one of the tragic heroines of the silent films of the period.

After removing her black leather gloves, she closed her eyes momentarily to concentrate her mind, took a deep breath and, with her head held high, prepared herself for the ordeal ahead.

Curtis-Bennett now handed Edith copies of the letters which had been submitted in evidence. As these letters were the only evidence against her, he had decided to pre-empt the prosecution and invite her to explain their meaning and intentions, and by so doing to spike their guns. Ambiguities and misconceptions would be erased and the sinister interpretations attributed to them would be nullified. This, at least, was the intention as he began his examination.

After taking her through the early years of her marriage, he asked her this:

'Have you at any time, from your marriage until the death of your husband, ever done anything to injure him personally?'

'Never.'

'Have you ever been in possession of poison?' he asked.

'Not to my knowledge.'

'Have you ever administered poison to your husband?'

'No.'

'Have you ever given him ground glass in his food?'

'Never.'

'Have you ever broken up an electric light bulb and given him that?'

'Never.'

Curtis-Bennett held up one of the letters.

'Let me read you this, Mrs Thompson. *"I had the wrong porridge today, but I don't suppose it will matter, I don't seem to care much either way..."* The suggestion here is that you had, from time to time, put things in your husband's porridge - glass for instance.'

Edith shook her head. 'I had not done so.'

'Can you give us any explanation of what you had in mind when you said you had the *wrong* porridge?'

Edith hesitated. 'We had...talked about that sort of thing,' she said slowly, 'and I had previously said: "Oh yes, I will give him something one of these days."'

It was an unguarded remark, and it prompted the judge to ask: 'Do you mean that you had talked about *poison*?'

Edith again hesitated before replying. She realized she was now in dangerous waters. 'We...had talked about making my husband ill,' she said.

Her counsel was taken unawares. Instead of dismissing it as a flippant remark, it had now taken on slightly disturbing undertones.

Curtis-Bennett was quick to respond.

'Did you ever give him anything?' he asked.

'Nothing whatsoever,' Edith replied. 'The porridge was always prepared by Mrs

Lester anyway, never by me.'

'What about this?' Curtis-Bennett then read an extract from another letter. ' *"I used the light bulb three times - but the third time he found a piece..."* Was there ever an occasion when you husband found a piece of glass in his food?'

'Never.' Edith replied.

Curtis-Bennett produced another letter. 'This one is dated Monday, 2nd October, the day before the attack on your husband,' he said meaningfully. 'I shall read you the last line of the letter. *"Don't forget what we talked in the tea room. I'll still risk and try if you will."'*

He lowered the letter and looked at Edith. 'What had you discussed in the tea-room?'

'My freedom.'

'Had you, at any time, any desire for Bywaters to commit an injury to your husband?'

'None whatever,' she replied. Then, unprompted, continued: 'I saw him in Fuller's about five o'clock in the afternoon and stayed with him until about a quarter to seven, when I returned home.'

'Was there any mention or any indication of any possible assault being committed on your husband?'

'None whatever. On Tuesday, 3rd October, we had lunch together and I saw him again about a quarter past five for about a quarter of an hour. After leaving him I met my husband and we went together to the West End where we had a meal together before going to the theatre.'

They were now at a critical point in Edith's evidence and Curtis-Bennett chose his words with care.

'Did you anticipate, or had you any reason to think that you would see Bywaters again that day?'

'None whatever,' Edith replied firmly. 'I had made arrangements to see him the *following* day at lunch time.'

Curtis-Bennett continued to speak slowly and deliberately.

'Had anything been said at all at your meeting with Bywaters on that Tuesday about seeing him again that night?'

Edith shook her head. 'No, nothing at all.'

'Had he made any *reference* to your husband?'

'No, none at all.'

At this point, Edith began to relate the events that took place after she and her husband had left the train at Ilford station. Less than half way through the story she broke down in tears and the packed court watched and waited in silence as she struggled to control her emotions.

Curtis-Bennett was in no hurry to continue. It did his client no harm at all to be seen weeping at the untimely death of her husband.

When she had finished her account of the fatal attack, Curtis-Bennett again waited for Edith to compose herself before going on.

'Had Bywaters *ever*, at any time, said anything to even suggest that he was likely to stab your husband?' he asked.

Edith shook her head, wiping away more tears. 'Never,' she said. 'I did not know that he possessed a knife. I had never seen it until it was produced in these proceedings.'

'After the scuffle, did you see someone running away?'

Curtis-Bennett's questioning was gentle but firm.

'Yes,' Edith said. 'I saw somebody running away and I recognized the coat and hat.'

'Was that the coat and hat of the prisoner, Bywaters?'

'Yes. Mr Bywaters.'

'Why,' Curtis-Bennett asked, 'did you tell the police officer you had not seen anyone about in Belgrave Road?'

It was a question the Crown were certain to ask and he had forestalled them.

'I was very agitated,' Edith said, 'and I did not want to say anything against Mr Bywaters; I wanted to shield him.'

There it was. No evasions, no excuses, the truth: "I wanted to shield him." What she had done could not be condoned nor excused but could, perhaps, be understood.

'Had you the remotest idea,' Curtis-Bennett asked, 'that any attack was going to be made on your husband that night?'

'None whatever.'

'Or at any time?'

'Never at any time.'

Curtis-Bennett sat down. The case for the defence was concluded.

Edith remained in the witness-box feeling she had given a good account of herself. The gentle questioning of Curtis-Bennett had raised her spirits and left her feeling optimistic.

It was three o'clock when the Solicitor General rose to cross-examine.

He adjusted his robe, shuffled his papers and polished his glasses before speaking - a ploy he often used to distract a defendant.

'Mrs Thompson,' he said crisply. 'Have you any recollection *now* of what happened when your husband was killed?'

'Only what I have said,' Edith replied. 'I was dazed.'

Inskip brandished a copy of Edith's statement.

'Here is the statement you made to the police! I shall read it to you. *"We were coming along Belgrave Road and just past the corner of Endsleigh Gardens when I heard him call out 'Oo'er' and he fell up against me. I put out my arm to save him and found blood which I thought was coming from his mouth. I tried to hold him up. He staggered for several yards towards Kensington Gardens and then fell against the wall and slid down. I felt him and found his clothing wet with blood. he never moved after he fell. We had no quarrel on the way. We were quite happy together. Immediately I saw the blood I ran across the road to a doctor's. I appealed to a lady and gentleman who were passing and the gentleman also went to the doctor's. The doctor came and told me my husband was dead. Just before he fell down I was walking on his right hand side on the inside of the pavement nearest the wall. We were side by side. I did not see anybody about at the time. My husband and I were talking about going to a dance".*

'Now,' Inskip said. 'Did you intend to tell an untruth *then* about the incident?'

'Yes,' Edith said.

'Was it to shield Bywaters?'

'It was.'

Inskip referred to the statement again. 'In your statement you say: *"We were coming along Belgrave Road and just past the corner of Endsleigh Gardens when I heard him call out 'Oo'er' and he fell up against me."* Does that not suggest,' he said sardonically,' that he was taken ill and that nobody was present?'

'Yes.'

'Did you intend when you said that, to tell an untruth?'

'That is so,' Edith agreed.

'It was an untruth in so far as it suggests that that was the first thing that happened?'

'That is so.'

'Was that again to shield Bywaters?'

'It was.'

'At the time you made this statement to the police, you knew it was Bywaters who had done it?'

Edith hesitated. 'I do not know what you mean by 'done it',' she said. 'I did not know *then* that anything was actually *done*. When I say I knew it was Bywaters, I mean I recognized his coat and hat - going away.'

'Then you *left out* the truth in order to shield Bywaters?'

'Yes, that is so,' Edith admitted.

'You knew, did you not, that if you told the truth, Bywaters would be suspected?'

'I did.'

Inskip allowed the suspicion of a smile to hover about his lips for a moment before continuing.

Looking again at the statement he said: 'You say, *"I was dazed for a moment. When I recovered I saw my husband scuffling with a man."* Is that the truth?'

'It is.'

'Did you see either of them strike a blow?'

'It was dark. 'I could not see.'

Inskip adjusted his spectacles. 'Here is another sentence from your statement,' he said. ' *"The man I know as Freddy Bywaters was running away. He was wearing a blue overcoat and a grey hat. I knew it was him although I did not see his face."* Do you mean by that that you recognized this man, whom you only saw at a distance, in he dark in front of you - that you recognized him by his overcoat and hat?'

'I did. By his back.'

Inskip looked at Edith, again with the hint of a smile.

'Do you *really* suggest that?' he said.

'I do.'

'Did you know right from the beginning that it was Bywaters?'

'I had no idea,' Edith said tersely.

Inskip was beginning to rattle Edith with his pedantic manner and persistent questioning. This wasn't how she imagined it would be.

'May we take it then,' Inskip said blandly, 'that when you made this statement, you left out Bywaters's name in order to shield him?'

The trap was set.

'I did so, yes,' Edith replied.

The trap was sprung.

'Why?' Inskip demanded. 'What were you afraid of if you did not know your husband had been stabbed?'

Edith swallowed hard.

'I was not afraid of anything,' she said quietly.

Inskip's voice took on a sharper edge. 'Were you not going to shield him from a charge of having murdered your husband?' he said grimly.

'I did not know my husband *was* murdered,' Edith protested.

'You did not know that your husband had been assaulted and murdered?' Inskip's brow was furrowed with disbelief.

'No...the inspector told me, but I did not realize, even at the time, that he was dead.'

'Are you saying that when you told those untruths, and left out Bywaters, you were *not* attempting to shield him from a charge of having murdered your husband?'

'I did not even know my husband *had* been murdered. I did not...realize it.'

Edith was beginning to flounder.

Inskip regarded her disdainfully for a moment

'I will ask you again, Mrs Thompson,' he said sternly. 'What were you attempting to shield the prisoner Bywaters from?'

Edith was becoming unsettled and confused.

'From...being connected with me,' she said falteringly. 'His name being brought into...anything.'

Inskip leaned toward her, eyes glinting behind his spectacles. 'Mrs Thompson,' he said scathingly, 'is it not a fact that you *knew* Bywaters was going to do something that evening and that these two false statements were an attempt to prevent the police getting wind of it?'

'That is not true!' Edith's voice was shrill and quivering with nervous tension.

Inskip watched impassively as Edith fumbled in her bag, took out a handkerchief and dabbed her eyes.

Having achieved his aim of disconcerting her, Inskip decided to change tack.

'Let me take you back to the early stages of your relationship with Bywaters,' he said dryly. 'Do you agree with me that it was June of 1921 that you first fell in love with Bywaters?'

Knowing that Freddy had already, on oath, declared that it was not until September, Edith felt constrained to follow suit.

'No, I do not,' she said defiantly.

'Where *do* you put it then?' he asked.

'September of that year.'

'Let me read you one of your letters to Bywaters dated August 1922,' he said. ' *"Fourteen months have gone by now, darlint, it's so terribly long. Neither you nor I thought we would have to wait all that long time."* Does that not satisfy you that you and Bywaters declared your love to each other in *June* 1921?'

'Not at all,' Edith replied.

Inskip raised an expressive eyebrow. 'You deny that?' he said incredulously.

'I do.'

'Then when *did* you first begin to address him as your lover? he asked patronisingly.

'It is just what you mean by "your lover"?' Edith asked.

Again there was the merest hint of a disdainful smile from Inskip. 'The terms in which a woman does not write to any man except her husband,' he said acidly.

'I can't remember,' Edith said shaking her head.

Inskip picked up another of the letters.

'What was the risk you were running. The risk you so often mentioned to Bywaters. Let me read you this: *"Why aren't you sending me something? I wanted you to - you never do what I ask you darlint - you still have your own way always - if I don't mind the risk why should you?"* What risk was that?' Inskip asked smoothly.

'The risk of Mr Bywaters sending me something instead of bringing something.'

'Why was that a risk?'

'Well, it would be a risk for me to receive anything.'

'Why,' Inskip persisted, 'should there be a risk in a friend - or even a lover - sending you a letter, or a present?'

'I did not say it was a letter.'

Edith was becoming more and more irritated by Inskip's manner.

"What was it then?' he asked.

'Something...Mr Bywaters suggested,' she replied.

'Did he suggest it was a dangerous thing?'

'No.'

'Then why did you think it *was* a dangerous thing?'

'I did *not* think it was a dangerous thing!'

Exasperation was beginning to show in Edith's voice.

'Then why did you think it was a risk?'

'There was a risk,' Edith said with growing confusion, 'to anything sent to me that did not come to my hands first.'

'You were afraid somebody might have thought there were improper relations between you and him?' Inskip asked sarcastically. 'Is that what you are saying?'

'No, no!'

'In the passage I have just read to you, you were asking Bywaters to send you something which he had said, according to you, he was going to *bring*. What was it?'

'I have no idea.'

'You have no idea?'

'Except what he told me.'

'What did he tell you?'

'That he would...bring me something.'

'He did not say what the something was?'

'No, he did not mention anything.'

Inskip persisted. 'What did he lead you to *think* it was?'

Edith hesitated.

'Something to give to my husband.'

This was the opening Inskip had been waiting for.

'With a view to poisoning your husband?' he said sharply.

'No, that was not the idea, that was not what I expected,' Edith protested.

'Something to give your husband that would hurt him then?'

'To make him ill,' Edith corrected.

'And you were urging Bywaters to send it instead of bringing it?'

'That is so.'

'Was that in order that it might be put into use more quickly?'

It was a loaded question and Edith had to choose her words carefully.

'I wrote that,' she said slowly, 'in order to make him think I was willing to do anything he might suggest...to enable me to retain his affections.'

Edith was having trouble focussing her mind. She knew she was treading on thin ice that could crack at any moment.

'Mrs Thompson,' Inskip said, 'is that a frank explanation of this urging him to send instead of bringing?'

'Absolutely,' Edith said. 'I wanted him to think I was eager to help him.'

Mr Justice Shearman leaned forward. 'Eager to do what?' he asked.

'Anything he suggested,' Edith replied.

Inskip pressed on.

'He suggested giving your husband something to hurt him?'

'He...had given me something.'

Edith was beginning to falter again.

'Did you welcome the suggestion that something should be given to your husband to make him ill?'

'I did not.'

Inskip put the question another way,

'Did you *object* to it?' he asked pointedly.

'I did at the time.'

It was another opening that Inskip swiftly seized upon. 'Yet although you objected to it you still urged Bywaters to send it more quickly than he intended. How do you explain that?'

Again Edith hesitated before answering. 'I objected at the time,' she said. 'Afterwards I acquiesced.'

Inskip picked up another letter and read an extract from it:

' "*I am going to try the glass again - when it is safe. I've got an electric light globe this time.*" When was it likely to be safe?' Inskip enquired.

'There was no question of it being safe or not; I was not going to try it.'

'Then why did you tell Bywaters you were going to try it when it was safe?'

The persistence of Inskip's questioning was beginning to wear Edith down.

'To let him think I was willing to do what he wanted.'

Edith realized that the impression she was giving was that of a foolish, besotted woman, willing to do almost anything to hold on to her young lover, but by now she was past caring.

Inskip's face was a picture of incredulity.

'You are representing that this young man...' he raised his arm and pointed dramatically at Bywaters, 'was seriously suggesting to you that you should poison your husband?'

Edith shook her head.

'I did not say that,' she said, near to tears.

'Then what *was* the suggestion?' Inskip asked tersely.

Edith felt trapped.

'He said he would give me something,' she said softly.

Again the judge intervened.

'Give him something in his food?' he asked querulously. 'You answered my question a little while ago that it was to give him something to make him ill.'

'That is what I surmised,' Edith said, 'that I should give him something so that when he had a heart attack he would not be able to resist it.'

At this incredible admission there was a concerted gasp of astonishment from the entire court followed by a susurration of urgent whispered conversation.

When the murmur had subsided, Mr Justice Shearman removed his pince nez, leaned forward and addressed Mrs Thompson. 'I do not want to be mistaken,' he said. 'Did I take you down rightly as saying: "I wanted him to think I was willing to take my husband's life"?'

'I wanted him to *think* I was willing to do what he suggested,' she replied.

'That is to take your husband's life?' the judge insisted.

'Not necessarily,' Edith said.

Inskip thanked the judge for his contribution and turned back to Mrs Thompson. 'To injure him then?'

'To make him ill.'

'What was the object of making him ill?'

'I had not discussed any special object.'

'Was not the object of making him ill that he should not recover from his heart attacks?'

'Yes,' Edith replied, 'that was certainly the impression.'

She was spared any further interrogation by the clock. Noting the lateness of the hour, Shearman adjourned the hearing until 10.30 the following morning.

As she left the witness-box Edith gave her defence counsel a strained smile as she passed and although he acknowledged her with a nod of encouragement, in his heart Curtis-Bennett knew that by going into the witness box his client had done herself irreparable harm. He would re-examine of course, but the damage had already been done. Thomas Inskip had managed to superimpose sinister and quite bogus interpretations on what were no more than the romantic dreams and fantasies of an impressionable, imaginative, besotted woman.

The point his client had failed to grasp was that it was up to the prosecution to prove her guilt, not for her to prove her innocence and, if it had been left to him, he would have made that proof impossible. Now, it was going to be an up-hill struggle.

On the morning of Saturday 9th December the crowd milling around outside the Old Bailey in Newgate Street had swelled to over two thousand for a trial that had captured the imagination of the people more than any other in living memory.

The heady mix of murder, intrigue, adulterous assignations and, above all, the letters chronicling their illicit love affair and containing references to poison and powdered glass, had turned it into a sensation.

Inside court Number One, Edith was back in to the witness box looking strained and apprehensive as she removed her gloves and prepared herself, once again, for the laying bare of her private life.

Inevitably the letters were produced, their contents scrutinized, interpretations advanced and insinuations made.

Finally Inskip came to the references to the novel *Bella Donna*.

'Is the story of *Bella Donna* about a woman who married and went to Egypt?' he enquired.

'Yes.'

'And when they were going to Egypt on the boat did they meet a man called Baroudi?'

'They did.'

'Did the woman, Mrs Chepstow, feel attracted to the comfort and pleasure that Baroudi could give her?'

'I believe she did.'

'Did she then arrange to poison her husband in order that she might be free to join Baroudi?'

'I cannot say she arranged it.'

'There is a plot, is there not, which is really the plot of the story, to poison her husband without anyone finding out what she was doing?'

'That is a matter of opinion,' Edith replied.

'At any rate,' Inskip went on, 'it was an important incident in the book that Mrs Chepstow should get rid of her husband, so that she might go to another man?'

'I do not remember that being mentioned in the book.' Edith felt on safer ground discussing books.

'Let me read you an extract from one of your letters dated 18th May 1922, which includes a direct quotation from the book, followed by a query from you: *"It must be remembered that digitalin is a cumulative poison and that the same dose, harmless if taken once, yet frequently repeated becomes deadly. Is it any use?"* Why,' Inskip asked, 'did you mention that particular passage to Bywaters?'

'I wanted him to think that I was still agreeing to fall in with the plan which he had suggested.'

'Were you going to deceive Bywaters and let him realize that you were no longer anxious to poison your husband?'

'I was *never* anxious to poison my husband,' Edith said reprovingly.

'What I am asking, Mrs Thompson, is this. Did you continue to let him believe that you were prepared to poison your husband?'

Edith considered for a moment.

'I suppose he must have thought I was still waiting to do so, yes.'

Thomas Inskip gathered up his papers. 'That is all I have to ask, M'lud,' he said. The time was now 11.30.

After Cecil Whiteley had declined to cross-examine Mrs Thompson, Curtis-Bennett rose to re-examine.

'You have been asked by my learned friend some questions about the book *Bella Donna,*' he said. 'Was Baroudi in the book a wealthy man or a poor man?'

'A very wealthy man.'

'And was Nigel, the husband of Bella Donna, a wealthy man or a poor man?'

'I believe his was a wealthy man.'

'As far as you know,' Curtis-Bennett continued, 'had Bywaters any money outside of his pay?'

'None at all.'

'Did you know how much that pay might be?' he asked.

'About two hundred pounds a year, I think.'

'Was your husband better off than that?'

'Not very much. I believe he got about six pounds a week.'

'Then, did *you* support yourself?' Curtis-Bennett asked.

'I did, absolutely.'

'What was *your* weekly wage?'

'I had been with Carlton & Prior for many years and my remuneration was a substantial one,' Edith said. 'Six pounds a week and bonuses.'

Curtis-Bennett now pressed home his point.

'If you *had* run away with Bywaters, would you have been able to remain at Carlton & Prior?' he asked.

'I think not.'

Curtis-Bennett glanced briefly at the jury before continuing. 'That being the position of you, Bywaters and your husband, as compared with Bella Donna, Baroudi and Mrs Chepstow's husband,' he said, 'I put to you your description of the woman Bella Donna in your letter of 14th July: *"She doesn't seem a woman to me - she seems abnormal - a monster, utterly selfish and self-living."'*

Curtis-Bennett put down the letter and grasped the lapels of his gown with both hands.

'Is that your *true* idea of that woman?' he asked dramatically.

'Absolutely,' Edith replied.

Having demolished any suggestion by the Crown that Edith was in any way similar, or sympathetic to the character in the book, Curtis-Bennett allowed himself a brief smile of satisfaction.

'When Bywaters was away from 9th June until 23rd September of this year, were you getting as many letters from him as previously?' he asked.

Edith shook her head. 'No.'

'What did you think from that?'

Edith bit her lip. 'I thought...he was gradually drifting away from me,' she said huskily.

'Did you love him very much?'

Asking such a painfully intimate question was not something Curtis-Bennett relished, but he felt he had to re-establish in the jury's minds how utterly infatuated Edith had been with her young lover.'

Her eyes brimming with tears, Edith lowered her head. 'I did,' she said in a voice barely audible.

Curtis-Bennett judiciously allowed the pregnant silence that followed this admission to continue for a few moments before speaking again.

'Just one or two questions about the night of 3rd October and early morning of the 4th,' he said gently. 'You told my learned friend that you were pushed aside and fell down.'

'Yes,' Edith said, wiping her eyes.

'When you fell down, did you receive an injury that you discovered later?'

'Yes, I had a large bump on the right hand side of my head.'

'Then you told my learned friend that when you looked down the street you saw your husband scuffling with someone?'

'That is so.'

'Did you recognize who the other person was?'

'I did not.'

'When was the first time that night that you saw something about that person which made you think who it was?'

'It was the coat and hat I recognized.'

'Had you any idea then that your husband had been stabbed?'

'None at all,' Edith replied.

'As far as you could, from the moment you got up to your husband, did you do everything you could for him?'

Edith nodded. 'Everything I possibly could,' she said. Then, overcome, put her head in her hands and wept.

After Edith had made a tearful exit from the witness box, Curtis-Bennett called his penultimate witness, Avis Graydon.

The contrast between the two sisters, often remarked upon, was now more obvious than ever. Avis had always been the practical, sensible, down-to-earth sibling; while Edith was ever the dreamer, the fantasist, the romantic, the actress. Standing erect in the witness box, her eyes ablaze with determination, Avis was totally convinced of her much-loved sister's innocence. And when she took the oath, her voice was clear and strong, carrying to the furthest corner of the oak-panelled courtroom.

'Miss Graydon,' Curtis-Bennett began, 'I want to read you a letter from Mrs Thompson to Bywaters, dated 13th June, *"I rang Avis yesterday and she said that*

Percy came down there in a rage and told Dad everything - about the rows we have over you. Dad said it was a disgraceful thing that you should come between husband and wife and I ought to be ashamed.

"Darlint, I told you this is how they would look at it - they don't understand and they never will, any of them.

"Dad was going to talk to me, Avis said - but I went down and nothing whatever was said by any of them. I told Avis I'd tell them off if they said anything to me, I didn't go whining to my people when he *did things I didn't approve of, and I didn't expect him to - however nothing was said at all."'*

Curtis-Bennett put down the letter and addressed Avis Graydon. 'Is there any truth in that at all?' he asked in ringing tones.

'There is none whatever,' Avis replied forcefully.

'Did you *ever* tell her anything like that at all?'

'I did not.'

At this point Mr Justice Shearman interjected.

'It follows, therefore,' he said, 'that your sister invented the whole of this?'

Avis took a deep breath. 'Yes. It is pure imagination on my sister's part.'

The last witness to be called for the defence was Mrs Graydon. Dressed entirely in black, care-worn and stooped, she cut a pitiable figure as she slowly made her way to the witness box.

The trial with its sensational revelations, the scandal-mongering by some sections of the press and the ever-present threat of the gallows hanging over her daughter had been a cross too heavy for her to bear, and she had lately taken to her bed.

Aware of the frailty of his witness, Curtis-Bennett did not intend to detain her very long - just one question in fact. He wished to support Edith's statement that she had not seen the fight between Percy and Freddy because she was badly affected by the fall.

'Mrs Graydon,' he said, 'while you were with your daughter at Ilford police station on 4th and 5th of October did she complain of a bump on her forehead?'

'Yes, she complained to me two or three times about a bump on her head. I put my hand over the place where she told me it was, and I felt a bump there.'

After excusing the witness Curtis-Bennett turned to the judge. 'That is the case for Mrs Thompson,' he said.

A few minutes later Cecil Whiteley rose to make his closing speech on behalf of Freddy Bywaters.

.

He was not an advocate renowned for his oratory but the speech that followed greatly surprised his colleagues and impressed the jury with its reasoned argument and, above all, its *passion*.

In it, he not only pleaded for his client, but for Mrs Thompson as well.

He chided the prosecution for using letters written by an infatuated woman in a hysterical state of mind - the contents of which had nothing to do with the murder - but not pursuing the four other charges on which she was indicted and which *were* relevant to the letters.

'Members of the jury,' he said, 'the tragedy in this case, the poignant tragedy so far as Bywaters is concerned, is that there is sitting next to him in that box one who is charged jointly with him, one who is dearer to him than his own life. You may have noticed,' he went on, 'that I asked no questions of Mrs Thompson, although I was entitled to do so. Why did I not? For this simple reason: my instructions were that neither by word nor deed, in conducting this case, should a word be said, or any action taken, which would in any way hamper the defence of Mrs Thompson.

He spoke of the letters written by Edith and urged the jury when considering them to separate fact from fiction - the imagining from the real.

He dealt with Freddy's futile claim, that Percy had attacked him, with an air of confidence which belied his inner belief that it was untrue.

His was a task of damage limitation and to save Freddy from the gallows.

After criticising the dubious method of the confrontation used by the police at Ilford police station to induce the two damning confessions, he once again raised the point of the unfairness of the right of last address by the Solicitor General and said: 'I am conscious that the interests of Bywaters may suffer from the fact that the Crown has the last word.'

He finished dramatically and his words clearly reached everyone in the court room.

'I challenge the prosecution to point to one stable piece of evidence, to any evidence, on which you can rely, on which you can say that that man agreed with Mrs Thompson to do some harm or some violence to Percy Thompson. Judge this young man as you yourselves would be judged. One life has already been sacrificed in this sordid and horrible drama. Is there to be yet another? Frederick Bywaters makes his last appeal to you through me, and he says to you, "It is true, only too true, that I have been weak, extremely weak. It is true, only too true, that I allowed myself to drift into this dishonourable entanglement and intrigue with a married woman living with her husband. It is true that I had not the moral courage to cut myself adrift from it and end it all. It is true, only too true, that she confided in me, that I was flattered that she should come to me, a young man of nineteen, and confide in me. It is true that I pitied her, and that my pity turned to love. I did not realize, I did not know, I had not enough experience in this life to know, that true love must mean self-sacrifice. All this is true," he says, "but I ask you to believe, and by your verdict to proclaim to this whole world that in all this history I am not an assassin! I am no murderer!"'

When Curtis-Bennett rose to speak for Edith Thompson an expectant hush fell upon the crowded court. His reputation as an orator was well known and his closing speeches were already the stuff of legend. He was not about to disappoint them.

After yet another tussle with the obdurate Justice Shearman over the propriety of Edith being charged with Freddy's crime, Curtis-Bennett simplified the matter.

'If you come to the conclusion that she conspired with Bywaters to murder her husband on that night, then you will convict her on that indictment. At this moment, however, she sits in the dock charged with being a murderess on the night of October 3rd, and it is for the prosecution to satisfy you that she is guilty. I contend that every single action of Mrs Thompson upon the night when the killing took place, shows that she knew nothing of what was going to happen.'

He went on. 'This is no *ordinary* case you are trying. These are not *ordinary* people. This is not an ordinary charge of murder. This is not an *ordinary* charge against *ordinary* people. It is very difficult to get into the atmosphere of a play or an opera, but you have to do it in this case. Am I right or wrong in saying that this woman is one of the most extraordinary personalities that you or I have ever met? She is a woman who lived the sort of life I don't suppose any of you live in - an extraordinary life of make-believe. She is always living an extraordinary life of novels. She reads a book and then imagines herself as one of the characters in that book.

'This is the woman you have to deal with, not some *ordinary* woman. She is one of the most striking personalities, met with from time to time, who stand out for some reason or another. I ask you again to get into the atmosphere of the life of Mrs Thompson. I do not care whether it is described as an "amazing passion" to use an expression of the Solicitor General, or as an adulterous intercourse.

'Thank God,' he told the jury, 'this is not a court of morals, because if everybody immoral was brought here I would never be out of it, and neither would you.'

Having painted a very accurate picture of Edith's extraordinary character he then set about explaining how, in fact, the letters showed her innocence not her guilt.

'The two lovers agreed to wait five years to be with each other. Can you say that such a wait is the arrangement of murderers, of two people who have made up their minds upon a certain date to murder a man? The very last letter, which was made so much of by the prosecution, stated: "There are only three and three quarter years left." Yet it is said that the person who wrote that letter on the 2nd of October was a murderess, by inference, not because she struck any blow as a murderess, but because she was planning murder *the very next night.*'

Referring to the letters Curtis-Bennett went on: 'I ask you not to forget that although they have been combed and combed by the prosecution to find anything that might suggest that Mrs Thompson is a murderess, they have not done so. There is nothing in the letters to show anything but that Mrs Thompson was desirous of impressing on Bywaters that she was prepared to go to any length to retain his affection. It is easy,' he continued, 'to take extracts from letters and to put them before a jury without their context and without the mentality of the writer and say to the jury: "What does that mean?" It is scarcely fair to do so. If you take the letters and read them through, as I was so anxious you should do, what does it come to? At the most it might possibly make that woman guilty of one of the charges in the second indictment. They certainly do not make her a principal in the killing of Percy Thompson on the night of 3rd October.'

He again reminded the jury of the *"I had the wrong porridge today..."* passage from one of the letters and asked them to remember it was Mrs Lester who prepared the porridge every morning. He went on:

'The prosecution thought that the only way for them to prove whether those statements in the letters were true or untrue was to have the body of Thompson exhumed. And what did they find? They found no possible trace of any sort of poison. They found no trace of glass having been administered in the body. And having found that the result of the post-mortem examination was consistent with the suggestion I am now putting to you *that the statements were absolutely untrue that she had administered anything* - the prosecution are not generous enough to say: "We will let you have the whole benefit of that, there is no corroboration that you ever gave poison or glass to your husband." But no. When Dr Spilsbury was in the witness-box, the prosecution got him to give an answer to a question which was obvious to all before he said it. "Oh, of course, it *may* be that poison was given and disappeared. There are certain poisons that do not leave any trace." How is one going to deal with a case if it is going to put that way?

'The real truth about Mrs Thompson, as borne out by her letters, was that she was a woman who would go on telling any lies so long as she could keep her lover Bywaters.

'This woman was eight years older than the man, and she realized that she might be losing him. Listen to the following sentence in which she writes, *"It was a lie - I would tell heaps and heaps to help you, but darlint do you think I like telling them?"*

'Bywaters knew the sort of woman she was, and he has described her to you as 'living in books'. You will remember the references to the book *Bella Donna* in her letters. I hope that most of you gentlemen of the jury who have read the book have seen the play.'

It was at this point that the judge made another of his querulous interjections. Frowning over the top of his pince-nez he asked: 'Are you going to put in the book? If you do,' he added pointedly, 'the jury will have to read the whole of it.'

'I do not wish to do that,' Curtis-Bennett replied. 'But I will, if necessary, put the book in.'

Shearman gave an exasperated sigh.

'Surely not,' he said crossly. 'I don't think that is necessary. I hope not - I hope you will not put it in.' Adding 'You can deal with anything that has been given in evidence about it.'

To Curtis-Bennett this was an altogether improper direction. Here was a woman on trial for her life and the judge was virtually telling her defence not to introduce something that could help her.

After sardonically thanking the judge for his valuable comments, Curtis-Bennett returned to the novel *Bella Donna*.

'Is it suggested that Mrs Thompson was slowly poisoning her husband? There is no evidence of it. Is it suggested that any one, at her instigation, was doing it, so that she might go off with Bywaters? Again, there is no evidence of it.'

Picking up another of the letters he read: ' *"The third time he found a piece of glass."'* Turning to the jury, Curtis-Bennett said: 'I ask you to imagine what effect such a piece of glass would have in passing through the intestines. Did she *ever* use it three times? The evidence is that there is no trace of anybody ever having administered anything of the sort to Mr Thompson.'

It was at this high point in his address, when the medical evidence of an expert, showed what had been written by Edith Thompson to be nonsense, that Mr Justice Shearman once again intervened to the detriment of the defence.

Although the courtroom clock showed only twenty minutes past four o'clock, he decided to cut short the afternoon session by brusquely announcing the adjournment of the court until Monday morning.

Interrupted once again whilst in full flow, Curtis-Bennett felt justifiably aggrieved.

But worse was to come.

Before releasing the jury, the judge had this to say to them: 'Before the Court rises for the day I wish to offer you, members of the jury, this advice. Of course, you will not make up your minds until you have heard the whole case.

'The only other thing is, having regard to the surroundings for so many days, by all means look at the atmosphere and try to understand what the letters mean, but you should not forget that you are in a Court of Justice trying a vulgar and common crime. You are not listening to a play from the stalls of a theatre. When you are thinking it over, you should think it over in that way.'

Curtis-Bennett was aghast. To describe the case before him as "vulgar and common" was wholly improper, blatantly prejudicial to the two prisoners, and undermining to his own attempt to get the jury to try to understand the mind of Edith Thompson. 'A vulgar and common crime' was the picture that the jury would have in its mind till Monday morning when the trial resumed.

At least Curtis-Bennett knew where he stood. The judge had made it plain he was openly hostile to his client. He knew he would have to be at his persuasive best when he resumed his address on Monday morning.

That night, after dining alone at the Beefsteak Club, Curtis-Bennett was making his way to the bar when he spotted his old friend and colleague, Marshall-Hall. Indeed, standing as he did at six feet three, Sir Edward Marshall-Hall. KC. was a difficult man to miss.

Later, ensconced in two leather armchairs either side of a crackling log-fire, the two most eminent KC's of the day were discussing the case over brandy and cigars.

After railing against the prejudice and downright rudeness shown by the judge during the trial, Curtis-Bennett lapsed into a pensive mood.

Marshall-Hall swirled his brandy around in the glass.

'You mustn't let that curmudgeonly old bugger, Shearman, get you down, old chap,' he said. 'He's just peeved that you've got your knighthood before he has.'

Curtis-Bennett exhaled a plume of cigar smoke.

'I have a feeling, Edward,' he said thoughtfully, 'that I may well have lost this case.'

'If I may say so,' Marshall-Hall ventured, 'allowing Mrs Thompson to give evidence was, to say the least, well...unwise.'

'Couldn't stop her,' Curtis-Bennett said ruefully. 'She was determined to have her say.'

The two men smoked their cigars in silence for a moment before Marshall-Hall spoke.

'The supreme irony of this case as I see it, is that in his desperate efforts to protect Mrs Thompson at all costs, young Bywaters might well have done her chance of acquittal irreparable harm. Because if *he* goes down *she* must go down with him!'

Curtis-Bennett looked enquiringly across at his old adversary.

Marshall-Hall took a sip of brandy before setting the glass down on the table beside him.

'You see, here we have a twenty year old youth of unblemished reputation; a personable, upright sort of young fellow, good to his mother, hard working and, in the eyes of the law, still a minor.

'If his defence had been that he was totally besotted by an older woman who led him to believe that the biggest stumbling block to their future happiness together was her husband, and having taken too much drink, he had accosted Thompson in the street to ask him to give his wife a divorce, and a fight had ensued, resulting in Thompson's death; then I firmly believe, taking into account his youth and previous good character, the jury may well have been persuaded to return a verdict of manslaughter. Which means that Mrs Thompson would walk free because she could not be an accomplice to an unpremeditated act.

'Furthermore,' he went on, 'even if they were *both* found guilty of murder, *in these circumstances* Bywaters would almost certainly be reprieved which would mean that neither he nor Mrs Thompson would hang.

'It is ironic,' he mused, 'that in his refusal to implicate Mrs Thompson, young Bywaters may well have condemned her to death.'

There was a long silence as Curtis-Bennett considered his friend's argument. 'By God, Edward!' he said. 'I hope you're wrong.

Marshall-Hall drew deeply on his cigar. 'So do I, old chap,' he said solemnly. 'So do I.'

In the early hours of Monday, as Edith turned restlessly in her narrow bed, a queue was already forming in the icy morning mists that curled around the Old Bailey for what everyone assumed would be the final day and which might, with a bit of luck, even produce a verdict.

On this, the last day of the most talked about murder case since the trial of Dr Crippen in the same court, so great was the hysteria the case had aroused among the general public, tickets to the public gallery were already changing hands for five pounds or more.

At 10.30 on that Monday morning as Curtis-Bennett rose to continue with his interrupted closing speech he was acutely aware of the heavy burden of responsibility he was carrying but was well prepared.

'When we adjourned on Saturday,' he began, 'I had almost finished dealing with the letters. I now wish to deal with a letter written on 12th September.

'"*This time everything seems different. I don't hear from you so much, you don't talk to me by letter and help me, and I don't even know if I am going to see you.*" Does that not show,' he asked, 'what I have been putting before you, that Mrs Thompson had in her mind that Bywaters was not so fond of her as he had been, and that she was anxious to show him that she would go to any extremes to keep his love?'

Curtis-Bennett picked up another letter. 'Look now at the letter of 20th September,' he said. ' "*You are jealous of him - but I want you to be - he has the right by law to all that you have the right to by nature and love - yes darlint be jealous, so much that you will do something desperate.*"

'Start at the end of the story with the death,' he told the jury, ' and work back to that, and you can make what is an absolutely innocent expression in a letter, appear to be a guilty one. Work back, as the prosecution have done, from the tragedy, and come to a letter written a fortnight before and, because in that letter there is this phrase "*do something desperate*", that means that the woman was asking the man to murder her husband. Are you, because of the prejudice created by the reading of extracts from these letters, going to say there is any evidence from them that this woman was a principal, a fortnight afterwards, in the murder of her husband?

'I come now,' he went on, 'to a letter written by Mrs Thompson on 2nd October. This letter is one of the strongest documents that you could have against the suggestion that these two persons made a prior agreement, on the very day before the tragedy took place, that Mr Thompson should be murdered.

' *"Darlingest lover of mine, thank you, thank you, oh thank you a thousand times for Friday...I tried so hard to find a way out tonight darlingest but he was suspicious and still is - I suppose we must make a study of this deceit for some time longer. I hate it. I hate every lie I have to tell to see you because lies seem such small, mean things...but until we have funds we can do nothing."'*

Curtis-Bennett put down the letter and looked along the row of jurors.

'Do the prosecution say,' he declaimed, 'that this letter, written on the 2nd October, is evidence that these two people were intending murder *the very next day*, or the day after, or the week after? No, this woman is saying, on the 2nd October, "it is funds we want, and until we have funds we can do nothing". They wanted funds for the purpose of living together, because if Mrs Thompson ran away with Bywaters, she would have to leave her job.'

Curtis-Bennett paused for a moment to allow the jury to consider what he had just said.

'The next passage in the letters is, *"Don't forget what we talked in the tearoom, I'll still risk and try if you will."'*

Curtis-Bennett again considered the jury before continuing.

'The suggestion of the prosecution - and they have no evidence at all of it - is that in that tearoom in Aldersgate Street, these two people were plotting murder. There is not one scrap of evidence. But having put all those letters before you, the prosecution then say, "The night of 3rd October Thompson dies", and add "Don't forget what we talked about in the tearoom", and you, members of the jury, are urged to believe that they were talking about murder. Look at the last words of the letter,' he asked the jury, ' *"We have only three and three-quarter years left, darlingest; try and help, Peidi."* It is almost inconceivable,' he thundered, ' that it can be suggested in that letter that it shows these two people were plotting murder. If the story put before you by the prosecution be true, do you not think that you would find in these letters some references egging-on, inciting, soliciting Bywaters to commit this murder? In my submission you would find exactly the opposite. There is not one reference in these letters which anyone in this country dare say shows that the suggestion made by the prosecution is true.'

Curtis-Bennett then turned to the night of the murder.

'The evidence is,' he said, 'that Mr and Mrs Thompson were at the Criterion Theatre with Mr and Mrs Laxton, and according to Mr Laxton, were happy and normal. Do you believe,' he asked the jury, 'that that woman could have sat with her husband and the Laxtons the whole evening, happy and in normal condition, if there was to her knowledge going to happen the tragedy which *did* happen to her husband?' He shook his head forcefully.

'The suggestion of the prosecution is that on the journey home, Mrs Thompson *knew* that at some spot her husband was to be attacked and murdered. I venture to point out that there is not a bit of evidence to show that she knew anything of the sort. The prosecution declared that the tragedy took place at a dark spot, but as a matter of fact the spot was similarly lighted to the neighbourhood around. It was the proper and best way home that the Thompsons took after coming from the theatre. She did not lure her husband into some dark byway when a murder could be committed. Are you going to cast those facts aside? Where is the evidence that this was the result of a conspiracy between the two, and that she was party that night to what happened?

'I suggest that Bywaters made up his mind on the spur of the moment to see Thompson and settle the question of leaving his wife. Test the evidence; don't be satisfied with guesswork. Yes, Mrs Thompson did try to conceal Bywaters's name, but we have, after all, to deal with human nature here. Of course one should always tell the truth, the whole truth, and nothing but the truth. But when, in a murder case, two people are sitting in the dock awaiting your verdict, is there anything in the fact that both kept from the police, until a certain moment, information about the other? Bywaters would not have been a man if he had not tried to shield the woman. Mrs Thompson would not have been a woman if she had not tried to shield her lover.

'It will be for you to say,' he went on, 'whether the arguments I have put forward for your consideration are well founded or not. It will be for you to say, when you have heard the Solicitor General address you again on behalf of the Crown, whether the prosecution have proved that either of these people is guilty of murder. I am only concerned with Mrs Thompson. It will be for you to say whether she is guilty of murder, or whether all the prosecution have done is show you a cloud of prejudice.'

The emotion in his voice was beginning to show and Curtis-Bennett paused for a moment to collect himself.

'I am loth to leave this discussion,' he admitted, 'because I am anxious to feel and know that I have dealt properly with the whole case as it is put against Mrs Thompson.'

Again he paused before continuing.

'I know,' he said to the jury, ' I have risked your displeasure in taking up your time at such length, but surely you do not begrudge a few hours one way or the other spent on something which means..eternity.

'Of course, I cannot see what is in your minds, because I cannot tell whether the matters I have been discussing are matters that you don't want to discuss because you have made up your minds. But in asking the question I know one thing: I shall get your answer, and the answer to the question I have put is the answer that Mrs Thompson is not guilty.'

As Curtis-Bennett's sat down, the tension in the court was at fever pitch.

It had been, by any standards, a performance of consummate skill, immense authority and impassioned eloquence, but Inskip, aware that Curtis-Bennett would be a difficult act to follow, was well prepared.

In his final address he began by referring to Bywaters's submission that on the night of the murder he was in fear of his life.

'I ask you,' he said directly to the jury, 'is there any evidence upon which you can reasonably come to the conclusion that he was acting in self-defence?

At least four or five deep and probably fatal blows were inflicted. They were delivered with a weapon which could hardly be used without running the grievous risk of immediate death.

Inskip paused for a moment to allow the jury time to consider his words.

'How does the case stand against Mrs Thompson? he asked rhetorically. 'I suggest that if she and Bywaters agreed to kill Mr Thompson, and the husband was killed in pursuance of that agreement, then there must be a verdict of murder against Mrs Thompson as well as Bywaters. I agree with my learned friends for the defence, that in order for you to arrive at a verdict of murder against Mrs Thompson you must be satisfied that the persuasion lasted right up to the murder.

'If you think that the expressions in the letters, however criminal and foolish, were not really the cause of the murder, then of course it is not a case of murder against Mrs Thompson.'

Inskip re-adjusted his glasses which had slipped down his nose, picked up one of the letters and read a passage from it.

' "...At least it will disarm any suspicion he might have if we have to take drastic measures."

'It has been suggested,' he said wryly, 'that the "drastic measures" meant leaving her husband.' He paused just long enough to allow the jury to register the look of scepticism on his face before adding, with a shrug, 'but you, gentlemen, must be the judge of that.'

He then held up a bundle of Edith's letters.

'When you review all these letters,' he said raising his voice slightly, 'you are driven to the conclusion that right up to the end she allowed Bywaters to think that she was prepared to co-operate with him in poisoning her husband. In trying to reconstruct the conversations between Bywaters and Mrs Thompson you can only draw inferences by giving Bywaters and Mrs Thompson any benefit of the doubt there may be. Nothing I have said should give you reason to think that I wish to impress a single phrase, a single letter, beyond its proper importance.'

Now he turned to the night of the murder.

Describing the events leading up to it and the subsequent struggle, he touched on the fact that Bywaters was carrying a knife on that night.

'You have seen the knife,' he reminded the jury, 'and it is for you to decide whether it was a handy or convenient thing to carry around with him. But not a single witness,' he went on, 'has been called to say that Bywaters was in the habit of carrying it.

'The case for the Crown,' he said, 'is that there was an agreement between these two persons to get rid of Mr Thompson, or that, if there was not an actual agreement in terms, there was an instigation by Mrs Thompson to get rid of him, on which Bywaters acted so as to kill him. Then you must consider Mrs Thompson's position and, weighing everything carefully, say whether she is not guilty of murder. The prosecution are under no duty to press anything beyond its fair value, but it is my duty to ask you not to shirk for one moment to give reasonable construction of those letters and to every incident in the case, even though it results in your returning a verdict of wilful murder against the woman as well as the man.'

As the Solicitor General resumed his seat at the end of his peroration, the consensus of opinion among those present was that it had been a relatively lacklustre performance containing several inaccuracies and misrepresentations. However, by exercising his right to speak last, Inskip had effectively hamstrung the defence in that they were unable to challenge any misleading statements made by the Crown in its closing address.

As Mr Justice Shearman clasped his hands together and looked sternly over the top of his pince-nez at the jury, the court settled down in anticipation of the final act of the drama.

'Members of the jury,' he said sonorously, 'there are several indictments in this case, only one of which is before you and that is the indictment of this man and this woman for wilful murder. The case represented is that these two, by arrangement between each other, agreed to murder this man, and the murder was effected by the man.

'Unless you are satisfied that they did it by arrangement, there would be no case against the woman. With regard to the man, if you are satisfied that, without any arrangements with the woman, he intended to murder, then, of course, you can find him guilty of that.

'There is one thing I would like to say,' he went on. 'We are in a Court of Justice, and Courts of Justice in this country are very properly open to the public. It is inevitable,' he continued, 'that you should have been surrounded in this case by a different atmosphere from that which prevails in the ordinary humdrum of the Courts, and you must throw that aside, because this charge really is - I am not saying whether it is proved - a common or ordinary charge of a wife and an adulterer murdering her husband.'

Having given the jury the benefit of his opinion on how they should approach the case, he went on:

'These cases are not uncommon. There are always cases of husbands who want to get rid of a wife, and of wives who want to get rid of the husband.

'Now I have an observation to make about Sir Henry Curtis-Bennett,' he said with a glint of malice in his eye. 'He said he "thanked God that you had to decide this case and not he". We are dealing with the law and justice here and I do not like invocations to the Diety.'

What Curtis-Bennett had actually said was, "Thank God this is not a court of morals", but by deliberately misquoting him, Shearman had lessened the effectiveness of Sir Henry's closing speech.

'You will,' he instructed the jury, 'apply the ordinary principals of common sense and I will tell you exactly when there is any law.'

'There is only one other observation I am going to make,' he told the jury. 'You have been told this is a case of "great love". Well, let us take one of the letters as a test. At the end of a letter comes this; *"He has the right by law to all that you have the right to by nature and love."'* Shearman made no attempt to disguise the look of contempt on his face. 'Gentlemen,' he said wrinkling his nose, 'if that nonsense means anything it means that the love of a husband for his wife is something improper because marriage is acknowledged by the law, and that the love of a woman for her lover, illicit and clandestine, is something great and noble. I am certain,' he said fixing the jury with a glare of righteous indignation, 'that you, like any other right-minded persons, will be filled with disgust at such a notion. So let us get rid of all that atmosphere, and try this case in an ordinary and common sense way.'

Having made plain his views on Edith's morals he returned to the letters.

'I am sure you know these letters by now and recollect the whole of them. However in exhibit 62 you find this: *"Yesterday I met a woman who had lost three husbands in eleven years, and not through the war: two were drowned and one committed suicide - and some people I know cannot lose one. How unfair everything is."*

'I am not going to comment,' he assured the jury, 'I am only going to call your attention to the facts. Of course,' he pointed out, 'you know these letters are full of the outpourings of a silly but, at the same time, wicked affection.'

He read from many more, each time quoting a passage out of context and apparently showing Edith's desire to be rid of Percy or her actual attempts to fulfil that desire..

Once again, *Bella Donna* was produced and, looking directly at the jury, the judge said: 'This book is about so-called heroes and heroines, probably wicked people, which no doubt accounts for many of the great tragedies.'

Quite what Mr Justice Shearman meant by that strange remark is not clear. But one thing is certain, it was not meant to assist the defence of Edith Thompson.

'Gentlemen,' he went on, 'that is really the whole of the case. I ask your earnest consideration of it. I shall say no more, other than to repeat that if you find the man guilty of murder, then you have got to consider: was this woman an active party to it? Did she direct him to go? Did she know he was coming? And are we satisfied that she was implicated directly in it?

'You know exactly what was was done before the act. You know the fact of all the letters, and you know that her evidence is now that she knew nothing about it. She says she is quite innocent of this matter, and that she is shocked at everything that has happened, and had nothing to do with it.' Shearman paused to allow the jury to note the look of disbelief on his face before continuing.

'You will not convict her,' he said, 'unless you are satisfied that she and he agreed that this man should be murdered, that she knew he was going to do it, and directed him to do it. If you are not satisfied of that you will acquit her. However, if you *are* satisfied of that it will be your duty to convict her.'

At the end of what had been a biased and less than impartial summing-up, the jury retired, taking with them the knife, Freddy's bloodstained overcoat and copies of the statements made by the two defendants.

The time was 3.32pm.

Edith could feel the abrasive, hot sand between her toes as she walked, barefoot, along the water's edge of a deserted, sunlit beach.

She was wearing a white cotton frock and her head was bare. The sun was warm, the breeze gentle, and the salt sea cool and refreshing as it lapped around her feet. In the distance she could hear a brass band playing while, out at sea, right on the horizon and shimmering in the heat-haze bouncing off the water was a steam ship, its single funnel staining the aquamarine sky with a streamer of black smoke.

As she watched the ship disappear from view, a woman's voice began urgently calling: "Mrs Thompson! Mrs Thompson?" and Edith was suddenly gripped by a deep and irrational fear. As she tried to ignore the voice it became closer and more insistent. She felt a heavy hand on her shoulder and, with a gasp of alarm...awoke.

Leaning over her was one of the wardresses.

'The jury's coming back, Mrs Thompson,' she said. 'Time to go.'

Blinking in the unkind glare of the overhead electric light Edith sat up and shook her head as the stomach-churning, grim reality of her situation became all too evident.

As Edith was putting on her hat, she asked the time.

'Twenty to six,' the wardress replied. Then, as she helped Edith on with her coat, whispered in her ear 'Good luck!'

Up above in the courtroom the jury filed back and resumed their seats to a buzz of excited speculation.

Next into court was the judge, who glanced briefly at the jury over his pince-nez before gathering his ermined robe about him and sitting down.

First into the dock was Freddy, flanked by two police officers. His face was taut with apprehension but he held himself erect and stared straight ahead.

Edith came next with a wardress either side. Her face was deathly pale and her hands trembled as she gripped the rail of the dock to steady herself.

All Edith's family were in court, convinced that in a short while they would be taking her home with them and all the anguish and doubt would be over.

As the Clerk of the Court rose to his feet, a pin-drop silence descended on the packed court.

'Members of the jury,' he said gravely, 'have you agreed upon your verdict?'

The foreman of the jury stood up.

'We have,' he said, trying to control the nervousness in his voice.

'Do you find the prisoner, Frederick Edward Bywaters guilty or not guilty of the murder of Percy Thompson?' he asked, enunciating every word carefully.

'Guilty, sir.'

A ripple of whispered comment swept through the court.

Freddy, still standing erect, showed no emotion as the Clerk of the Court continued:

'Do you find the prisoner, Edith Jessie Thompson, guilty or not guilty of the murder of Percy Thompson?'

The jury Foreman swallowed hard.

'Guilty!' he said.

Immediately there was uproar in court with gasps of astonishment, disbelief or shock from all corners of the room.

Edith swayed momentarily as if about to faint, and was quickly supported on either side by a wardress.

During the hubbub, the sole woman juror was seen to wipe tears from her eyes, while the other members looked down at the floor or up at the ceiling - anywhere but at the two young people they had just condemned.

As the two defence counsels sat, stunned with disbelief, the Clerk of the Court continued with his duties.

'You say that they are severally guilty, and that is the verdict of you all?'

'It is,' the Foreman replied.

The Clerk turned to the two accused.

Frederick Bywaters and Edith Thompson,' he said, 'you severally stand convicted of murder. Have you, or either of you, anything to say why the Court should not give you judgement of death according to law?'

Freddy spoke first, his voice firm but charged with emotion.

'I say the verdict of the jury is *wrong*,' he said defiantly. 'Edith Thompson is not guilty. I am no murderer! I am no assassin!'

Edith, in a barely audible voice whispered, 'I am not guilty.'

The Court chaplain then placed the square of black silk upon the judge's head for the ritual of sentencing to begin.

'Frederick Edward Francis Bywaters, the sentence of this Court upon you is that you be taken from this place to a prison of lawful execution where, on the appointed day, you will be hanged by the neck until you be dead. And may the Lord have mercy on your soul.'

After a muttered 'Amen' from the chaplain, Shearman turned to Edith.

Edith was slumped in the chair provided for her, her face contorted with agony, her eyes staring but unseeing.

'Edith Jessie Thompson,' Shearman's voice was devoid of any emotion, 'the sentence of this Court is that you be taken from here to a place of lawful execution where, on the appointed day, you will be hanged by the neck until you are dead. And may the Lord have mercy on your soul.'

The Clerk of the Court asked: 'Edith Jessie Thompson, have you anything to say in stay of execution?'

Edith was helped to her feet and stood, swaying slightly, gripping the rail of the dock tightly with both hands.

'I am not guilty.' Her voice was high-pitched and quavering. 'Oh, *God*. I am not guilty!'

As the warders took Freddy by the arms, he cast one last anguished look at the woman he loved before being bundled down the stairs.

Now it was Edith's turn, and the wardresses had to prise her fingers from the dock rail and carry her over to the stairs. As they descended, Edith emitted a wail of anguish, pain and despair which, in the confined space on the cramped stairway, was greatly amplified imbuing it with a weird, almost unearthly quality.

In the awed silence that followed after the last echo had died away, Edith's mother at last found her voice after having been literally dumbstruck by the verdict. A low moan escaped her lips followed by a piteous cry 'She is my child!' she wailed. 'They *dare* not harm her!'

As she was led sobbing from the court, and Mr Justice Shearman prepared to address the jury for the last time, several well-dressed women in the public gallery were seen to be weeping as the peep-show they had paid good money to watch had turned into an unbearable tragedy.

'Gentlemen,' Shearman said .'I thank you for your patient attention to a long and difficult case.'

The legal trial of Edith Thompson and Freddy Bywaters was over, and a trial of a different kind was about to begin.

Chapter 15

"It is not within my powers of realisation that this
sentence must stand, for something I have not
done, something I did not know of, either
previously or at the time."

From now on, frantic preparations were put in hand to secure a reprieve for the two condemned prisoners. Freddy, still determined to protect Edith, once again instructed Whiteley to exclude from his appeal anything that might reflect badly upon her.

As for Edith, she was now in the relatively comfortable and more relaxed regime of the hospital wing, and although still weak and under sedation, was slowly beginning to recover her strength and, more importantly, her determination.

Outside her parents' home at 231 Shakespeare Crescent, a large group of reporters and press photographers gathered daily in the hope of a comment from one of the family or a picture for the next morning's front page - all of which were either politely refused or studiously ignored, except one.

The editor of the *Daily Sketch* had asked for permission to print photographs of the family in their campaign to save Edith.

The Graydons knew that this gesture was not entirely altruistic but, after a long, soul-searching family conference, they decided it would be in Edith's best interests if they participated.

Consequently, on Wednesday 13th December, the *Daily Sketch* printed on its front page a prominent picture of the family, self-consciously reading telegrams from wellwishers, inset with a picture of a young, smiling Edith.

They also printed a personal appeal from Mrs Bywaters, headlined:

"A Mother's Appeal to the Mothers of the Nation".

'I am appealing to the hearts of all the mothers of the nation to give me their help in getting a reprieve for my boy. You who have dear boys of your own will I am sure understand the terrible agony I am now suffering, and my great anxiety for his life to be spared. His father gave his life for you and yours, don't let them take my boy away from me.

From a brokenhearted mother.'

The same evening, a young man made his way along Shakespeare Crescent. As he walked past the lighted windows in that suburban street, he could see Christmas decorations festooning the walls and ceilings, with the odd Christmas tree twinkling away in the corner. He passed a small group of children, muffled and swathed against the cold night air, singing *'Good King Wenceslas'* in tuneless, piping voices before finally came to a halt outside number 231.

In stark contrast to the other houses in the street, the Graydon's house stood dark and unwelcoming, and the young man hesitated for a moment before approaching the front door.

Just down from Cambridge, Beverley Nichols had secured a job as a reporter with the *Weekly Despatch* and his first assignment had been to cover the trial where he had watched in disbelief as Edith was sentenced to death. So appalled was he that he had talked his editor into making an offer to help the family financially in return for the story of Edith Thompson's life.

As he tugged on the bell-pull he was not at all sure that his mission would be successful. From what he could gather, the Graydons were a closely-knit, highly respectable family who might consider what he was about to suggest beneath their dignity.

The door was opened by Mr Graydon, looking tired and careworn.

'I'm sorry to disturb you at this hour, Mr Graydon,' Nichols said. 'My name is Nichols, I work for the *Weekly Despatch* and I...'

Mr Graydon sighed. 'I'm sorry,' he said. 'I have nothing more to say.'

'If you would let me in for a few minutes, I could explain how the *Despatch* can help you in your campaign for a reprieve.'

Mr Graydon thought for a moment, then nodded. 'Come in,' he said, stepping aside to allow the young man to pass. 'Come through to the sitting room.'

As they walked down the passage, Mrs Graydon called from upstairs. 'Will, who is it?'

'It's alright, dear,' he called back. 'Nothing to worry about.'

The sitting room was comfortably furnished with a round table in the centre covered by a dark green chenile cloth on which stood an aspidistra. There was a coal fire burning in the grate, and on the mantelshelf above, a framed photograph of a young and smiling Edith.

'My wife has taken to her bed, I'm afraid,' Mr Graydon said apologetically. 'This dreadful business has rather laid her low. Won't you sit down, Mr ..?'

'Nichols. Yes, thank you,' he said, sitting on a chair by the table.

'It's Edith's birthday on Christmas Day,' Mr Graydon said wistfully. 'Twenty-nine she'll be - prime of her life.' He shook his head sadly.

'That *this* should happen to people like *us*,' he said, still unable to come to terms with the tragedy that had shattered his family.

'I'll get straight to the point, Mr Graydon,' Nichols said. 'The *Despatch* is prepared to offer you a substantial sum of money to help in your campaign to secure a reprieve for your daughter. In return, we ask you to give us the story of

Edith's life; what she was like as a child, her schooldays, all the happy memories you have of her and all the good and positive things you remember about her. We would need photographs, school reports, things like that.' He paused for a moment aware of the doubt on Mr Graydon's face. 'With your help,' he said earnestly, 'I think we can bring about a change of heart in the powers-that-be and secure the reprieve that the whole country is praying for and your daughter so obviously deserves.'

Mr Graydon, impressed by the young man's sincerity and good manners, promised he would talk it over with the rest of the family.

As he was being shown out, Nichols turned to Mr Graydon. 'Did you know that Mr Edgar Wallace has written a letter to *The Times* supporting your daughter's cause?'

Mr Graydon smiled sadly. 'Every little helps,' he said.

A week later, the *Despatch* began publishing the first of a series of articles written by Nichols based on information supplied by Mr Graydon.

Meanwhile, Dr Morton, the governor of Holloway, had the unpleasant duty of giving Edith the grim news that the execution date had been fixed for Wednesday 3rd January. It was a most painful duty but, to his immense relief, Edith made it easy for him by accepting the dread tidings calmly and even thanking him for his consideration.

The following day, Sir Henry Curtis-Bennett visited Edith in Holloway prison to discuss her appeal; the date for which had been set for December 21st.

Seeing Sir Henry again, immediately lifted Edith's spirits and, in her fragile mental condition, she quickly began to get over-excited at the prospect of another hearing of her case. So much so that Curtis-Bennett felt constrained to explain to his client the exact function of an Appeal Court.

'You must understand, Mrs Thompson,' he said gently, 'this is *not* a re-trial. A Court of Appeal has the power to revise a sentence or quash a conviction only on the grounds that the verdict was unsafe or unsatisfactory, or that the judgement of the trial judge was wrong in law, or that there was a material irregularity during the course of the trial.'

But Curtis-Bennett's strictures were falling on deaf ears as Edith's febrile imagination began to take flight. Now more than ever she was convinced that away from the emotion-charged atmosphere of the Old Bailey, with three eminent judges deliberating her case in a calm, unbiased, thoughtful manner, there would be, could be, only one possible outcome.

On the morning of 15th December the *Daily Sketch*, now with the bit firmly between its teeth and sales soaring, headlined its edition for the day: *"Bywaters*

Must Not be Hanged", and proudly informed its readers that over 10,000 letters had already arrived in support of the campaign and that a huge queue had formed outside their offices in Shoe Lane to sign the petition.

Indeed, most of the popular press had by now climbed onto the bandwagon set in motion by the *Sketch*, adding their strident voices to the rising clamour for a reprieve for Freddy Bywaters which, if granted, would ensure that Edith Thompson would not hang.

For the moment though, all Edith's hopes were pinned on her the appeal - a hearing she felt sure must finally vindicate her, rectify the wrongs done, and put an end to all her suffering.

Chapter 16

"The smallest ray of hope seems so futile
that I can hardly make myself keep it alive."

On Thursday 21st December, in the court of the Lord Chief Justice in the Strand, three eminent judges took their places to hear the appeals of first, Frederick Bywaters, followed later by that of Edith Thompson. Freddy had elected to attend the hearing while Edith, unable to face another court, had chosen to forgo that right.

The Triumvirate, consisting of Lord Hewart, the Lord Chief Justice, Mr Justice Salter and Mr Justice Darling, indicated that they were ready to hear the appeal on behalf of Bywaters.

Cecil Whiteley's argument was threefold.

Firstly he protested about the refusal of the Court to allow separate trials for the two accused, arguing that the evidence given by one could adversely have affected the case of the other. Secondly, he submitted that the letters, although potential evidence against Mrs Thompson, were not evidence against *his* client and that they had been prejudicial to his case. Finally, he reiterated his belief that, by exercising its right to address the jury last, the Crown had seriously damaged his client's defence.

He had spoken for almost an hour and a half but, after he sat down, it took the judges less than five minutes to dismiss the appeal on all grounds.

Freddy, stoical as ever, took the verdict calmly, even managing to smile at his distraught mother before being ushered out and returned to Pentonville prison.

With such ill-disposed members of the judiciary sitting in judgement, Curtis-Bennett did not entertain very high hopes for Edith Thompson's chances. He was not about to be disabused.

After speaking with great eloquence and clarity of thought for over three hours, it took the judges just eight minutes to dismiss Edith Thompson's appeal on all grounds.

In his summing up, Hewart referred to a 'commonplace and unedifying case', and to the letters as 'deplorable correspondence of the most mischievous and venomous kind', adding that in his view the letters had been quite properly submitted, and concluded with these words: 'This sordid affair exhibits from beginning to end no redeeming feature whatsoever.'

The voice of the law, in all its pomp and bigotry, had spoken.

When the news was relayed to the governor of Holloway, it fell to him once again to be the bearer of bad tidings.

In her cell, Edith was knitting a scarf while chatting to her 'two prison flowers', Rose and Lily, the wardresses assigned to watch over her, both of whom had become quite taken with Edith's charm, grace and intelligence - qualities not often to be found within the walls of one of His Majesty's prisons.

Before he left, the governor had to tell her that, because of the appeal, her execution would now take place on 9th January.

Again, all Edith could do was to nod her head in silent acceptance of her fate.

After he had left, Edith sat quietly weeping for a minute or two as Rose and Lily, both saddened by the news, looked on helplessly.

Eventually she recovered her composure and asked for a pen and paper. She was now desperate to talk to someone, and drying her eyes, she penned a letter to her parents.

Dearest Mother and Dad.

Today seems the end of everything. I can't think - I just seem up against a black, thick wall, through which neither my eyes nor my thoughts can penetrate.

It is not within my powers of realisation that this sentence must stand for something which I have not done, something I did not know of, either previously or at the time. I know you both know this. I know you both have known and believed it all along.

However, I suppose it is only another landmark in my life - there have been so many when I look back, but somehow they are not landmarks until I look back upon the journey, and then I know that certain events were landmarks.

I've tried to unravel this tangle of my existence, this existence that we all call life. It is only at these times that we do think about it.

It has been an existence, that's all, just a 'passing through', meeting trials, and shocks and surprises with a smiling face and an aching heart, and eventually being submerged and facing Death, that thing there is no escaping - no hope of defeating.

You both must be feeling as bad and perhaps worse than I do today, and I do hope this will not make things harder to bear, but I really felt that I should like to talk to you both for just a little while, after I was told the result. Even now, I cannot realise all it means; but, dearest mother and dad, you must both bear up - just think that I am trying to do the same, and I am sure that thought will help you.

Love.

Edith.

As Christmas approached, Edith was dismayed to learn that she would be allowed no more visitors for three days. It was an imposition she found hard to bear since, Christmas Day being her birthday, the family would normally get together to mark the double event.

On Christmas morning, Rose and Lily wished her a happy Christmas and a happy birthday in the certain knowledge that it would be, could be, no such thing for the sad, desolate woman in their charge.

Her Christmas dinner, which she was obliged to eat with a wooden spoon, to prevent any possible suicide attempt, was roast chicken and fruit salad.

As she toyed with her food, the bells of nearby St Luke's church began ringing out their joyful, festive message. Edith suddenly pushed her plate away and cried: 'What a Christmas!' then began to weep and wail hysterically.

The doctor was summoned and, held down by the wardresses, she was injected with a sedative which quickly, and mercifully, put her to sleep.

Over at Pentonville, Freddy was in better spirits and, after a visit to the prison chapel, sat down to a hearty meal of roast beef and plum pudding.

Boxing Day dawned with gusting winds and lashing rain but, having slept for almost fourteen hours, Edith was in a calmer and more positive state of mind. Once again requesting a pen and paper, she sat down and wrote a letter to her childhood friend, Bessie Akam, who had been to see her a few times and had recently written commiserating with her at the failure of her appeal.

Dear Bessie

I wanted to write to you yesterday and yet I couldn't. I could do nothing but sit and think. Who was it who said: 'Some days we sits and thinks, and some days we simply sits'? Well, yesterday was a 'sitting and thinking' day.

I got your little letter on Saturday. Yes, the result of the appeal was a great shock - I had such hopes of it - not only hopes for mercy, but hopes for justice; but I realise how very difficult it is to fight prejudice.

If you have facts to fight, and you fail, you seem more reconciled, but when it's only prejudice - oh, it's awful.

You talk about not having to suffer the extreme penalty. Do you know that I don't dread that at all? I feel that would be far easier than banishment - wrongful banishment for life.

I feel no apprehension of what might lie ahead after this life.

Yesterday I was twenty-nine; it's not really very old I suppose, and yet it seems so to me.

I suppose when you're happy, age doesn't count. It doesn't seem to matter. It's when you're not that the years seem so frightening.

Yesterday I was thinking about everything that has ever happened, it seems to help in all sorts of ways when I do this. I realize what a mysterious thing life is. We all imagine we can mould our own lives - we seldom can, they are moulded for us - just by the laws and rules and conventions of this world, and if we break any of these, we only have to look forward to a formidable and unattractive wilderness.

I've often thought how good it would be to talk, to pour out everything, it might have pained as well, but it would be pain that comes with sudden relief of intolerable hurt.

However, I am going to forget all that now, I'm going to hope - because everybody tells me so. I am going to live in those enormous moments when the whole of life seems bound up in absolute necessity to win.

Thank you so much for writing to me, and helping to keep me cheerful.

Edith.

When visits were resumed, Edith was joined by members of her family all of them buoyed up by the news that the magic figure of one million signatures been reached in the *Daily Sketch* petition, and that the Home Secretary, William Bridgeman, had had a meeting with the Prime Minister. Hopes had never been higher.

Edith was so exhilarated by the news, and so reassured by the scores of letters of support arriving by every post from home and abroad, that her spirits had begun to take wing.

Meanwhile, it was decided among family and friends that all it would need to achieve the longed for, prayed for, reprieve, would be one last big, concerted effort.

To this end, Mrs Graydon wrote a moving letter to Queen Mary, 'as one mother to another', pleading for her to intercede on her daughter's behalf and ending with these words: *'I hope in your Royal mercy and graciousness you will not fail to hear this cry from the heart of a grief-stricken mother in her hour of need, all of whose sons served their country in its hour of need.*

'I have the honour to remain Your Majesty's most faithful subject and dutiful servant.
Ethel J. Graydon.'

On the same day Avis wrote a long, rambling and at times, incoherent letter to the Prime Minister, Bonar Law. In it she pleaded Edith's innocence of any poisoning attempts and her ignorance of Freddy's movements on the night of the murder, going on to describe her sister as an overwrought, unhappy woman long before she met Bywaters.

Then in what can only be described as the desperation of an emotionally disturbed woman, she attempted to blacken her brother-in-law's good name, describing him as a man with no friends of his own who disliked and disapproved of all Edith's friends.

Quite what bearing this had on the case is unclear, but such was Avis's state of mind at this, the eleventh hour, that she would have done or said anything to save her sister. 'The man is dead,' she wrote coldly of Percy, 'but why should he die blameless?'

In one final, desperate attempt to procure the Prime Minister's intervention, she even called into question the state of Edith's mind.

'Could it be that my sister is insane?' she asked. 'Is this question having the prison doctor's attention?'

She ended the letter by saying: 'I beg you to show mercy on her, for her parents' sake. You are a father therefore you understand their feelings at this time.

'We are helpless and know she is not guilty.

'May the Great Judge of all guide you in coming to your final decision, to which the family are just clinging, as the last hope.

'Committing the above to your kind attention,

'I remain in anticipation

Avis E. Graydon. (Miss)'

Towards midnight on New Year's Eve, Edith Thompson lay awake in her cell straining to catch any sounds of the world outside the confines of the prison walls.

She could hear a late tram clanking its way along Parkhurst Road on its way to Finsbury Park, or perhaps down towards Camden Town. Later, she heard a group of drunken revellers singing tunelessly, their raucous voices carrying in the stillness of the night.

Then, at midnight, when the bells began to ring in the New Year, people all over the country would be hugging and kissing each other, drinking champagne, dancing or falling into fountains as they excitedly discarded the old and welcomed in the new.

It was an achingly poignant moment for Edith as she contemplated her impending fate. It fell to very few to know even the *year* of their death, let alone the actual day and the exact time.

Would she *really* die in nine days? Cease to exist? Be no more? She could not bring herself to believe her life would end in such a ghastly fashion.

It was over sixteen years since a female had been executed, and the natural revulsion felt by most civilized people about hanging a woman would, must, convince the Home Secretary to exercise his prerogative of mercy and grant her a reprieve.

It was around 3am, that sleep at last enfolded Edith, bringing a brief respite to her grievously troubled mind.

In Pentonville, Freddy was bearing up well, buoyed by in the knowledge that public opinion was on his side.

In an effort to transfer his optimism to Edith, whom he suspected to be in very low spirits after the denial of her appeal, he wrote to her:

Edie - I want to ask you not to give up hope. I know and you know also, that you should not be in the position that you find yourself. I'm still hoping that the powers that be will exercise some common sense and displace their suppositions with facts. I know this must be a terrible strain on you, but Peidi mia, don't lose heart - BB (Be Brave)

...If you are able, will you write? I want to say a lot, but cannot. You understand? I can only hope and trust that some time in the future we will be able to talk to one another.

Goodbye, Peidi mia. BB
Always,
Freddy.

This letter, like others he had written, never reached Edith. Unknown to both of them, their letters to one another were routinely intercepted and retained by the authorities - correspondence between two convicted murderers being forbidden under prison regulations.

In one last attempt to save Edith, Freddy wrote a letter to the Home Secretary.

'Sir

I am writing to ask you to use your power to avert a great catastrophe and also rectify a grave injustice. Edith Thompson & I have been found guilty & today stand condemned upon a charge of which we are innocent.

'In the first instance I wish to speak to you of Edith Thompson. The case for the prosecution was based entirely upon a series of extracts from letters written by her to me. There were, mentioned in these letters, names of some poisons & broken glass. It was suggested that Mrs Thompson was committed for trial on the charge of having administered poison to her husband. I am asking you to believe me, sir, because what I say is the truth, that Mrs Thompson never had any intention or the slightest inclination to poison her husband or kill him in any way. The only way to treat those letters is the way in which I read them. She is an hysterical & highly-strung woman & when writing letters to me she did not study sentences and phrases before transferring them to paper, but as different thoughts, no matter what momentarily flashed through her mind, so they were committed to paper. Sometimes, even I could not understand her. Now, sir, if I had for one moment, thought or imagined, that there was anything contained in Mrs Thompson's letters to me that could at any time harm her, would I not have destroyed them?

'I was astounded when I heard the sinister translation the prosecution had put to certain phrases which were written quite innocently. Those letters were the outpourings of an hysterical woman's mind, to relieve the tension & strain caused

by the agony she was suffering. If you like, sir, merely melodrama.

'Furthermore I wish to say that she never suggested to me that I should kill her husband. She is not only unjustly condemned but it is wicked & vile to suggest that she incited me to murder. God knows that I speak the truth when I say that there was no plan or agreement between Mrs Thompson & I to murder her husband. I can do no more, sir, than ask you to believe me - the truth - & then it is for you to proclaim to the whole world that Edith Thompson is 'Not Guilty' & so remove the stain that is on her name.

'It was said by an officer of the law, when the result of the exhumation was known, 'The case against Mrs Thompson had failed.' Why then, sir, was she committed for trial? I ask you, I implore you, sir, in the name of humanity and justice, to order the release of Edith Jessie Thompson.

'I have not much space, sir, so will try to be as concise as possible in laying before you my case. I wish to bring to your notice that the evidence against me is only that which has been supplied by myself. I was asked at Ilford if there had been a fight and I said yes. I was not asked for details & I received no caution. When I saw my solicitor on Oct 7th I told him exactly what had happened the same as I did at the inquest at Ilford. I was advised by a law officer to get the charge against me reduced. I mentioned that to my solicitor who said it would be best to say nothing until the trial at the Old Bailey. You now know, sir, why my explanation was not made known before.

'Mr Justice Shearman suggested to the Jury that my knife was in my pocket for one reason only - namely that I had agreed with Mrs Thompson to murder her husband on Oct 3rd. I saw Mrs Thompson at midday on Oct 3rd & it was then, for the first time, I learned that she was going to the Criterion Theatre that evening. My knife was in my pocket then & it had been there since 23rd Sept. I was in the habit of always carrying either a knife or a revolver

'At the inquest, Dr Drought in his evidence stated that the first blow had been delivered from the front. That is quite untrue, you have my statement made in the witness-box at the Old Bailey. If I could speak to you I could explain any point you might wish, more fully but my space here is limited.

'I ask you to accept my word, sir, or perhaps you can show me some way in which I can prove to you that I am speaking the truth.

'I hope & trust that this will receive your careful & favourable consideration, sir, & that you will order another hearing of this case.

I am, sir

Yours respectfully,

Frederick E. F. Bywaters.'

But there was to be no reprieve for Edith Thompson or Freddy Bywaters. The million signatures on the *Daily Sketch* petition meant nothing; the heartfelt pleas of family, friends, church leaders and eminent people were ignored. The executions were to go ahead on January 9th.

Telegrams were despatched to the country's chief executioner, John Ellis of Rochdale and William Willis of Manchester, the deputy hangman. They in turn notified their two assistants, Robert Baker of Hereford and Thomas Phillips of Bolton. Ellis was appointed for Edith's execution and Willis for Freddy's.

As the executioners were travelling down to London, Mrs Graydon and Lily Laxton were visiting Edith in Holloway, unaware that the young woman they both loved so dearly was already standing in the shadow of the gallows.

They found Edith surprisingly cheerful and forthcoming. She told them she had had a letter from Mrs Bywaters which had cheered her up and told them how nice Dora Walker, the new lady Assistant Medical Officer was towards her, adding, 'I have been weighed as many as three times a day', blithely unaware that it was all part of the grisly ritual of execution.

Mrs Graydon had brought her daughter a special present.

Back in September, Edith had taken a small picture to be framed. It was a pencil sketch, drawn by Freddy, of his ship, the *SS Morea*, and Mrs Graydon, finding the receipt among Edith's things, had collected it for her.

Edith was so overjoyed to have it that throughout the entire visit she kept the picture clasped to her bosom.

After her loved ones had left, Edith sat on her bed gazing wistfully at the small drawing, blinking back tears as she remembered how blissfully happy she had been just three brief months ago.

As Mrs Graydon and Lily Laxton walked towards the junction of Parkhurst Road and Holloway Road to catch their trams home they could hear a newspaper boy calling out, but it wasn't until they got closer that the dreadful news burst upon them. A young lad in a cloth cap was yelling in a sing-song voice: 'No reprieve for Thompson and Bywaters. Read all about it. Get your paper 'ere'. The placard he was holding in front of him proclaiming: "No Reprieve. Thompson and Bywaters to hang on Tuesday".

The Star, the *Evening News* and the *Evening Standard* had all rushed out special editions.

It took fully ten minutes for Ethel Graydon to tear herself away from her sister's tearful embrace and make her doleful way back to Manor Park.

When she reached her house a large group of reporters and photographers were milling around outside hoping for some sort of comment but, upon seeing Mrs Graydon's deep distress, they stood silently aside, allowing her to pass through unmolested..

Once inside, she went round closing the curtains in every room. 231 Shakespeare Crescent was now a house in mourning.

It was a little after 3pm when the governor of Holloway entered Edith's cell to inform her of the Home Secretary's final decision. To Dr Morton's relief, she appeared to take the news calmly, but it was simply her traumatised mind refusing to accept the awful implications of what she had just been told.

She sat for a while motionless and glassy-eyed, until a sudden spasm shook her body as a maelstrom of emotion began to take hold. She began to sweat profusely as the appalling reality of what was to happen finally broke through the barriers her mind had erected.

In four days time they were going to drop her through a trap-door, bound hand and foot, with a rope around her neck and a hood covering her face.

Edith suddenly leapt to her feet screaming. 'I never did it!' and began shaking her head violently in a demented manner. As the two wardresses restrained her, Dr Morton was hurriedly re-called to inject her with morphia. It took a short while for the opiate to take effect, but within five minutes, Edith Thompson had lapsed into a deep, coma-like sleep.

The following day, Edith was sitting up in bed, still in a semi-drugged state when entire family came to see her.

It was to be a difficult, emotion-charged visit with their once delightful, vivacious, fun-loving daughter and sister now a sad-eyed, whey-faced, forlorn shadow of the woman she once was; answering questions in monosyllables and constantly gazing up at the barred window of her cell, on the outside of which the sun was shining.

When the half hour was up, the farewells were particularly painful. With no visiting allowed on Sundays, it would be Monday before they could see her again and offer what comfort they could.

That same afternoon, in Pentonville, Freddy was visited by his mother, his sisters Lilian and Florence and a cousin, Mary Simmons. It was the saddest of occasions for everyone because they realized that after three months of optimism and steely resolve, Freddy had at last accepted his fate. He would die at 9am on Tuesday; nothing could change that now.

Looking pale and tense he made what amounted to a full confession. Realizing what he was about to say might be important, his cousin, Mary Simmons, took it upon herself to write it down.

'I don't care for myself,' he began. 'I lost my temper. He always made her life Hell, and he used to say if she ever left him he would make it worse than ever for her. I didn't know what I was doing. I had no intention of killing him, and I don't remember what happened. I just went blind and killed him.

'The judge's summing up was just, if you like, but it was cruel. It never gave me a chance. I did it, though, and I can't complain.

'I can't believe they will hang her as a criminal. I swear she is completely innocent. She never knew that I was going to meet them that night. If only we could die together now it wouldn't be so bad, but for her to be hanged as a criminal is too awful. She didn't commit the murder, I did. She never planned it. She never knew about it. She is innocent, innocent, absolutely innocent. I can't *believe* that they will hang her.'

At this point, for the first time, he broke down sobbing while the four heartbroken women looked on, unable even to hold his hand.

Just before they left, his mother asked him if he would like to see his younger brother, Frankie.

'No, mother,' he said, drying his eyes. 'Let him remember me as I was. Bring him up to be a man.' As his family bid their distraught goodbyes, he said, 'Do everything you can to save Edith. I have not met with justice in this world, but I shall in the next. I hope I shall die like a gentleman. I have nothing to fear.'

Realizing what Freddy had said might help Edith's cause, Mary Simmons took a taxi to the offices of the *Daily Express* in Fleet Street where the editor, Beverley Baxter, an ardent opponent of capital punishment, had campaigned tirelessly for Edith's reprieve.

When he read the confession made by Freddy with all hope of his own reprieve abandoned, he decided on one last-ditch effort to save Edith.

Fired by the thought that even at this late stage, an intervention by the Home Secretary might still be possible, he telephoned the Home Office and discovered that William Bridgeman was at his country estate at Minsterley in Shropshire. He then telephoned Mr Stern, who immediately agreed to go to Minsterley to put Edith's case to the Home Secretary.

With the bit now firmly between his teeth, and with the possibility of a sensational scoop on the cards, Baxter chartered a four-seater light aeroplane and despatched Mr Stern and two of his reporters to Minsterley.

It was almost 10pm when the plane landed at a small aerodrome outside Shrewsbury where a car was waiting to take the three men to the Home Secretary's residence.

Not best pleased at having been roused from his bed, Bridgeman, nevertheless, received the deputation with courtesy in the library of his country house sitting in his dressing gown and pyjamas as he read Freddy's 'confession'.

Having read the statement through a couple of times, Bridgeman removed his glasses and looked up.

'It is not unknown of course,' he said 'that when two criminals are found guilty of a serious crime, for one of them, in an effort to exculpate their partner in that crime, takes all the blame himself. I must be honest with you, gentlemen, I have followed this case very closely and studied all the transcripts of the trial assiduously. But I must tell you I have been unable to find any mitigating circumstances which would prompt me to interfere with the due process of the law.' He rose to his feet ' And that, I'm afraid, is my final decision on the matter.

'Thank you for bringing this to my attention,' he said as he walked to the door. 'My man will see you out. Good night, gentlemen.'

On the day before the executions both Edith and Freddy were visited by the Bishop of Stepney. After visiting Pentonville, he arrived at Holloway around midday and stayed with Edith for an hour, passing on a message from Freddy. During this time, as well as offering spiritual support, he was able to tell her that Freddy had told him that he would never stop loving her, and to be brave, and that they would be together soon.

Before he left he asked Edith if there was anything she wanted to confess. Edith shook her head. 'I am prepared,' she said calmly. 'I have nothing on my soul.'

In the interim between the Bishop's departure and her family's arrival, Edith sat down to pen the last letter she would ever write, addressed to her mother.

In it she told her of her deep love for her family, her sadness at being the cause of their grief and suffering, and to bid them each a last, sad farewell.

When she had finished the letter she was so distressed that, to ensure her last visit passed off without incident, Dr Morton decided to inject Edith with a strong sedative.

When her family arrived, accompanied by Lily Laxton, they were shocked at Edith's appearance and demeanour, seeing a marked deterioration, even from the pathetic figure she had presented the previous Saturday. She was pale-faced and listless,, Her hair, now flecked with grey, was unbrushed and her clothing dishevelled.

They tried valiantly to engage her attention and to get her to respond but it was a lost cause - the spark had gone. Edith was already withdrawing from the world around her and beginning the journey she would have to make alone.

When the time came for them to leave, their sense of loss and desolation was overwhelming. As her loved ones each bid their last goodbyes, Edith stared with fierce intensity into each of their faces as if committing them to memory, before turning away and sinking down on her bed, where she sat completely motionless, hands clenched tightly together, her eyes unfocussed and staring.

She was still sitting in the same position when the prison governor arrived to supervise her removal to the death cell.

Because of her confused state of mind, and much to the governor's relief, the transfer was completed with the minimum of fuss and emotional upset.

It was not until Edith began to look around her new surroundings that she became distressed. There were now *two* doors to her cell and *four* wardresses accompanying her.

As she sat on the narrow bed, her numbed mind trying to understand what it all meant, Dr Morton was obliged to read to her the Home Secretary's final communication, ending with the chilling words, *'...after full consideration of all the representations made to me, I regret to say I found no grounds for departing from my decision.'* It was then that the dreadful truth finally dawned, and Edith began to scream and struggle violently. Rose and Lily managed to hold her writhing body still long enough for Dr Morton to inject her with another shot of morphia, after which her struggles gradually subsided.

Meanwhile, in Pentonville Freddy, while awaiting the arrival of his family, had written several last letters to friends and relations, one to his cousin concluded with these lines:

'I want you, now that you know Edith (Mrs Thompson), always to love and cherish her memory as a brave-hearted, noble, and loyal woman. You can understand what she has suffered. Don't pity her, but love her. We will be together, and what was not to be on this sordid planet, this land of cowards and curs, will be in another world.'

At 2.30pm Mrs Bywaters arrived for her last visit, with Freddy's two sisters, one of the sister's fiance, and Mary Simmons and her daughter.

From the outset Mrs Bywaters could barely contain her grief, unable to fully accept that this would be the last time she would ever look upon her dear son's face, and never again hear him call her 'mum'.

In spite of his comparative youth, Freddy Bywaters had greatly impressed the prison governor and his warders with his maturity, stoicism and courage, but never more so than now as he comforted his mother and sisters, saying he was going to be alright and telling them not to worry about him.

The only moment of doubt came when he spoke of Edith. Taking his mother's hands in his he asked: 'Why can't I be with her?' His mother, utterly overcome and could only shake her head. 'Poor girl,' he said, his eyes misting up. 'It must be terrible for her.' Choked with emotion, all his mother could do was nod her head in dumb agreement.

Lilian and Florence did what they could to relieve the tension by recalling their happy childhood in Manor Park, with their carefree school days and summer holidays in Southend and on Canvey Island until it was time to go.

When they took their leave, Mrs Bywaters had to be supported by her two daughters as she kissed her son goodbye for the last time. After hugging his mother, Freddy held her at arms length and, looked intently into her eyes. 'Give my love to Edith,' he said knowing that such a thing was not possible but hoping his mother might convey his last words to the Graydon family and let them know that his last thoughts were of Edith.

That night, Major Blake was sitting in his office thinking about the prisoner Bywaters and his appointment with the hangman in the morning. He had always held the conviction that British law should be amended to allow for degrees of murder, as it did in the USA. Had such a law been on the statute book, he believed young Bywaters would almost certainly be facing a prison sentence instead of awaiting execution.

On an impulse he dispatched a prison officer to bring Freddy to his office. On this, the last night of his young life, he felt he must offer the lad what solace and comfort he could.

The major was a compassionate man; a professional soldier for twenty-five years who had served with distinction on the Western front in the war, before retiring from the army in 1919.

Fired with a sense of vocation, he had entered the prison service intent on humanising the penal system. It had been a slow process, but in his three years as governor of Pentonville, he had gradually introduced a less rigid, more tolerant regime; a transition that had earned him the respect of the inmates and the suspicion of some of the prison staff.

Since Freddy had arrived, a bond had developed between them. The major found Freddy a likable, upright young fellow, unfailingly polite and grateful for any small privileges he was allowed. For his part, Freddy looked upon the governor as a kind of father-figure - someone he could turn to for help and advice.

When Freddy arrived at his office, in direct contravention of prison regulations, Blake sent the warder out of the room, leaving the two men to talk in private. They sat talking well into the night, a prisoner and his gaoler, sharing reminiscences about their lives.

Freddy talked a lot about Edith, repeating again and again that they were going to hang an innocent woman, and voicing his anguish and despair at having brought the woman he loved to such a ghastly end.

It was well after midnight when Freddy finally stood up to leave. As they shook hands, Blake asked Freddy if he had any last request to make.

'Actually I have, sir,' he said. 'In the stamp pocket of my wallet there's a sixpence wrapped in tissue paper. It's my lucky tanner. I'd very much like to have it with me when...the time comes. If that's alright?'

Blake nodded.

'I'll see to it,' he said.

'Thank you very much, sir.'

'Anything else?'

'If you wouldn't mind, sir,' he said. 'In that same wallet there is a small photograph of Mrs Thompson. I should very much like it to be buried with me.'

Major Blake put his hand on Freddy's shoulder.

'I will make sure it is.'

As a warder entered to escort the prisoner back to his cell, Freddy again extended his hand.

'Thank you for all you have done for me, sir,' he said earnestly. 'I shall never forget it.'

Then he smiled briefly, nodded his head, turned and left the room.

Chapter 17

*"We ourselves die and live in the books we read while we
are reading them and then, when we have finished,
the books die and we live...until when? Who knows..?
We are not the shapers of our destinies."*

At 8am on Tuesday 9th January 1923, two male prison officers, Young and
Wood, arrived at Holloway prison to assist with the hanging of Edith Thompson,
it being considered much too harrowing for female officers to undertake.

Young immediately went to the death cell and looked at the woman he would
almost certainly have to carry to the scaffold. When he peeped through the spy-
hole he could see her sitting on her bed weeping and being comforted by the
prison chaplain.

Fifteen minutes later, Dr Morton entered the condemned cell and injected an
unresisting Edith with a shot of morphia after which she sank into a comatose
state.

At exactly 8.59am Ellis, the hangman, entered with his assistant through one
door while P.O. Young entered through the other.

Young immediately lifted Edith's limp body to an upright position so that Ellis
could pinion her arms behind her back. As he did so, Edith came to momentarily
and looked uncomprehendingly into his face. 'Come on, mate,' he whispered in
her ear, 'it'll soon be over.'

By now Ellis had tied Edith's skirt around her legs and bound her ankles. Then,
with the chaplain walking beside them intoning the burial service, she was carried
across the rain-swept prison yard to the brick shed that housed the gallows.

While still being held upright by Young, Ellis lifted Edith's drooping head, put
on the white hood and fastened the noose around her neck with the knot just below
her left ear. Then with a nod to Young, who let go of Edith's body, Ellis stepped
back and kicked the lever that operated the trap-door. With one last choking gasp
Edith was consigned to the abyss.

While the rope began gently swaying and creaking as the body suspended from
it twitched and slowly rotated, the stench of the excrement and urine that had been
released from Edith's bowels and bladder began to permeate the room.

She hung there for another hour before Dr Morton and Dr Walker went down
into the pit to check for a heartbeat. Satisfied that life was extinct, the two men
hurriedly left the execution chamber holding handkerchiefs to their noses.

As he sat awaiting his fate, Freddy was praying with the chaplain, his 'lucky tanner' clasped in his left hand.

When Willis, the hangman, entered his cell Freddy stood up, squared his shoulders, shook hands with his executioner, and calmly allowed his arms to be pinioned behind his back. Then, accompanied by Major Blake, two warders, and the chaplain, he started out for the scaffold.

As they arrived, Freddy ran up the steps and stood waiting with his head held high. He was going to die as he had said he would, like a gentleman

The hood was placed over his head, the noose tightened and the trap-door sprung, committing him to eternity.

The violent jolt at the rope's end which broke his neck also forced open his clenched fist, and a bright, 1916 sixpenny piece dropped onto the concrete floor eighteen inches below his swinging body and rolled into a corner.

At 11am, Edith body was winched up and taken to the mortuary where the soiled undergarments were removed and burned and the body washed and redressed. Then they brushed her hair, closed her eyes, covered her bruised neck with a piece of white silk, and lowered her body into a plain, elm coffin, after which they folded her arms across her breast and placed a small bunch of white lilies at her feet.

At 231 Shakespeare Crescent, Mrs Graydon had been prostrate with grief throughout the previous night, with none of the family able to sleep. At a few minutes to 9am, they gathered round Mrs Graydon's bedside where, with hands clasped and heads lowered in silent prayer, they mourned the untimely passing of their beloved Edith.

Sadly, there was still one more heart-rending duty for the family to perform; the formal identification of Edith's body.

The group that left 231 later that day for Holloway prison consisted of Mr and Mrs Graydon, Avis, and Bessie Akam - the three brothers being too distraught to attend.

When they arrived at Holloway, a huge crowd consisting mostly of women had gathered outside the prison gates, foremost among them Violet Van Der Elst, an implacable opponent of capital punishment and a lifelong campaigner for its abolition. Some carried placards denouncing the barbarism of legal execution, whilst others bore religious texts urging sinners to repent and warning 'The End Is Nigh'.

The same scene was repeated outside Pentonville Prison where, in spite of the steadily falling rain, another large crowd had gathered, with two mounted policemen on hand in case of trouble.

As the Graydons gathered round Edith's coffin, they were overcome with grief as they looked down for the very last time on the woman they loved, her face, so clouded with unimaginable suffering for the last few months of her life, now at peace in death.

After each of them had kissed the forehead of the dead woman, Mr Graydon was handed his daughter's fur coat and wedding ring. Then, with arms around each other, the stricken family slowly left the room, leaving behind the one thing they had loved most in this world.

As soon as they had gone, lime was poured over the body and the lid screwed down and sealed. Ten minutes later the coffin was lowered into a freshly-dug hole in the prison graveyard and covered over, with nothing to mark the last resting place of Edith Thompson.

In Pentonville, Freddy's body had been taken down and laid out. With his mother and sisters too distraught to identify him, Detective Inspector Francis Hall, the man who had arranged the 'accidental' meeting of Thompson and Bywaters at Ilford police station which had sealed their fate, stepped in to complete the formality.

Freddy was buried in lot number 38 in Pentonville cemetery.

Less than a mile apart, the two ill-starred lovers were finally united in death.

"I will always love you; if you are dead, if you have left me,
even if you don't still love me, I always shall you."

EPILOGUE

In the days following Edith Thompson's execution, the newspapers were filled with lurid accounts of her death describing how she had had to be carried to the gallows and was unconscious when she was hanged and that her 'insides had fallen out' in the process. One paper even went so far as to suggest that a foetus had been found in the pit below the gallows and hastily burnt.

There was no doubt the execution had had a profound effect on those present that morning. Many of the prison staff involved asked to be excused attendance at any further executions and Dr Morton took early retirement one year later. In 1928, John Ellis, the hangman, who had retired fourteen months after the execution, attempted suicide. He eventually succeeded some years later.

In the last week of Edith's life, William Graydon, unable to continue the weekly articles for Beverley Nichols, returned his fee to the *Weekly Despatch*. On Sunday January 14th the *Despatch* printed the following letter from him.

'Sir

'I had hoped that after the execution of my unhappy daughter, I should have been able to retire into obscurity and try, if not to forget, at any rate to be forgotten.

'Certain sections of the press, however, are still engaged in publishing intimate details of my daughter's life.

'May I through your columns, protest against this?

'Mrs Thompson sinned and she paid the penalty. How great that penalty was, only those who knew and loved her can tell. Surely the decent thing is to let the past bury itself, if not out of pity for her, out of consideration for those she left behind.

'Wherever I or any member of my family goes we are pointed at, stared at, photographed. My house is besieged all day and every day by anybody who is the victim of morbid curiosity.

'During all these terrible weeks we have had no privacy, and now that we desire to go away for a brief period, we are haunted always by the thought that we shall

be known and followed.
'To continue to rake up the past is only to prolong the agony. And when that past is almost entirely fictitious I feel bound to protest.
'Nine tenths of what has been written about my daughter has been completely untrue.
'Now that she is dead, cannot these lies cease? Cannot we be left to the privacy which I used to think was the right of all Englishmen to enjoy?

'I am, Sir, yours faithfully
W.E. Graydon.'

On Monday January 15th, Sir Ernley Blackwell dictated a letter in reply to a letter from the MP for Stratford, Mr T.E. Groves, who was concerned about the manner of Edith Thompson's execution.

'Dear Sir
'In reply to your letter of the 10th instant, I am desired by the Home Secretary to say that from reports he has received he is satisfied that the execution of Mrs Thompson was carried out in the most humane manner possible. The statement that the prisoner was 'in a state of collapse practically all through the previous night' is without foundation.
'She slept soundly for several hours. As for the suggestion that she had to be carried to the scaffold, it was thought to be more humane to spare her the necessity of walking from her cell, but she was not unconscious.'

The Graydon family stayed on at 231 Shakespeare Crescent. The three boys married and moved away.

Mrs Graydon died in January 1938, aged 65, without achieving her dearest wish - to have her daughter's remains disinterred and re-buried in the family plot at the City of London Cemetery in Ilford.

In 1941, Mr Graydon died in Gants Hill a broken man. He and Avis had moved there in 1939. With so much of that which he held most dear now gone, he had lost the will to live.

He was buried beside his wife.

In 1924 Avis embraced the Roman Catholic church and was a regular worshipper at St. Francis Church in Stratford where, to this day, on the 9th of January every year, a memorial service is held for Edith Thompson.

Avis died on 6th August 1977, and is buried at St Patrick's Roman Catholic Cemetery in Leytonstone. She was 81 years of age and had remained a spinster, convinced that the notoriety surrounding her family would preclude any hope of marriage.

Richard Thompson continued the family vendetta against Edith and the Graydons, continually writing scurrilous letters to the press and defaming Edith's morals and memory on many occasions.
He died in 1952.

At an auction held at 41 Kensington Gardens on Tuesday 27th September 1923, the household effects of the Thompsons were sold by B. Bailey & Co.
So large was the attendance, that the auction was conducted through the bay window of the Thompsons' living room while the bidders stood in the front garden and the street.
Small items like earthenware pots from the garden and kitchen utensils fetched large bids. The highest bid was for the Thompsons' mahogany bedroom suite.
When the sale was over, the privet bushes round the garden had been stripped bare by souvenir hunters.

The letters which condemned Edith Thompson together with those she wrote to Freddy, suppressed while she was in Holloway Prison, were last seen in 1924. Their current whereabouts is unknown.

In 1971, the remains of Edith Thompson, together with three other executed women, were removed from the prison graveyard at Holloway and re-buried in an unmarked grave at Brookwood Cemetery in Woking, Surrey.
In 1993, after a long campaign by a small group of sympathizers, chief among them René Weis, author of *Criminal Justice. The True Story of Edith Thompson*, the grave was identified as plot 117.
On Saturday 13th November of that year, justice of a kind was finally done to Edith Thompson.
In a short, moving ceremony, the Reverend Barry Arscott, vicar of St Barnabas Church, Manor Park, where Edith and Percy had married, blessed the ground under which Edith lay.
Two days later, a memorial stone was placed at the site which reads:

Edith Jessie Thompson
25th December 1893.
9th January 1923.

"Sleep on beloved.
Her Death Was A Legal Formality."

After seventy years, Edith was finally resting in consecrated ground.
Freddy Bywaters still lies in an unmarked burial plot at Pentonville prison.

BIBLIOGRAPHY

A POLICE CONSTABLE'S GUIDE TO DAILY WORK
Sup't B.M. Bragg and J.C. McGrath **1922**

THE TRIAL OF FREDERICK BYWATERS AND EDITH THOMPSON
Edited by Filson Young **1923**

THE CASE OF THOMPSON AND BYWATERS
Published by Geo Newnes **c1925**

GREAT STORIES OF TRUE LIFE
Edited by Max Pemberton **c1926**

BLACK CAP
Murder Will Out
W and L Townsend **1930**

FORTY YEARS AT SCOTLAND YARD
Frederick Porter Wensley **1930**

FAMOUS CRIMES c1930

NOTABLE TRIALS
Difficult Cases
R. Storry Deans **1932**

A PIN TO SEE THE PEEPSHOW
F. Tennyson Jesse **1934**

ROGUE'S MARCH
George Dilnot **1934**

ON THE GALLOWS
Violet Van der Elst **1937**

CURTIS
The Life of Sir Henry Curtis-Bennett K.C.
Roland Wild and Derek Curtis-Bennett **1937**

GREAT CASES OF SIR HENRY CURTIS-BENNETT K.C.
Edward Grice **1937**

BRIEF LIFE
Cecil Whiteley K.C., D.L. **1942**
THE LIFE AND TIMES OF JUSTICE HUMPHREYS
Stanley Jackson **1951**

BERNARD SPILSBURY
His Life and Cases
Douglas G. Browne and E.V. Tullet **1951**

THE INNOCENCE OF EDITH THOMPSON
A Study in Old Bailey Justice
Lewis Broad **1952**

HANGMAN'S CLUTCH
Nigel Moreland **1954**

UNITED IN CRIME
Montgomery Hyde **1955**

SHOULD WOMEN HANG?
Bernard O'Donnell **1956**

THE SWEET AND TWENTIES
Beverly Nichols **1958**

THE WALL IS STRONG
Life of a Prison Governor
Cap't Gerold Fancourt Clayton **1958**

THE CHIEF
The Biography of Gordon Hewart
Lord Chief Justice of England 1922-1940
Robert Jackson **1959**

THE MURDER AND THE TRIAL
Edgar Lustgarten **1960**

HANGED IN ERROR
Leslie Hall **1961**

HOLLOWAY PRISON
The Place and people
John Camp **1974**

CRIMINAL JUSTICE
The True Story of Edith Thompson
René J.A. Weis **1988**